Mysterious Seed

ANOTHER DESTINY IMAGE BOOK BY BOB MUMFORD

Agape Road

Mysterious Seed

MATURING IN FATHER'S LOVE

BOB MUMFORD

DESTINY IMAGE® PUBLISHERS, INC.

P.O. Box 310, Shippensburg, PA 17257-0310

"Promoting Inspired Lives."

This book and all other Destiny Image, Revival Press, MercyPlace, Fresh Bread, Destiny Image Fiction, and Treasure House books are available at Christian bookstores and distributors worldwide.

For a U.S. bookstore nearest you, call **1-800-722-6774.**

For more information on foreign distributors, call **717-532-3040.**

Reach us on the Internet: **www.destinyimage.com.**

ISBN 13 TP: 978-0-7684-3897-0

ISBN 13 Ebook: 978-0-7684-8958-3

For Worldwide Distribution, Printed in the U.S.A.

1 2 3 4 5 6 7 8 9 10 11 / 13 12 11

Endorsements

It was not until I heard Bob Mumford's illustration of the acorn and the supernatural impregnation of God's mysterious Seed within us that I began to believe there was personal hope to become human as God intended. All the focus of my nearly 40 years of Christianity had been on performance and outward change, trying to overcome sin and out-perform flesh through causes and gifts. Needless to say, it was a set up for eventual failure. Now I know what Paul meant when he said to imitate God. Now I understand how God has given His DNA in seed form to change our very nature from the inside out, maturing us on this journey into His likeness. I have been forever transformed by His Seed and by *Agape*—His supernatural love.

David VanCronkhite
Friend

It has been an indescribable privilege to observe, from a front-row seat, the Lord cultivating His sacrificial, self-giving Love in the man Bob Mumford over many years. Through him, the Lord has laid a foundation of the knowledge of God—the life in *Agape* that the Trinity has shared together from eternity. Discovering the Seed of Their essential life within us—"Christ in you the hope of glory"—and understanding it by faith is causing the love of God to grow in me in practical ways. I am confident that *The Mysterious Seed* will greatly enhance your participation in daily fellowship with the Father, Son, and Spirit.

Eric Mumford
Bob's son and president of Lifechangers

I know that everyone who has tried to follow Jesus for very long is anticipating some kind of massive change in the Body of Christ and how it operates. This book, *The Mysterious Seed*, offers more health food for change than anything I've read. Clearly Bob's experiences, education, pain, and more experiences have left him scared with love (*Agape*), and we can now reap the benefits of that knowledge. This has already become my daily devotional.

Don Potter

I believe it was Providence that brought Bob and I together in the late '90s. I'm a firm believer that at every stage of life one needs a mentor. Bob has been that to me—watering, nurturing, and nourishing the mysterious Kingdom Seed in me but never getting in the way of Father who makes all things grow. His latest book, *The Mysterious Seed*, continues the process of providing guidance and encouragement as I muddle my way along on the Kingdom journey.

McDaniel E. Phillips
Missionary, TWR International (formerly Trans World Radio)

I was 19 years old the first time I heard Bob Mumford teach. My father and grandfather were both ministers, but as I listened that day, the words from John 7:46 came to my mind: "No one ever spoke the way this man does"! That was 42 years ago, and that man, Bob Mumford, has planted Kingdom Seeds in my life from that day until this. As Bob's spiritual son, I can say that the words in this book, like seeds, will absolutely bring life and transformation to those who receive it on fertile soil.

Darrell Scott
President and Founder, Rachel's Challenge

Staying right at the center of God's love,
keeping your arms open and outstretched,
ready for the mercy of our Master, Jesus Christ.
This is the unending life, the real life!

(Jude 21 TM).

By Love Doth Love Grow Mighty In Its Love
I am a little weary of my life—
Not thy life, blessed Father! Or the blood
Too slowly laves the coral shores of thought,
Or I am weary of weariness and strife.
Open my soul-gates to thy living flood;
I ask not larger heart-throbs, vigor-fraught,
I pray thy presence, with strong patience rife.

—George MacDonald, *Diary of an Old Soul*, November 30

Contents

Part II Journey to the Father

Part III *Eros* and *Agape*

Part VI Intentionality

Part VII Fallen King

Part VIII Pride and Rage

Foreword

I don't remember the day I first believed in God. I have always believed in Him. My Papa has been planting and cultivating the seeds of the Kingdom in my life since I was born and watering those seeds with his tears ever since. When I was a toddler, he taught me to be grateful and give Father the evening sacrifice. I remember my sister and I kneeling in prayer with Dad Christmas morning 1960 to thank God for the gifts we were about to open. As an independent teenager, I gave my dad a lot of practice in praying that the imperishable seed planted in me would take firm root and grow. After numerous occasions in the Rubber Room, I realized that the Seed really is indestructible. There have been thousands of other seeds that my Papa has planted in me, like the importance of being prepared to pull the King's carriage, how to stand in the midst of a whirlwind, and what it meant to be a priest and bear someone's burden. Throughout my life, one theme has always been consistent: being conformed to the image of God's Son so I can become a full-grown, symmetrical tree that provides shade and bears fruit.

This book came out of three week-long teaching sessions with a group of dear friends in the mountains of North Carolina. All of us in those sessions were seasoned believers, some having walked with the Lord for many decades, some in full-time ministry. As a papa, Bob asked each of us to set aside our belief systems for a few days so we could see through rather than look at Kingdom issues. By the time Papa finished teaching, every one of us had a completely new foundation in our Christian life. We saw how water baptism is an act of warfare, and many of us chose to be rebaptized in the pond on the property. We learned about being givers rather than takers and how to transition from being a sheriff with bullets to a gardener with seeds. We saw darkness in its raw and ugly state and only then began to understand Light. We learned that we really are fallen kings and the only way to freedom is to act against ourselves. It is only *Agape* that can keep us from stumbling and make our lives count. *The Mysterious Seed* and Papa's next book, *Nourishing the Seed*, are the fruit of those sessions.

God's Kingdom really is like seed thrown on the fields of our hearts. We have no idea what was even planted until it begins to sprout and grow. May the Seeds of *Agape* take deep root through this book and produce a healthy harvest in each of us so that we can become fully mature, producing fruit for generations to come.

Keren Mumford Kilgore

Preface

CARLSON, my college music teacher, hosted an early-morning prayer meeting at his home, which my wife, Judith, and I often attended. Even though Carlson was an accomplished classic pianist, he rarely played during our worship times. "I can hear more music in my soul than I can express on the keys," he used to explain, "and if I try and play what I hear, I only frustrate myself for the rest of the day!"

I can fully identify with Carlson. I see and sense more of the Kingdom of God than I have the ability to express, and I feel like my circuits are completely inadequate. My goal in this book is to express the manner in which God Himself comes to us. There have been times in my walk with the Lord when I did not think I could take another step, but I knew if I stumbled, at least I was pointing in the right direction. The two objectives in this book are to expand our capacity to be loved and expand our capacity to love God as He desires to be loved.

Therefore, rather than offering a systematic presentation from my unfolding journey in the love of God, I simply want to pass on to you what Father has given me—a *bag of seed*. When God chose to express Himself to us, He did not send us a text book entitled *How to Know God*. Rather, He told us stories, He painted us pictures, and He planted seeds of Himself in our minds and hearts.

The marvel and mystery of these seeds is their absolute ability to do what the Creator intended—produce a harvest of fruit after its nature. Jesus told

His disciples that after the seed is planted, we go about the normal functions of life, and the seed of the Kingdom sprouts, grows, and produces a harvest in a way we cannot understand (see Mark 4:26-28). As we consider the mystery of the Kingdom Seed, it is my intent to release the mystery into your life so it can do its marvelous work. The DNA of the acorn enables it to become all that God the Father intended—a huge, symmetrical, and fully formed oak tree. The Father's Seed in us comes to maturity in the same way.

In keeping with the seed format, I will be presenting individual sessions that have been born out of the fruit of the Kingdom as I have experienced it. Though they are often linked by a theme, each will stand on its own to be received, cultivated, and nurtured in your person. I suggest you read one a day and receive it into your being, allowing it to work in you for the next 24 hours. When possible, look up the biblical references; reading directly from the Word will "fertilize" each concept and help the seed to sprout and grow.

Taking one section a day may seem slow at first, but remember—you can't rush a garden! I am sharing my seed with you in confidence that the Seed, which is uncreated, eternal, and unshakable, will germinate and grow into the fruit of *Agape*, producing in you your full inheritance in the Kingdom of God. May the Lord grant you the grace to be a good farmer!

Bob Mumford

50 Cents and a Well-Spent Life

*Therefore, since we have so great a cloud of witnesses surrounding us, let us
also lay aside every encumbrance and the sin which so easily entangles us,
and let us run with endurance the race that is set before us* (Hebrews 12:1).

WHEN I came back to the Lord after 12 years of backsliding, I went
to Bible college and worked at a gas station during a summer break.
As I was handing a customer a 50-cent piece in change the Lord said, "You
have 50 years of ministry. Each year equals one cent. Let Me spend you the
way I want to spend you, and I'll give you a good return on your investment."

A few years later as a young, successful Bible teacher, God was moving
through my ministry, and I could see He was spending my 50 cents well!
Then one day the Lord told me, "I want you to go to the Episcopal Seminary
in Philadelphia for three years and get your Master's Degree."

"Three years! I can't spend three years doing that—the world is dying!
People need my ministry! Jesus is coming!"

His response was simple: "Jesus was a nine-month baby."

Even though the world was dying when Jesus was born, God didn't shorten
His gestation time to six months. Neither did He rush Jesus into ministry
when He was 25 years old. The Father's focus was never on the needs of the
moment but always on nurturing and bringing His seed in Jesus to maturity.

Throughout my life, I have had to learn that everything comes in the
fullness of time rather than being defined by my needs and the needs around
me *today!* I always say, "I'm ready, God, let's go!" However, Jesus was never

motivated by external circumstances. The impetus for His every action was the fullness of His Father's purposes. The intoxication of ministry can seduce anyone out of the fullness of the Father's time and into a spiritual wasteland from which, tragically, they may fail to return.

When I met the Lord at 12 years of age, the Father inseminated me with the DNA of Jesus. His seed was mostly dormant during my 12 years of backsliding, but it never died because it contained the power of an indestructible life (see Heb. 7:16). In the Father's time, it sprouted and began to grow. During my life, there have been seasons of growth, rest, pruning, and fruitfulness. Each season has been part of the Father's sovereign process in my life.

The ability to have some longevity in our mindset is important in order to finish our race well. God's seed has faithfully grown and matured in my life through five decades. I can testify that God has wisely spent my 50 cents! March 16, 2011, was my 57th year in ministry, and I'm living on the promised return of that 50 cents. By His grace, I've got another 20 years to go!

If you allow God to spend you—three years here, a year there, five years somewhere else—your allotment of years will be well spent. Take hold of this, and you will never fight God whether He tells you to serve tables at a local recovery mission, spend five years getting a degree, or take a season away from your job or ministry. Keeping a 50-year perspective is very healthy.

Thoughts and Questions

- Describe some of the seasons God has brought into your life.
- How have you resisted and/or cooperated with the Father in these seasons?
- Can you define your present season and how the Lord is "spending your time"?

PART I

Mysterious Seed

Growth of the Mysterious Eternal Seed

God's kingdom is like seed thrown on a field by a man who then goes to bed and forgets about it. The seed sprouts and grows—he has no idea how it happens. The earth does it all without his help: first a green stem of grass, then a bud, then the ripened grain (Mark 4:26-29 TM).

IT is a mystery how anything can grow out of a pile of dirt. When I was a kid, there was a huge maple tree in front of our house, and one of the seeds dropped into the crack in the sidewalk. Eventually, that seed grew until the whole sidewalk was pushed up. I can remember flying over the concrete ramp that the roots created on my scooter made out of orange crates and old skates.

Jesus compares the Kingdom of God to a seed. In so doing, He reveals several aspects of the Kingdom that will help us know the Father's ways and move with them. It is always fascinating to see how the four Gospels amplify and clarify different aspects of the Kingdom of God. The parable of the sower is pivotal, far-reaching, and monumental in helping us understand the Kingdom mystery. Mark, after recording this parable, adds important and fundamental insights:

1. *Casting Seed.* This implies that our confidence is in the Seed and that it contains all that is necessary to produce fruit.

2. *The growth of the Seed is a mystery.* We sleep or rest with full confidence in the power of the Seed, and we embrace the mystery that we do not really know how the growth occurs.

3. *The Seed bears fruit in its season.* The earth brings forth fruit from the Seed by some "automatic" process. It grows and produces

fruit by itself. We can cultivate, water, and nourish, but we cannot make the fruit grow.

4. *Harvest of fruit.* The harvest cannot happen until or unless the fruit has appeared.

What a beautiful picture Mark gives us of how the Kingdom fruit does not emerge fully mature. As the crop grows, we first see a green stem of grass, then the bud, and then the ripened grain—and only when the crop permits is it harvested for use. Every farmer knows the futility of forcing a seed to grow. He also knows it is not possible to plant watermelon seeds today and get watermelons tomorrow. The farmer quickly learns not to give him or herself a spiritual hernia trying to make the seed grow or reap a crop before it is ready.

Thoughts and Questions

- What does the nature of the Seed tell you about Father's ways?
- In what areas of your life have you cultivated, watered, and nourished the Seed and are now waiting for fruit?
- In what ways have you given yourself a spiritual hernia trying to produce some characteristic or spiritual attribute?

READING 2

The Nature of *Agape*

Love never disappears (1 Corinthians 13:8, Moffatt).

IN order to understand the mysterious Seed, we must have a grasp of *Agape* and *Eros*. We will look at *Agape* first and *Eros* afterward.

Agape (Strong's #25) is a Greek word for love and is an exercise of the divine will in deliberate choice made without assignable cause, save that which lies in the nature of God Himself (see Deut. 7:7-8). It is a quality of life and is used as both a noun and a verb. *Agape* unfolds in three progressive steps, none of which can be omitted: *1. Love God* with all of my heart, soul, mind, and strength (see Mark 12:30). *2. Love myself* because God has given me value and worth by pouring His Own love into me while I was yet a sinner (see Rom. 5:8). *3. Love others*, even my enemies, in the same manner and degree that He has loved me and gave Himself for me (see Matt. 5:43-48).

God Himself is *Agape* (see 1 John 4:8). His love—covenantally faithful, unconditional, and self-giving—is depicted as a straight arrow. *Agape* is God's absolute by which He judges all things and is His Nature, His DNA, or as we have seen, His communicable attributes that are imparted to His own. *Agape* is ultimate reality. In 1 Corinthians 13, the famous chapter on love, we can see several aspects of the nature of *Agape*.

Agape creates community. It brings us to *being* rather than *doing*. We can know all mysteries and all knowledge, but if we do not *have* love, we are nothing (see 1 Cor. 13:3). The reason we are nothing is because it is *Agape* that gives us identity, revealing us to ourselves and to each other. Because *Agape* is relational, we would have to say, "It is God's *Agape*, given to me freely in the person of Christ that imparts to me value and identity." Apart from Christ's act, we would remain dead and incapable of the *Agape* responses that God desires. God has given us *His* capacity to love, but that capacity must be brought to its full end so we can love as He loves.

Agape loves without being self-referential. We can even give all our possessions to feed the poor and still be self-referential, expecting to get something from God in return. God's *Agape* goes out to a hurting world without seeking return and comes to us from God, as Father, without personal advantage or selfish gain.

Agape is the single cohesive factor for the entire body of Christ and the social fabric of the universe. It is by the instrumental means of *Agape* that the body builds itself up in love (see Eph. 4:16).

Thoughts and Questions

🦌 From personal experience, how would you interpret the statement "If I do not have love, I am nothing"?

🦌 How does putting *Agape* into action affect your relationships?

🦌 What are the three progressive stages in which *Agape* grows?

The Nature of *Eros*

But if your eye is unsound, your whole body will be full of darkness. If then the very light in you [your conscience] is darkened, how dense is that darkness! (Matthew 6:23 AMP)

EROS is a Greek word, but it is not used in the New Testament because of its sexual corruption. The essential meaning of *Eros* is the desire or intention to possess, acquire, or control. *Eros* does not seek to be accepted by its object, but to gain possession of it.[1] *Eros* has an appetite or yearning desire that is aroused by the attractive qualities of its object. *Eros,* in Greek philosophy, came to mean someone or something that is loved for the purpose of personal satisfaction. It is from this posture that the word *Eros* took on its sexual and ultimately pornographic connotation. The word is not primarily sexual but has more to do with living for our own personal advantage. The Greek word "evil" in many places in the New Testament is "*porneia*" (Strong's #4190), where we get the word pornography. Essentially *porneia* is a love that is bought and sold, which is no love at all.[2]

Porne is the link that joins *Eros* and original sin. Moffatt translates *porne*, the King James word for evil, as selfishness. Because the New Testament uses *porne* for its description of evil, it is saying something like, "all evil is love for God that has been twisted and sold for something else." Paul explained evil as fallen man exchanging God's glory for his or her own desires (see Rom. 1:23).

Eros is the mother of all sins. It can be recognized because it is *always* self-referential. It is not only self-centered, but it also becomes self-consuming, turning increasingly inward upon itself in a tighter and tighter spiral.

Eros is a highly refined form of self-interest and self-seeking. It is a love that has become so distorted that its only purpose is to meet its own needs. When Jesus referred to religion that turned us in upon ourselves, He said, *"How great is that darkness"* (Matt. 6:22-23 KJV). He was talking about selfishness that leads to a form of darkness that has deadening results. Jesus challenged *Eros*-motivated religion with these words, *"But blessed are your eyes, because they see; and your ears, because they hear"* (Matt. 13:16).

The nature of evil is selling or sharing our love that belongs to God in an illegal manner. God jealously asks for all our love—heart, soul, mind, and strength—to the limit of our capacity because He knows it is the *one force* that releases us from ourselves and exerts the capacity to keep us from evil. We do, indeed, become what we love. We are faced with the inexorable truth that no one can set us free from that which we still love—especially an illegal love for ourselves!

Thoughts and Questions

- In what ways have you seen *Eros* functioning with the intention to possess, acquire, or control?
- Explain why *Eros* is always self-referential.
- Why does God ask for all our love—heart, soul, mind, and strength?

ENDNOTES

1. Anders Nygren, *Agape and Eros* (Philadelphia: Westminster Press), viii-xvi.

2. William Barclay, *Flesh and Spirit: An Examination of Galatians 5:9-23* (Nashville: Abingdon Press / SCM Press LTD, 1962), 23.

Agape and Preferential Choice

But I tell you, love your enemies and pray for those who persecute you
(Matthew 5:44).

*A*GAPE responds first. We love God because He first loved us (see 1 John 4:19). We respond effectively to God when, like a sponge, we absorb His love and return it to Him in as pure a form as we are capable. He instills in us the desire and then enjoys our response.

Agape requires preferential choice. In order to exhibit love that is patient and kind (see 1 Cor. 13:4), we must prefer *Agape* over anything else, even our reactions. We simply choose to accept God's love or resist it. Fortunately, *Agape* is not dependent on us. The very act of preferring *Agape* over everything else breaks the darkness of *Eros*.

Agape loves even our enemies. To be measured as authentic, *Agape* must reach even to our enemies (see Rom. 12:14). It does not act unbecomingly, does not seek its own, is not provoked, and does not take into account a wrong suffered (see 1 Cor. 13:5). We are not talking about our feelings or emotions for our enemies but our *intention* to do them good. *Agape* works like this: We discover in ourselves a new and unusual desire to do someone good. Increasingly, we are aware that this desire does not originate within ourselves. *Agape*, if authentic and present, must reveal itself in action. We now begin to look for opportunity to do others good. Fruit is appearing in the life of the believer!

Agape is Truth. It hates unrighteousness but loves truth (see 1 Cor. 13:6). Truth is one aspect of God's DNA that was imparted to us. In spite of antagonism from the world, Jesus revealed truth to both His friends and His enemies. The Psalmist beautifully stated, *"Love and truth meet in the street, right living and whole living embrace and kiss!"* (Ps. 85:10 TM).

Agape controls us (see 2 Cor. 5:14). *Agape* bears all things, believes all things, hopes all things, and endures all things (see 1 Cor. 13:7). It is not human will-power but *Agape* that controls our desires and governs our ability to reach out to others who are hurting in spite of our own pain or sense of failure.

Agape will never go away. Love never disappears. If I am manufacturing love, it will disappear. If love is the real thing, it will stand, continue, and never disappear because God *is Agape.* In Paul's well-known words in First Corinthians 13:13, *"these three remain: faith, hope, Agape."*

Thoughts and Questions

- Why would the act of preferring *Agape* over anything else break the power of *Eros*?

- Why must love include our enemies to be considered authentic?

- In what ways have you experienced *Agape* never disappearing?

READING 5

The Immortal Mysterious Eternal Seed

You have been regenerated (born again), not from a mortal origin (seed, sperm), but from one that is immortal by the ever living and lasting Word of God (1 Peter 1:23 AMP).

SINCE Jesus compares the Kingdom of God to a seed, understanding the reproductive nature of the Kingdom is essential.

The Seed reproduces after its kind. Apple trees produce apples, and peach trees produce peaches. The source of the Eternal Seed is not from the earth, nor is its origin mortal as in human sperm but from One who is immortal by the ever-living Word of God. Coming in Seed form, *Agape* is required to mature or be perfected so it can find expression and release. When the Kingdom Seed of *Agape* begins to grow, it brings forth characteristics of the Kingdom—it produces God's *Agape* as fruit after its kind. This is Paul's reasoning to the people in Galatia: If we depart from Christ, the fruit or manifestation will be fleshly behavior (see Gal. 5:19-21). If we abide in Christ and water, nourish, and cultivate that Eternal Seed, the fruit will be *Agape* (see Gal. 5:22-23). Many Greek expositors explain Galatians 5:22 as the fruit of the Spirit is *Agape*, out of which there appears joy, peace, longsuffering, kindness, godliness, faithfulness, meekness, and self-control.

The Seed is incorruptible. Agape enters our person in the form of the incorruptible Seed (see 1 Peter 1:22-23). Once the DNA is set, it cannot be changed. The Seed has remained the same in all of redemptive history in spite of the efforts of Satan to kill or corrupt it. The new creation and God's eternal purpose were established before the foundation of the world and are totally dependent on the Eternal Seed. Consequently, God gave us Himself, in the person of Christ, and that Seed of the Kingdom is uncreated, eternal, incorruptible, and unshakable. Thus, Peter says, *"But the word of the Lord endures forever"* (1 Peter 1:25).

While teaching in a prison one time, something significant happened in me. As I looked at the 60 prisoners in the room, I felt deep internal compassion moving my insides for these men. The Greek word for compassion is *splagchnon,* meaning bowels or to feel deeply, viscerally, or yearn. I felt my deep inner person move uncontrollably with *Agape* for them. This is the same love that came to us in imperishable and incorruptible Seed form when we were born again. This is what Scripture means by *"Christ lives in me"* (Gal. 2:20). The Seed is God's DNA brought to us in Jesus' incarnation and then inseminated in us when we *received* Christ, and it seeks to grow in us so He can express Himself to a hurting world.

Thoughts and Questions

- How is *Agape* an incorruptible Seed?
- What are some of the characteristics of the *Agape* Seed growing in you and your family?
- In what ways is the new creation and God's eternal purposes dependent upon the Eternal Seed?

READING 6

Cultivating the Seed in Ourselves

*And those sown on the good (well-adapted) soil are the ones who hear the
Word and receive and accept and welcome it and bear fruit—some thirty
times as much as was sown, some sixty times as much, and some [even] a
hundred times as much* (Mark 4:20 AMP).

MARK understood the principle of Kingdom fruitfulness. Cultivating
the Seed of *Agape* in ourselves involves three measurable steps.

First, we discover the internal desire to do others good. We were created
for good works (see Eph. 2:10). Our activities and responses, however, are not
human "works" but a fulfillment of that which was spoken of our Lord Jesus
Christ:

> *God anointed and consecrated Jesus of Nazareth with the [Holy]
> Spirit and with strength and ability and power; how He went
> about doing good and, in particular, curing all who were harassed
> and oppressed by [the power of] the devil, for God was with Him*
> (Acts 10:38 AMP).

When we recognize and respond to the Holy Spirit's promptings to do
good, however elementary and immature our response, we are on our way to
bringing forth the fruit of the Kingdom. Our good works are not the result
of our own human effort but the cooperation and expression of the Eternal
Seed of the Kingdom. When we respond to the Eternal Seed, our human
spirit comes alive, and we become one with the giving, resurrected Christ who
dwells within us.

Then we recognize that this desire does not originate within ourselves but is the result of the insemination of *Agape* as the Eternal Seed received at our new birth. When we soak ourselves in the water of God's Word, we nourish and strengthen our ability to see, hear, respond, and obey the promptings of the Holy Spirit. Paul's admonition was that those who are led by the Spirit are God's maturing children *"bearing fruit in every good work and steadily growing and increasing in and by the knowledge of God"* (Col. 1:10 AMP). As we respond to and obey the promptings of the Holy Spirit, we cultivate the Eternal Seed, and as it grows, it crowds out every other seed that is not *Agape*.

Finally, we seek opportunities or occasions to do others good. This is not religious effort but an expression of the new life within us. Doing others good involves spontaneity and risk, and the results are pure joy. Following Jesus involves seeking occasions and opportunities to give expression to others of that great and unlimited love that has entered our own life by means of the new birth.

It is important to grasp that we are now becoming who we already are: sons and daughters of the living God. This is living in the prophetic perfect, which we will look at next.

Thoughts and Questions

- In what ways can you see the three measurable steps in your own life?
- How can we know we are maturing and producing fruit?
- What is one of the ways we cultivate or nourish the Eternal Seed in ourselves?

READING 7

Prophetic Perfect

Even as [in His love] He chose us [actually picked us out for Himself as His own] in Christ before the foundation of the world, that we should be holy (consecrated and set apart for Him) and blameless in His sight, even above reproach, before Him in love (Ephesians 1:4 AMP).

ONLY the eternal, uncreated, omnipotent, and omniscient God has the capacity and willingness to declare a thing to be what it is years before it has even come into being. The Seed is God's inheritance in the form of the prophetic perfect. God speaks of the future as if it were already in the present and declares something complete because it is anchored in the *certainty* of God's intention to bring it to fulfillment. The results are well over the horizon, so we cannot see them yet. This is another way of saying, *"bringing many sons to glory"* (Heb. 2:10). There are many prophetic perfect statements in Scripture, such as, *"For the Lord has created a new thing in the earth"* (Jer. 31:22, 31-34).

God's confidence is in His ability to bring His own purpose into being. Because He knows the end from the beginning, He calls that which is naught as though it is. We can better understand the coming of the Kingdom as seen in Matthew 5-7 in this light. These chapters describe what we will be like when the Kingdom Seed has been cultivated and is fruitful in our own lives. Often travail is necessary to bring forth God's purposes (see Gal. 4:19; Rev. 12:2; Rom. 8:22). He knows what we will look like when He is done with us, and He speaks the prophetic perfect into each of us. We may not be able to see it yet, but we do see Him. Living in the prophetic perfect requires us to

36

see through rather than *look at* circumstances, because whatever God wants to do in us is already achieved.

The Eternal Seed falls into this prophetic perfect category. God's confidence is in His ability to bring His own purposes into being. Jesus told us that if we followed Him into His Kingdom, we would look like Him when we got there. We cannot make ourselves loving, but He can. He does so by means of imparting to us His nature in the form of *Agape* as the Eternal Seed.

Success is in generational transfer; it is not just what you can do but what you can get others to accomplish. We are to cultivate the *Agape* Seed in our own backyard and in the nations of the world. Jesus said He accomplished the work that the Father gave Him to do (see John 17:4). I always thought that was the crucifixion, but it primarily had to do with delivering the 11 disciples from their own *Eros* and bringing them into the governing principles of the Kingdom. The entire chapter of John 17 is Jesus praying for the 11 disciples. Jesus was going away, and everything depended on them. The disciples were His success or His generational transfer, and He spoke the prophetic perfect into their lives. *The Eternal Seed is destined to bring forth a disciple, not a convert.* Conformity to the image of God's Son is not inevitable; it takes cultivation in us and in others. Even when we can't see it, God is faithful to fulfill His Word.

Learning to cultivate, nourish, and prophetically speak to the Seed and call it forth into all God intended is what makes us farmers.

Thoughts and Questions

🌱 Explain how living in the prophetic perfect requires us to *see through* rather than *look at*.

🌱 Why does it take cultivation to be conformed into the image of God's Son?

🌱 How does the prophetic perfect result in generational transfer?

READING 8

Cultivating the Seed in Others

Your new life is not like your old life. Your old birth came from mortal sperm;
your new birth comes from God's living Word. Just think: a life
conceived by God himself! (1 Peter 1:23 TM)

THE Seed is eternal and incorruptible when it is inseminated into our person at our new birth in Christ. When the Seed permeates our deepest person and personality, something begins to happen because the Eternal Seed contains the mystery of the Kingdom. We do not know how God does it—that is a mystery—but something begins to grow. Our confidence is in the fact that He is the one who causes the Seed to sprout in each one of us. Remember, the nature of the Seed is that it produces after its kind; the Seed is eternal, and it produces eternal life.

We have a responsibility as Kingdom gardeners to bring forth God's inheritance. One evening after several days of intense ministry, I got on a plane to come home and did not want to talk to anybody, not even God. As I sat there, I felt mean, tired, and exhausted. It was a three-hour flight, and the plane was half-empty, so I prayed, "Please don't let anybody sit next to me." Down the aisle comes a young woman who chooses the seat right next to me. After we took off, I turned to her and said somewhat prophetically, "You used to know the Lord, but you're not walking with Him now." She burst into tears! We talked a long time, and I was able to minister to the Seed that had been inseminated into her person. When we see the incorruptible, imperishable, Eternal Seed, confidence begins to rise because we are called to be cultivators or farmers. We have been given the responsibility and capacity to water, nourish, guard, and speak edification and comfort to the person in whom the Seed has been inseminated.

Jesus, in His priestly prayer (see John 17), knew the importance of praying for the Seed as part of personal care. He was earnestly praying for the disciples because everything was resting on them. Judith and I have four children. Although we were far from perfect parents, all of our children, their mates, and our grandchildren are serving God. The sole reason is that we learned early how to pray for the Seed *in* them. We would pray over our children while they were sleeping, "There is a Seed in this daughter of ours. In Jesus' name, let it live!" And we would water it with our tears, knowing that it was eternal and incorruptible.

It is important to understand that all ministry is Seed cultivation. It roots back into the opportunity for God to reveal Himself as He is through you. We are cultivatable and can be cultivated to fruitfulness. Learn to cultivate the Seed in your rebellious son, your wayward daughter, a business deal, or the elder in your church who is such a pain. Tears are good fertilizer! Before long, the concrete sidewalk over the Seed begins to crack, and you will see the signs of it in your son or daughter. Suddenly the plant sprouts up and your daughter says, "Mom, I feel like I've really been unkind lately. Forgive me?" and we can say, "You're forgiven!" Take your eyes off the person and start interceding for and cultivating the Seed. When it starts to break through, they may not know what's happening, but we do because the power is in the Seed, not in the person!

Thoughts and Questions

- Why does something begin to happen in us when the Eternal Seed is implanted?

- Explain the importance of praying for the Seed as part personal care and edification.

- What are some ways we can cultivate the Seed in our children?

Bad Fruit

So every good tree bears good fruit, but the bad tree bears bad fruit.
A good tree cannot produce bad fruit, nor can a bad tree
produce good fruit (Matthew 7:17-18).

ONE of God's first instructions after He created the earth was *"be fruitful and multiply"* (Gen. 1:28). He expected seed to bear after its kind and bring forth life. *Agape* is not a gift; it is a fruit. Fruit is the result of the Eternal Seed that has been planted, cultivated, and brought to maturity in us. He planted His *Agape* Seed in us at our new birth, expects it to grow, and holds us responsible for the watering and nourishment of that Seed. *Agape* cannot be imitated or manufactured; it is something we learn and practice. We are instructed to *keep* ourselves in the *Agape* of God (see Jude 21). This is something we have to continually practice and cultivate so we have something of God's Seed to give to a hurting world. Fruit is a product of righteousness that is sown in peace (see James 3:17-18). No one is excluded from the expectation of producing fruit. The Kingdom is given to those who will bring forth the fruit of that Kingdom.

In Greek, the word for bad fruit is *porne,* meaning to take hold of someone in such a way as to do them injury. *Bad fruit* is described in Hosea 10:13, *"You have plowed wickedness, you have reaped injustice, you have eaten the fruit of lies. Because you have trusted in your way..."*. Bad fruit is when our life or testimony does injury or harm to ourselves, our neighbor, and Father's reputation in the earth. Bad fruit is a result of something inside us that has been twisted by *Eros.* We can eat the bad fruit of our own way and be satiated with our own devices (see Prov. 1:31) for many years. Absence of good fruit leaves a vacuum in which religious and ascetic behavior can flourish. Paul strongly encouraged us to *"not participate in the unfruitful deeds of darkness, but instead even expose them"* (Eph. 5:11).

Many people think anger is bad fruit, but anger is not the real issue; it is our response to anger that reveals the fruit. I remember checking into a hotel where I was to speak the next morning. The hotel did not give me the right room, and frankly, I was angry. One of the hotel staff got on the elevator as I was going up to my room, and I was so wrapped up in myself that I responded harshly to her. I have done this with my children, with my friends, and with people I've pastored. This was undeniable evidence of bad fruit in my life—no excuses and no shifting blame. The reality is that when bad fruit appears, we are accountable to ourselves and to the King and His Kingdom. Father has to show us how to expose unfruitful deeds of darkness and what it means to walk in light so we actually treat people with *Agape* even when we are irritated. This process begins with repentance. Jesus must take us out of *Eros* and teach us how to walk differently, which requires a reformation of our whole person. Freedom is walking into Light.

Thoughts and Questions

- Why is *Agape* not a gift but a fruit?
- What are some results of bad fruit?
- Describe how bad fruit has affected your own life.

Uncultivated Fruit

Is the seed still in the barn? (Haggai 2:19)

WHEN I was young, my dad took me to visit my grandfather. There was a lot of arguing between them, but I figured that was just how adults acted. Pork chops had been served for dinner, and there was one left on the plate in the middle of the table when an electrical storm hit and all the lights went out. In the dark, both my dad and my grandpa went for the last pork chop, but grandpa beat him to it and my dad ended up jabbing him in the back of his hand with his fork. Then, in my memory, all hell broke loose, my dad packed us up, and we went home. I assumed that because they were Christians they would act a certain way, so I was rather shocked that as soon as the lights went out *both of them acted in their own best interest.* I now understand that they had the Seed of God in them, but that Seed was essentially left uncultivated, so it never grew to the point of producing the fruit of *Agape*.

Uncultivated Seed is kept in the barn or under the clod (see Joel 1:17) rather than planted and never germinates. When the *Agape* seed remains uncultivated, it lays dormant in us. It has potential, rather than realization; theory, rather than experience; and doctrine in the place of fruit.

Unfruitful Seed falls into several categories: trampled, eaten by birds, withered because they had no roots, and choked by thorns (see Matt. 13:3-7). When seed is trampled on or eaten by birds, it cannot find soil deep enough to take root, or the soil is so shallow that is unsuitable to grow anything. The Seed can also be choked by thorns, meaning it is crowded out or overpowered by all kinds of legitimate things in our life. However, without fruit, we are considered useless and unproductive. One of the more frightening descriptions of being fruitless is: "...*men who are hidden reefs in your love feasts when they feast with you without fear, caring for themselves; clouds without water, carried along by winds; autumn trees without fruit, doubly dead, uprooted*" (Jude 12).

Most new believers with weak foundations or inadequate spiritual root systems have been battered beyond comprehension by inner voices and by God's own people using Scripture in an accusatory and condemning manner. Psychological techniques and the wrong use of Bible verses do not necessarily bring harmony, and neither are they able to effectively repair something in disarray. The Seed may yet be in the barn and not have experienced the necessary planting, death, and resurrection that releases the life of *Agape*.

Not all conflict we experience is about us; much of it surrounds the Seed that has been inseminated within us. The growing process can be painful as fruit is birthed (see John 16:20-21). This process is critical because the whole creation (see Rom. 8:19-21) is waiting for the *Agape* Seed to come to birth in us.

Thoughts and Questions

- Describe what it means to have uncultivated seed lying dormant in you.
- Why are we useless without fruit?
- Is there any unfruitful Seed in your life that Father is asking you to cultivate?

Good Fruit

Other [seed] fell on the good soil and yielded a crop, some a hundredfold, some sixty, and some thirty (Matthew 13:8).

IN spite of adversity and inherent dangers, some seed does manage to grow and conquer *in this present life*—some 30, some 60 and some 100-fold. Thirty-fold is considered fruitful and 60-fold very fruitful. It is seed bearing after its kind. This kind of fruitfulness is what it means by the verse *"you will know them by their fruits"* (Matt. 7:16). Hundredfold fruit can be seen in the fruit of the Spirit, which is love, joy, peace, patience, kindness, goodness, faithfulness, gentleness, and self-control (see Gal. 5:22-23). Peter told us that if these qualities are yours and are increasing, they render you neither useless nor unfruitful in the true knowledge of our Lord Jesus Christ (see 2 Peter 1:8).

Reaping good fruit requires time, cultivation, and weeding. God puts various people in our lives to help cultivate the seed. Paul said, *"I planted, Apollos watered, but God was causing the growth"* (1 Cor. 3:6). We must let the Seed grow on its own accord; we cannot demand or expect fruit before its season (see Mark 11:13).

God designed repentance to make room for *Agape* to grow (see Matt. 3:8). It is repentance that allows us to move toward being perfect (*telios*), meaning complete and fruitful in the manner in which the Creator intended. *Fruit is Agape, and Agape is behavioral.* Good fruit fulfills the whole law and does no injury to another. If our behavior doesn't change, *Agape* is not being cultivated, so it is impossible to manifest good fruit. To be good farmers, we must *"be imitators of God [copy Him and follow His example], as well-beloved children [imitate their father]. And walk in love, [esteeming and delighting in one another] as Christ loved us and gave Himself up for us"* (Eph. 5:1-2 AMP). Note the three uses of *Agape* in these verses: well-beloved, walk in love, and Christ loved us. Jesus described the good fruit of *Agape* as feeding the hungry; giving water to the thirsty; welcoming, lodging, and entertaining the stranger; clothing the naked; giving help and ministering care to the sick; and visiting the prisoner—and doing so *as if we were doing it to Him* (see Matt. 25:34-40). It is evident that walking in *Agape* has to do with behavior, not doctrine; it changes the way we conduct our life, the way we speak to our family; it changes us on the inside.

As sons and daughters of the Kingdom, Father seeks to replicate His own love in His own people. The evidence of Christ-like behavior becomes the measurement or standard that we are of Christ and not engaged in some cultic or religious activity. *"You will fully know them by their fruits"* (Matt. 7:20). It is clear in the New Testament that the ultimate way in which a person or doctrine is to be measured is by the amount of fruit produced.

Thoughts and Questions

- How would you describe 100-fold fruit?
- Explain why fruit is *Agape* and *Agape* is behavioral.
- What is our job as sons and daughters of the Kingdom?

Givers and Takers

Do not merely look out for your own personal interests,
but also for the interests of others (Philippians 2:4).

THE most basic philosophy in all of life is the concept of givers and takers. Most people fall into one of two categories: we are either givers looking out for the interests of others as exemplified by our Lord Jesus or takers who only seek their own interests (see Phil. 2:21). These two effectively transcend all other categories of religion, race, caste systems, ethnicity, social standing, and education. Father is a giver, but the whole world *"lies in the power of the evil one"* (1 John 5:19). In the Garden, Eve was a taker—she sought her own interests, which resulted in the original sin of mankind. Fortunately, our Heavenly Father intervened on our behalf.

As we begin to mature spiritually, we are often a *mixture* of givers and takers, which is the source of untold conflict. The disciples were a tremendous mixture. John wanted Jesus to do whatever he asked of Him (see Mark 10:35). Most churches are serious mixtures. A friend of mine faithfully supported a church for 14 years and then finally decided it wasn't working anymore. He met with the pastor and told him that after much anguish and prayer, he decided to find another church. The pastor's only response was a total absence of relational integrity and *Agape*: "Don't you own the front end-loader outside? Could you finish the back-fill before you leave?"

Takers are full of *Eros*—they love for what they can get out of someone. "Good to see you, Greg! Do you still have your sailboat?" The moment he sells his sailboat, he isn't needed anymore. If our relationship is built on *Agape*, we love Greg regardless of whether the sailboat sells, sinks, or burns.

The Holy Spirit is unbelievably faithful to prompt us internally when we cease being a giver and start becoming a taker. Givers can be seen in these Scriptures:

> *Let no one seek his own good, but that of his neighbor* (1 Corinthians 10:24).

> *Just as I also please all men in all things, not seeking my own profit, but the profit of the many, that they may be saved* (1 Corinthians 10:33).

> *[Love] does not act unbecomingly; it does not seek its own, is not provoked, does not take into account a wrong suffered* (1 Corinthians 13:5).

> *I urged Titus to go, and sent the brother with him. Titus did not take any advantage of you, did he? Did we not conduct ourselves in the same spirit and walk in the same steps?* (2 Corinthians 12:18).

It requires the presence of *Agape*, which includes spontaneity and risk, for us to be transformed from a taker to a giver. The love of God is never our possession; it is God's—His love comes to us, then *through* us to a hurting world. If there is a logjam, it is in us. We love because He first loved us.

Thoughts and Questions

- Why was Eve's original sin an act of being a taker?
- Would you categorize yourself as a giver or a taker? Why?
- When someone has approached you as a taker, how did you feel?

READING 13

Bullets or Seeds

I'm after mercy, not religion (Matthew 9:13 TM).

DURING Bible college and seminary days, we were taught to recite Scripture like cowboys in a fast-draw contest: John 3:16; Romans 3:23; Ephesians 2:8-9. I made a painful discovery in my journey—wherever the most Scripture was preached, it seemed that I found the least amount of *Agape*! One day while watching the news, a reporter was interviewing a person in line to see the movie *The Last Temptation of Christ* when a middle-aged woman walked up to him. The camera swung around to capture a close up of her contorted face screaming, "If you go in that movie, you're going to hell!" Although I did not advocate the movie, this awful thought swept over me: I'd rather go to the movie with him than go to church with her!

As evangelicals, we have not been taught to listen; we have been taught the biblical fast draw. A man once said, "I quoted Scripture to my wife, and I didn't see her for two weeks—because my eyes were swollen shut." I hope that all of us have learned enough to not quote Scripture to our spouse and children! In the Gospels, the Pharisees always had their hands on their guns; Jesus had His in His bag of Seed.

The more Scripture we are taught without *Agape*, the more loaded guns we carry. We start with a BB gun, then we need a shotgun, and then our memory verses are like two pistols. Sheriffs that are more serious get a Glock® Nine with 14 rounds in the chamber so they can straighten out the world with Bible verses. When Jesus was being arrested in the Garden, Peter whipped out his sword, cutting off the soldier's ear. All of us have cut off a few ears in our time. I used memory verses like two pearl-handled six guns. Then the Lord asked me, "Are the Scriptures bullets or are they seeds?"

The answer to this question determines whether we see ourselves as a sheriff or a gardener. A sheriff tries to keep everybody straight; a gardener lets the tares and weeds grow with the wheat, allowing God to sort out the good from the worthless at harvest time. City dwellers demand tare-free fields, but farmers know this is not possible. Every church has tares. There is no pure church—just real church with real people and real problems. A sign in the doctor's office said, "Please do not exchange symptoms, it confuses the doctor." If you have three people attending church, you have six problems because they not only have their own problems, but they get together with others and combine problems to make new ones.

The church suffers badly from evangelical sheriffs. To the sheriff, judgment will be merciless because he has shown no mercy (see James 2:13). I have been the sheriff on too many occasions. We need government, but it must be tempered with mercy. Unfortunately, many new Christians who were recently filled with the love of God often encounter a church full of gun-slingers. If we could learn how to bless and not curse and allow our Bible verses to produce fruit in ourselves, we would soon learn to share the love of an eternal Father with a hurting world. God intends for us to be gardeners showing compassion and mercy.

Thoughts and Questions

- Have you been taught to memorize and recite Bible verses to hurting people? What was the result?

- Explain why we need to allow the weeds to grow with the wheat.

- Why would a sheriff want to see immediate change while a gardener would want to show mercy?

Transition From Sheriff to Gardener

He cuts off every branch of me that doesn't bear grapes. And every branch
that is grape-bearing he prunes back so it will bear even more
(John 15:2 TM).

I made my transition from a sheriff to a gardener when I learned that Father Himself is a Gardener, not a sheriff. Father reserves the pruning for Himself; He does not let anyone else prune. The Greek word for vinedresser is *georgos,* meaning a farmer or husbandman who tills the ground. Our Father is the Farmer, and He knows something about cultivating and drawing out the Seed. If we could surrender our sheriff's badge and turn in our ankle holsters for gardener's cultivating tools, we could effectively love those who are hurting. With God's help, we can learn to be farmers rather than sheriffs because our confidence is in the Seed of the Kingdom.

We are capable of being cultivated, and Father seeks to cultivate us so that we can be fruitful. If we have fruit, He seeks more fruit. We also have the capacity to do the cultivating; it is our personal commission. Our job as farmers is to cultivate and bring forth fruit in ourselves and in others and do so with truth and grace. If we attempt this as a sheriff with assumed authority, we make irrational judgments and cut people off. The bottom line question: Is the Bible an ammo pouch or a seed bag?

Luke 13:6-9 gives us a powerful parable of the importance of cultivation:

And He began telling this parable: "A man had a fig tree which
had been planted in his vineyard; and he came looking for fruit on
it and did not find any.

"And he said to the vineyard-keeper, 'Behold, for three years I have come looking for fruit on this fig tree without finding any. Cut it down! Why does it even use up the ground?' "And he answered and said to him, 'Let it alone, sir, for this year too, until I dig around it and put in fertilizer; and if it bears fruit next year, fine; but if not, cut it down.'"

If we approach this scenario as a sheriff, we would write down the names of the more challenging members of our church and transfer their membership to another state. God gives us some people to practice on, and as farmers we should say, "Oh, please don't cut it down yet. I know they have missed it. I also know they really do seek to follow Christ. Allow me to fertilize and water and give them another year to bear fruit." I appeal to you—dig around the tree and cultivate the seed rather than cut it down. Pray and intercede for others. With God's grace, fruit will emerge when our confidence is in the Eternal Seed.

God expects us to develop the capacity to bless, nourish, guard, and cultivate the Seed. He gives us the nine tools of the Gardener for cultivating Kingdom fruit:

1. *Scriptures*: God's love letter to His own Bride

2. *Prayer*: Returning God's affection in as pure a form as possible

3. *Church*: Mutual encouragement, breaking individuality, producing community

4. *Lord's Table*: Giving and receiving the Bread of God and the wine of forgiveness

5. *Deliverance*: Release from cyclical behavior and ungoverned desires

6. *Worship*: Declaring our love privately and corporately

7. *Forgiveness*: Freely receiving and giving unlimited forgiveness

8. *Fasting*: Humbling our soul by governing food, talk, and activity

9. *Abiding*: Resting in faith and keeping ourselves in the *Agape* of God

Thoughts and Questions

❦ Explain why Father is a Gardener rather than a sheriff.

❦ Why is it necessary to turn in our sheriff's badges for gardening tools?

❦ In what ways has your Gardener cultivated fruit in your life?

READING 15

Owners or Stewards

But those farmhands saw their chance. They rubbed their hands together in greed and said, "This is the heir! Let's kill him and have it all for ourselves" (Mark 12:7 TM).

THERE is a critical difference between a steward and an owner. Mark 12 tells a story about some vine growers who refused to give the fruit of cultivation to the landowner. They beat and killed every person the landowner sent, even his beloved son. These vine-growers were not the owners; they were only stewards, yet they acted as if they owned the vineyard.

When we are an owner, we think that just because we have first dibs on something, it is essentially ours. I go to the gym three days a week in the early morning and use a certain cardio machine—the second one on the first row. That is *my* machine. Just as I was getting into my ownership routine, a woman started getting there a few minutes ahead of me. Every morning, she was on *my* machine. The Lord put me through many changes over that until I began to see the subtle and demanding nature of ownership.

In church, ownership takes many forms, including sitting in the third pew on the left. All the regular churchgoers know that is your seat, so they choose to sit elsewhere. We know we are an owner when we get all bent out of shape if a visitor takes our assigned seat. I knew a man who was one of the most powerful worship leaders, but he owned it. One day, the Lord just lifted the anointing from him not because of overt sin but because he began to be an owner. We are called to be stewards, not owners. It is not our church or our people; it is His church and His people. It is not our parking place or our particular privilege.

Ownership can be seen in offices and titles (i.e. apostle, prophet, pastor, teacher). When someone goes by Apostle Smith or Prophet Jones, there is a good chance he or she feels some ownership of the position. Someone once introduced me as Dr. Mumford, and when I got up to speak I said, "I'm not a doctor. I'm not even a nurse." I was seeking to avoid illegal ownership. The minute we start owning anything or anyone, we have abandoned our call to be stewards.

Several years ago, we sent our son, Eric, into another country to build a family home for orphans. Once established, Eric appointed a steward to help oversee the work there. This steward slowly began to take ownership of the home. Once he felt he was the owner, he began to assassinate Eric's character by giving false reports to the media and social workers and eventually took Eric to court for custody of the children in the home. The social workers believed the media stories, and soon Eric was forced to abandon the work he started there. Essentially, this steward beat up our son and kicked him and his family out of the vineyard.[1]

We don't own our reputation, our occupation, or our children. As King-dom men and women, we are placed in these positions as stewards of Father's House. The moment we start seeking to own something, whether it's anoint-ing, title, ministry, or our kids, the life is squeezed out and God's *Agape* begins to dissipate. How do we know whether we are an owner or a steward? Just let God touch whatever we think we are stewarding. If the Lord gives it, He can take it.

Thoughts and Questions

- Describe the difference between an owner and a steward.
- In what ways have you experienced being an owner?
- What has God called you to steward? Can your stewardship be improved in any way?

ENDNOTE

1. For more on this principle, I recommend Eric's *Plumbline* entitled "Sonship Keeps Lifting Me," available through Lifechangers.

READING 16

Nine Seeds of *Agape*

We have come to know and have believed the Agape that God has for us
(1 John 4:16).

IT is personally amazing to me that John would instruct us to both "know that love" and learn to "believe that love." His next statement is, "God *is Agape.*" When known and believed, the following nine aspects of *Agape* become seeds that will begin to birth in us a new understanding of Christ and His Kingdom:

1. God is *Agape*, therefore, *Agape* is uncreated, eternal, and unshakable.

2. *Agape* is God. If we know and embrace *Agape*, then we know we are on the road that takes us to the Father, aligning us with His own nature.

3. The essence of the Kingdom is *Agape* applied in practical, everyday relationships with people. It is the Father's *Agape* being replicated in us.

4. The Kingdom—uncreated, eternal, and unshakable—is *Agape* in action. If we want the supernatural, this is the route. If we genuinely love people, Father will give us the supernatural to accomplish His own purposes.

5. *Agape* never fails or disappears because it is eternal; it is God's nature.

6. *Agape* is the solitary, epistemological evidence of our having embraced Christ.

7. *Agape*, in contrast to *Eros*, makes the definitive difference between being an owner and a steward. I know of nothing more serious in the body of Christ than seeking to own what belongs to God.

8. *Agape* alone, when cultivated and replicated, has the power and strength to restore and transform Father's *reputation* in the earth. We must pick up the burden to change the way God is perceived. He is the most maligned and falsely accused of all beings in the universe.

9. *Agape* is the solitary answer to Jesus' prayer that we would be one with the Father just as He is and that we would be made perfect so the world would know the Father (see John 17:21-26).

Thoughts and Questions

- In what ways do you *know and believe* the *Agape* God has for you?

- In your own words, explain the essence of the Kingdom.

- How have you found *Agape* to be the definitive difference between being an owner and a steward?

PART II

Journey to the Father

READING 17

Use of the Name

I AM has sent me to you (Exodus 3:14 AMP).

I AM is used 6,800 times in the Old Testament. It is a play on the verb *to be* and is essentially untranslatable. The best workable translation is, "I will become what I need to become in order to meet the needs of My people." The I AM is God revealing Himself in the Incarnation and becoming a Man in order to meet the needs of His people. Jesus referred to Himself as I AM at least eight times. He said, *"I AM the way, the truth, and the life," "I AM the good Shepherd,"* and *"Before Abraham was, I AM."* In the garden, the Roman guards were all knocked off their feet by His saying, *"I AM He."* The I AM is God in Christ, reconciling the world to Himself.

Because the name is above every name (see Phil. 2:9), it becomes the source of healing, deliverance, and release. Use of His name becomes a sign of the Kingdom, meaning its real presence, and an insight into the reason for its coming. Jesus requested that we go into all the earth to pray for the sick, cast out demons, and raise the dead in His Name. His intention is to bring a manifestation of Father's redemptive nature to those who are yet in bondage to alien forces (see Acts 10:38).

For several years, the Lord instructed me on how to minister using the power of His name—the I AM. On one occasion, a hurting mother asked me whether her child could be healed. The Lord had told her that if Bob Mumford said her daughter could be healed, He would give her the faith for it. As she asked me this, I had not yet laid eyes on the child. I stood there and asked the Father, who is the I AM, what His response was to this woman's request.

I had a clear impression that He had spoken to her, so I said, "Yes, your child can be healed. The Father wants you to have confidence in His nature." She went back to her husband and got the 4-year-old child and brought her to me. She had strong physical evidence of Down's syndrome. When I saw her, it shook me because I did not want to make a false promise. I took the little girl in my arms and said to the child and the mother, "I commend you to God the Father and Jesus Christ His Son, who is the expression of the I AM. His purpose and nature is that we should be well and whole." I put the little girl down, and she ran back to her dad.

The following year, I spoke at the same conference and had totally forgotten about the instance. After one of the meetings, the mother walked up with the little girl, and I recognized her. Her facial features and ability to speak were 90 percent healed. The mother told me she was no longer in special education. The I AM had manifested Himself to this child, her mother, and me, proving that He wants to be what we need Him to be in the real situations of life.

I challenge you to begin to think about an increased perception and use of the Name. Hurting people need the name as the expression of God's love because *Agape* is the route to the supernatural.

Thoughts and Questions

- What does I AM, the name of God mean?
- What are some other uses of I AM in Scripture?
- In what ways can you see the name as an expression of God's love?

The Name of Christ

Therefore let the whole house of Israel recognize beyond all doubt and acknowledge assuredly that God has made Him both Lord and Christ (the Messiah)—this Jesus Whom you crucified (Acts 2:36 AMP).

WHEN Jesus was given a human name, its significance meant, "God Saves." His name includes every aspect of our life—physical, mental, spiritual, and emotional. Hastings Dictionary makes some important comments on the name:

> To know God's Name or declare His Name is to know or declare His character, His Person, i.e. all that is known of Him. To call upon His name signifies worship as He is revealed (compassionate and gracious, slow to anger, and abounding in lovingkindness and truth; who keeps loving-kindness for thousands, who forgives iniquity, transgression and sin). The Name of Christ means our willingness and determination to offer worship to Christ as He is self-revealed, i.e., only begotten of the Father. Christ's Name represents the total revelation of God to man.
>
> To be gathered in His name signifies our uniting with Him in a common attitude to Himself and to His Person as revealed in His life, death and resurrection.[1]

Jesus said, *"For wherever two or three are gathered (drawn together as My followers) in (into) My name, there I AM in the midst of them"* (Matt. 18:20

AMP). The use of the name I AM is the source of our union and cohesion. When we learn to see through, our capacity to perceive His Presence in our gatherings and participate in the benefits of getting to know Him and each other are dramatically increased.

I have a friend named Charles who does not like to be called Charlie. While talking with a mutual friend, the man referred to Charles and said, "Oh, I know Charlie well!" Immediately I knew that he did not know Charles very well at all; he was only name dropping. We do this with God all the time—we say we know Him but do not understand His preferences; fail to grasp His purpose; and repeatedly misrepresent Him. Like Paul, our desperate prayer is that I might know Him. As we come to know Him, we are more perceptive of His nature and intentions. When the spiritual or perceptive person uses the name "Jesus," you are aware that he really does know the Person he is speaking of.

The Scriptures have two different words for knowing. The first is objective knowledge, which includes the facts or circumstances surrounding the issue or person. For example, we know Don Shula was the coach of the Miami Dolphins, but we may not personally know him. The second is a more sophisticated form of knowing, one that is spiritual and subjective. In the high priestly prayer, John identifies spiritual and objective knowing as *"eternal life: [it means] to know (to perceive, recognize, become acquainted with, and understand) You, the only true and real God, and [likewise] to know Him, Jesus [as the] Christ (the Anointed One, the Messiah), Whom You have sent"* (John 17:3 AMP).

Thoughts and Questions

- ❦ Why do you think it is important not to use the name carelessly?

- ❦ How have you seen people using the name in a name-dropping manner?

 In what ways do you perceive, recognize, and understand the name?

ENDNOTE

1. Hatings, James, *A Dictionary of the Bible,* Vol. 4, (Charles Scribner's Sons, New York, NY. 1902) Pg. 489.

READING 19

Jesus' Personal Preference

Have this attitude in yourselves which was also in Christ Jesus, who, although He existed in the form of God, did not regard equality with God a thing to be grasped, but emptied Himself, taking the form of a bond-servant, and being made in the likeness of men. Being found in appearance as a man, He humbled Himself by becoming obedient to the point of death, even death on a cross (Phil. 2:5-8).

IT never entered my mind that Jesus would have a personal preference, but He did and intentionally set it aside. Gethsemane was an unqualified surrender of His preference and a serious embrace of Father's will. His surrender of personal preference can also be detected in His statement in John:

> *For I have come down from heaven not to do My own will and purpose but to do the will and purpose of Him Who sent Me. And this is the will of Him Who sent Me, that I should not lose any of all that He has given Me, but that I should give new life and raise [them all] up at the last day"* (John 6:38–39 AMP).

Jesus starts with the fact that no one can come to Him unless the Father draws him, which is a delightful Kingdom principle of surrender of personal preference. It can be summarized like this: *I am here to do Father's will. He is the one who draws people to me. If I did not particularly like that person, it would not matter, for I did not come to do my own will but the will of Him who sent me. I will not cast out or reject anyone on my personal preference, but I will hold you as a steward of Father's purpose and raise you up on that last day.* Think of this principle in terms of prisoners and addicts who have done some very ugly things. Learning that Father is the one who has drawn them and that Jesus, and consequently those of us who have surrendered our personal preference, will not reject them.

Henry Blackaby, in *Experiencing God*, says that walking with God means finding out where He is going and going with Him. That is seeking first His Kingdom (see Matt. 6:33) and is motion and direction. When Peter made the choice (personal preference) toward self-preservation, he could not expect more than he could ask or think. The moment Peter's personal preference was God's Kingdom, he experienced an *Agape* conversion. *"When you are converted,"* Jesus says to Peter, *"strengthen your brothers"* (Luke 22:32). Self-preservation is the curse of the Church.

We are simply unable to take God's yoke or seek His Kingdom without first surrendering personal preference, because when His Kingdom comes, our kingdom is terminated. Although the term "will" has been denigrated and shopworn, it still means personal preference. I would prefer a Buick rather than a Volkswagen. So, when the Lord gives me a Volkswagen, He is looking for is a proper response—to set my *Agape* on Him and learn to love it as Father's gift to me. Such a response frees the Father to give and bless and do whatever He wants because I am honestly learning to love what He loves. Surrender of personal preference is radical Christianity. It is nothing less than a serious attempt to follow Jesus, doing what He did and acting in a similar manner and for the same reasons!

Thoughts and Questions

- 🐝 Find other occasions in Scripture when Jesus gave up His own personal preference.
- 🐝 Describe how important this concept is to those who have been rejected.
- 🐝 Why is surrender of personal preference radical Christianity?

READING 20

Re-Laying Our Foundations

Therefore let us go on and get past the elementary stage in the teachings and doctrine of Christ (the Messiah), advancing steadily toward the completeness and perfection that belong to spiritual maturity. Let us not again be laying the foundation of repentance and abandonment of dead works (dead formalism) and of the faith [by which you turned] to God (Heb. 6:1 AMP).

A S a medic in the Navy, I was on duty late one night at a hospital when a middle-aged officer came in the sick bay hemorrhaging from the nose. At first, the medical doctor on duty and I thought a simple nose bleed couldn't be much of a problem. However, we were not able to stop the bleeding. Finally, it became so serious that we gave him two pints of whole blood and called for an emergency ear, nose, and throat surgeon. Before they took him into emergency surgery, I sat talking with him by his bed trying to keep his spirits up. After a while he said, "This is not fatal, is it?" In my ignorance I said, "Ahh, you can't die of a nose bleed. In just a little while we'll have this fixed up. It can't be anything that serious." Meanwhile, he continued to hemorrhage down his throat and out his nose while the surgical specialists were working on him. A very rare aneurysm in the artery behind the nose had ruptured, causing his life blood to pump out of him. As I sat with him, I watched him turn white and die.

The church is called to be both priest and physician—to sit at the bedside of a very sick patient—our nation and other nations. However, the Church is as sick as the patient. We are unaware of how serious the hemorrhaging is; we flippantly think that no one can die of a nosebleed. Hurting nations need to know if the doctor can help. We know that as goes the Church, so goes the nation. My urgent concern is to present the *Agape* paradigm as the needed remedy to that which is self-referential and self-serving in the Church so we can bring cessation to the hemorrhage.

Elizabeth Kubler Ross, in her book *On Death and Dying*, wrote about the five progressive stages of dying: denial, anger, bargaining, depression, and acceptance. As a nation, what stage do you think we are in? It seems most people, including believers, are incapable of facing the ugly reality. If the Church has so lost its Kingdom agenda as to present itself as a rubber crutch and unable to provide real and workable answers, then we are headed toward great disillusion and offense. In order to bring healing to a hurting nation, it is essential that we become established in the clear foundation of the uncreated and eternal Gospel of the Kingdom. We must be certain that we know who He is and cultivate an unshakeable relationship with Him.

Jesus said to the disciples, *"You are already clean because of the word which I have spoken to you"* (John 15:3). Peter was on the rooftop when he saw a vision of a sheet full of all kinds of animals and creatures being lowered from the sky. Twice a voice said to him, *"What God has cleansed, no longer consider unholy"* (Acts 10:15; 11:9). What God was communicating was the need of faith alone, Christ alone, and Scripture alone as the means of our salvation. Our foundation can be built on nothing less than *Agape* alone. It is our only hope to stop the hemorrhage and heal the patient.

Thoughts and Questions

- In what ways can you see a hurting world hemorrhaging and the Church without answers?
- Why is it essential that we become established in a foundation of faith?
- If you struggle with guilt, consider taking a hard look at your foundation of faith.

READING 21

The Way, Truth, and Life

I am the way, and the truth, and the life;
no one comes to the Father but through Me (John 14:6).

J ESUS' job description is to lead us into an intimate love relationship with God. At the same time, the Father is reaching for us through His Son, Jesus Christ. Ponder for a moment an inconceivable thought—God Himself passionately desires an intimate relationship with each of us! The path that leads to an open connection with God is called the *Agape* road. It is a path of

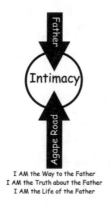

I AM the Way to the Father
I AM the Truth about the Father
I AM the Life of the Father

love He laid out to bring us to Himself, one that Jesus pioneered during His earthly life. He invites us to journey this path to knowing and loving God as Father, but the choice is ours. It is important to understand that heaven is not the goal. If you are a Christian and you die, you have to go to heaven; there is no place else to go! The goal is knowing the Father Himself.

When we choose to follow Jesus and we give our hearts to Him, we *do* experience some intimacy with God. However, it is often sporadic and inconsistent. Let me illustrate this from my own life. I was sitting on my back porch when I heard God clearly say to me, *I want you to love Me with all your heart, soul, mind, and strength, and I want you to love others. This will require spontaneity and risk.*

The more I thought about God asking me to love others, the more I felt resentment, discomfort, and anger. I felt it was unfair for God to ask me to do what I could not do and, really, did not even want to do! I believed I might be able to love God—but not His kids! *I was simply too immature to know how to receive or give love on God's terms.* Without realizing it, I was initially attracted to God as Father because I wanted to use Him for my own comfort and success. Essentially, I wanted Him to do what I wanted, not have a free hand to do what He wanted with me.

When you think about this, it summarizes most people's initial experience with God. As I began to realize how much of my prayer life was centered on getting things from God, I was devastated. I found that I did not even know how to pray without attempting to *control* God. When my prayer life crashed, I took a pendulum swing to the other extreme and became afraid that if I really loved God and opened to Him, He would send me to some forgotten backwater to rot. In an effort to please Him, I basically lied to Him. I vowed, committed, and promised what I knew I could not give Him—my whole heart. Like Adam and Eve in the Garden of Eden, I ran, hid, and shifted blame—the essence of sin. Eventually, discouragement made me feel like Peter who said to the Lord, *"Depart from me for I am a sinful man"* (Luke 5:8 AMP). But Jesus was faithful to take me up the *Agape* road, where I found the grace to say, *"Abide with me, for I am a sinful man."*

When God tells us to love, the *ability* to give and receive love begins to grow. As we discover our *real* motives and attitudes and come to terms with the "real" us, Jesus will begin to walk us up the *Agape* road toward genuine love.

Thoughts and Questions

- In what ways has your intimacy with God been sporadic or interrupted?

- How do you feel about developing an intimate relationship with God?

- In what ways are your prayers aimed at getting God to do what you want?

How God Wants To Be Known

The Lord, the Lord God, compassionate and gracious, slow to anger, and abounding in lovingkindness and truth; who keeps lovingkindness for thousands, who forgives iniquity, transgression and sin (Exodus 34:6-7).

BECAUSE God is a Spirit, we cannot see or know Him unless He chooses to reveal Himself. God once let Moses see part of Himself. Moses had asked to see God's glory, which would be to see all of who God is. God explained to Moses that anyone who saw all of His glory would die. What a way to go! However, He let Moses see a specific aspect of His glory that He most wanted us to know (see Ex. 33:12-34:7).

What God showed Moses was the essence or the very heart of His *character.* I like to call this *God's DNA.* DNA (deoxyribonucleic acid) is the material inside the nucleus of all living cells that carries genetic information. It inexorably predetermines the physical, mental, and personality characteristics of offspring. God's DNA determines everything He does and contains the code to understanding who He is. God could have shown Moses His power and greatness, but He wanted Him to know the deepest part of His heart— the "real" Him.

If you want to truly know and understand who God is, then become familiar with these seven strands of God's DNA:

- Compassion
- Grace
- Slow to anger

- Mercy
- Truth
- Faithfulness
- Forgiveness of iniquity, transgression, and sin.

Our journey up the *Agape* road means being willing to be transformed by God's DNA until it becomes our DNA. One of the most difficult things about God's DNA is learning to receive and enjoy it. Our nature wants to earn, perform, and do religious things to gain His blessing because in our religious activity, we are really trying to control Him. My primary goal in writing this book is to increase your capacity to receive the love of God, to expand your experience in loving Him, and to see His love for others cultivated in you. We all have ideas about how we want God to love us—I challenge you to allow God to love you *the way He wants to!*

Christ came as a living picture of God's DNA. The only way the world can see God's hidden nature or what He is actually like is in a living person, Jesus Christ. In this age, the only visible repository of that DNA is in His people who have learned to walk the *Agape* road.

Thoughts and Questions

- When Moses asked to see God's glory, what do you think he was expecting?
- When we speak of seeing God's glory today, what do you think we mean by that?
- How do you think God expresses His DNA toward you?

God's Personality

The Lord is compassionate and gracious, slow to anger and
abounding in lovingkindness (Psalm 103:8).

L ET'S look more closely at the seven aspects of God's personality.

Compassion is the quality of understanding the suffering and weakness of others and wanting to do something about it. Compassion is more than pity or empathy; it is an inward affection and tender mercy. The Greek word from which compassion is derived means literally "from the bowels," denoting the seat of emotions, inner parts, or belly. It is a visceral heart reaction.[1]

Graciousness or *grace* is the very source of understanding God's person. It means to find favor, kindly, friendly, benevolent, courteous, disposed to show or dispense grace and forgive offenses, and to impart unmerited blessings. In the Bible, it is usually used of God in His relationship to the sins and shortcoming of humanity.

Slow to anger (longsuffering) is fortitude, forbearance, or patience. It means it really takes strenuous effort to get God ticked off! Most of us think God as edgy and slightly irritated with the way we mess up, hence our continual need to apologize for every little misstep. Few distortions of God's person are as pervasive, subtle, or numbing as this one.

Mercy is tenderness of heart and actions in which God looks past what is wrong in us and treats us better than we deserve. The Hebrew word is *hesed,* which means loving-kindness, steadfast love, loyalty, and faithfulness. It is compassion or forgiveness shown toward an enemy or person in one's power. Mercy is compassion in action.

Truth is conformity with fact or reality. The word also implies that which can be trusted to be steady and unchanging. Jesus said He is the Truth (see John 14:6). Truth is a person—one who shows us ultimate reality and can always be trusted to be the same.

Faithfulness is fixed, determined love, to be kept, guarded, watched over, and preserved. It is steadfastness, firm adherence to truth and duty, true to the facts or the original, allegiance, careful to observe all compacts, treaties, contracts, or vows, true to one's word. Faithfulness means that God will always do what He said and fulfill what He promised. This is a kind of faithfulness that does not come from a feeling but from God's determination to stick by us no matter what. He was so serious about it that He swore an oath and gave us His word that He would never change (see Heb. 6:13-20). Therefore, He has no choice but to show us mercy!

Forgiving means pardoning, remitting, disposed to forgive, and inclined to overlook offense, mild, merciful, and compassionate as a forgiving temperament. God pardons us when He could and should give judgment. God, as Father, took care of all our failures in His Son, Jesus. God forgives because it is His character. He forgives *iniquity, transgression,* and *sin,* which include every kind of sin—not only what we do but even who we are.

These seven things are not what Father God *does* but *who He is.* Receiving the Father as He is self-revealed and *wants* to be known is the first step on the *Agape* road.

Thoughts and Questions

- How has Jesus shown Himself to you as having God's nature?

- Think of someone who has hurt or offended you, and write a prayer using these qualities.

🐝 Describe how your relationships might be changed if these were practiced.

ENDNOTE

1. Ryken, L., Wilhoit, J., Longman, T., Duriez, C., Penney, D., and Reid, D. G. (2000, c1998). *Dictionary of Biblical Imagery* (elec. ed.) (424). Downers Grove, IL: InterVarsity Press.

READING 24

Jesus, Revealer of God's Glory

The Word became flesh and blood, and moved into the neighborhood. We saw the glory with our own eyes, the one-of-a-kind glory, like Father, like Son, generous inside and out, true from start to finish (John 1:14 TM).

JESUS plainly stated, *"Anyone who has seen Me has seen the Father"* (John 14:9 AMP). He came as *Agape* in the flesh for the express purpose of showing us what the Father is like. Hebrews tells us He was *"the radiance of His glory, the exact representation of His character"* (Heb. 1:3). Remember the

Compassion
Gracious
Slow to Anger
Mercy
Truth
Faithful
Forgiving

seven aspects of God's glory from our last session. Experiencing this glory leads us to knowing the Father the way He wants to be known. Jesus, as the Lord of the glory (see 1 Cor. 2:8), along with the Holy Spirit, takes on the task of teaching us how to continually walk in God's glory by leading us the way He went—up the *Agape* road.

This is what Jesus meant when He said that if we follow Him, He will take us to the Father. God's glory, as it was shown to Moses on the mountain, is revealed by every action and word of Jesus. When we see Jesus in the Gospels, we see God's compassion, grace, mercy, truth, faithfulness, and forgiveness walking and talking on the earth.

A son represents his father's name. If one of my boys was causing trouble or acting up, they would say, "Oh, that's Mumford's son," because he was connected with my name! Sometimes children act the way they do, both good and bad, simply because they carry their parents' DNA. That can be scary or comforting depending on the circumstances. Jesus did what He did because He carried His Father's DNA.

Every time we pray for someone in Jesus' name, we should be expressing at least one of His seven character traits. Ministry to others cannot happen without loving them with one of the seven aspects of God's glory because *Agape* must find a way to reach hurting people. God is *Agape* (see 1 John 4:16) and just as He chose to love the world through Jesus, He now desires to love the world through us! He gave us His Name (His reputation) and His glory (see John 17:22) for us to represent Him. When we use the authority of Jesus' name to pray for people, we are applying His DNA in our everyday lives.

Therefore, when the Bible says, *"all have sinned and fall short of the glory of God"* (Romans 3:23), it is not primarily referring to doing bad things. It is failing, neglecting, refusing, or perhaps even being ignorant of doing what we were created to do— to reflect God's glory, His DNA.

Thoughts and Questions

- ❦ Think of three or four incidents where Jesus demonstrated one of the seven characteristics of God's glory in what He did or said.

- ❦ With all seven aspects of God's DNA in mind, how might you specifically reveal God's glory to your family and those you encounter every day?

- ❦ Explain how our falling short of the glory of God hinders God reaching a hurting world.

READING 25

The Old Testament Seed of God's Glory

And their eyes were opened. And Jesus earnestly and sternly charged them, see that you let no one know about this (Matthew 9:30).

IN order to receive the major theme of God's glory in the Old and New Testaments, we must have spiritual eyes and an open heart. Once our eyes are open to the manner in which Father has chosen to make His glory known, the Scriptures come alive and life takes on new dimensions because glory and *Agape* work synergistically.

We know that God's glory consists of His hidden attributes: compassion; graciousness; slow to anger; mercy; truth; covenantal faithfulness; forgiveness. For whatever reason, this unfolding of His person has not been understood as the content of His glory. These hidden attributes can only be revealed to a hurting world by means of you and me. He has chosen to reveal Himself through His own people. We are His letters, known and read of all men (see 2 Cor. 3:2). It is by the replication of His *Agape* that we are identified as sons of the Father.

Christ shared His Glory with us, but we need to make a careful distinction between the attributes of God that are intended to be communicated for the purpose of restoring the image of God in man as contrasted with the attributes of God that were never designed to be given to man, such as uncreated, omnipotent, omniscient, and eternal.

It is difficult to express in some languages the concept of he also shared his glory with them. This may be expressed as "he gave them part of his majesty," "he gave them some of the wonderfulness which he had,' or 'he caused them to be glorious in some way similar to the way he is glorious."[1]

God's glory in the Old and New Testaments is formed in us in a progressive pattern as shown in this diagram. In Numbers 14:21, Israel had trans-

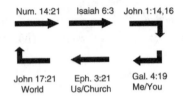

gressed badly, and defeat and embarrassment had come because they had "come short of God's glory." In that circumstance and climate of failure, God states His intention with an oath: "as I live, all the earth shall be filled with the glory of the Lord." He uses the phrase "as I live" 26 times in the Old Testament. Similarly, in Isaiah, Israel has failed badly and transgressed the covenant, and King Uzziah had died. In the midst of failure comes Father's similar declaration regarding His glory: *"Holy, Holy, Holy, is the Lord of hosts, the whole earth is full of His glory"* (Isaiah 6:3).[2] His eternal purpose is still in the process of being settled, and we progress toward the birth of Christ, of whom it is said in John 1:14, *"We beheld His glory."* This glory resident in Christ is imparted to us through the mysterious Seed.

Thoughts and Questions

- ☙ What does "He also shared His glory with them" mean to you?
- ☙ In what ways can you see God's glory as progressive through the Old Testament?
- ☙ In the remaining Scriptures in the diagram, how can you see the progression of God's glory?

ENDNOTE

1. Romans 8:30: Newman, B. M., and Nida, E. A. (1994). *A handbook on Paul's letter to the Romans*. UBS Handbook Series, (169). New York: United Bible Societies.

2. Among 194 uses of "glory" in the Old Testament; compare Deuteronomy 5:24, Psalm 8:5, Isaiah 60:1, and Daniel 7:14

READING 26

Jesus, the Seed of God's Glory

He is the sole expression of the glory of God [the Light-being, the out-raying or radiance of the divine], and He is the perfect imprint and very image of [God's] nature (Hebrews 1:3 AMP).

THE Seed of God's glory is waiting to be brought to maturity in us in the same manner as Christ saying: *"If you have seen Me, you have seen the Father"* (John 14:9). God came to us in Christ—Immanuel, God with us. Paul acknowledges this when he said, *"God was in Christ, reconciling the world to Himself"* (2 Cor. 5:19). Christ can only be understood as *Agape* incarnate because God is *Agape* and chose to incarnate Himself in His Son. We can see the progression of glory in the New Testament in the following Scriptures:

- Ephesians 1:17—*He is the Father of glory.* He came Himself to allow His Glory to be seen.

- 1 Corinthians 2:8—*He is the Lord of the glory.* The original language and the commentaries state the phrase "the Lord of the glory." This means Christ's primary job description is that of restoring and establishing God's glory in the earth. He was given the responsibility to see that the glory of the Lord is revealed and fills heaven and earth.

- 2 Corinthians 4:3—The *knowledge* of that glory is hidden from those who are lost. This changes and affects our approach to evangelism and counseling as well as how we relate to those who have turned away from God.

- 2 Corinthians 4:6—The *knowledge* of the glory of God is in the face of Christ. In John 1:14 we beheld His glory, and in Luke 9:32, we saw His glory. God is coming into view. We are getting to know Him as He promised.

- Romans 3:23—*All men have come short of the glory.* When we fail to live our lives out of the nature of God, the world cannot see His glory.

- James 2:1—*The Lord who is the glory.* It is God's glory that changes us deep inside.

- Hebrews 2:10—*Many sons to glory.* The new birth, the coming of the Holy Spirit, and the insemination of *Agape* that is brought to maturity carry the glory of God. When this Gospel of the Kingdom is proclaimed and cultivated, the end result is the glory of God.

We are increasingly able to see that God's glory is a refreshing new route to personal holiness (see 1 Cor.10:31; Eph. 1:18). In everything we do and say, in how we make decisions or what we wear or where we go, we must include one or more of the seven aspects of God's own nature. This is His glory. It is His nature being revealed in us, and our lives are to be given to making God's glory known in the earth. As the Seed of God's glory begins to grow in us, we experience a change in our *center*—from me and mine to a passion to see His glory fill the earth. This affects our family, work, and social relationships because our actions are motivated and overflowing with God's nature and person.

Thoughts and Questions

- Have you seen any change in your life due to the Seed of God's glory?

- What were the circumstances in your life before the change?

- Why do you think the Seed of God's glory changes something in our center?

Born of God's Seed

For you have been born again not of seed which is perishable but
imperishable, that is, through the living and enduring word of God
(1 Peter 1:23).

T HE Seed has the power to produce after its kind. Just as Jesus carried
the Father's DNA, so should we. Jesus lived a life of *Agape* because of
God's DNA. A more careful reading of this passage regarding the Eternal
Seed is helpful:

> *Since by your obedience to the Truth through the [Holy] Spirit*
> *you have purified your hearts for the sincere affection of the breth-*
> *ren, [see that you] love one another fervently from a pure heart.*
> *You have been regenerated (born again), not from a mortal origin*
> *(seed, sperm), but from one that is immortal by the ever living and*
> *lasting Word of God. For all flesh (mankind) is like grass, and all*
> *its glory (honor) like [the] flower of grass. The grass withers and*
> *the flower drops off* (1 Peter 1:22-24 AMP).

Peter's appeal is love (*Agape*) for one another due to the reception of the
eternal, incorruptible Seed that was given to us at the time of our new birth.
This incorruptible Seed must produce *"fruit after its kind"* according to the
laws of creation in Genesis.

The Word of God is Christ incarnate, who gave Himself in life, death,
burial, resurrection, and ascension so the Eternal Seed could come in spiritual
form: *"May Christ through your faith [actually] dwell (settle down, abide, make*
His permanent home) in your hearts! May you be rooted deep in love and founded

securely on love" (Eph. 3:17). When Christ is fully formed in our person, as Paul prays in Galatians 4:19, we discover that the Eternal Seed produces the fruit of *Agape*—love, joy, and peace (see Gal. 5:22-23). Father has provided Himself "sons unto glory"—men and women who are able to display His glory as the seven aspects of His DNA. It is the Father's intent that just as Jesus carried His DNA, so should we.

Thoughts and Questions

- In what ways can you see Peter's appeal for *Agape* in this Scripture?
- At what point does the Eternal Seed begin to produce fruit?
- Why is it important for us to be "sons unto glory"?

PART III

Eros and *Agape*

Profound Contrasts

Most of all, love each other as if your life depended on it. Love makes up for practically anything (1 Peter 4:8 TM).

IN order to better understand God's *Agape,* which is the Eternal Seed, we must grasp its opposite—*Eros.* In 1984, I picked up a book entitled *Eros and Agape* by Anders Nygren.[1] It was beyond my understanding, but the Lord kept sending me back to it, so I struggled through it about five times. Finally, I found this list, and I have never recovered. This is not the latest fad but basic Christianity. These are a little heady, but please do not run from them. We need to see that the contrast between *Eros* and *Agape* are two different worlds and two different kingdoms. The essential difference restores us to biblical experience and the Kingdom of God.

Eros is acquisitive desire and longing.	*Agape* is sacrificial giving.
Eros is an upward movement.	*Agape* comes down.
Eros is man's way to God.	*Agape* is God's way to man.
Eros is man's effort: it assumes that man's salvation is his own work.	*Agape* is God's grace: salvation is the word of divine love.

Eros is egocentric love, a form of self-assertion of the highest, noblest, and sublimest kind.	*Agape* is unselfish love, it "seeketh not its own," and it gives itself away.
Eros seeks to gain its life, a life divine, immortalized.	*Agape* lives the life of God, therefore dares to "lose it."
Eros is the will to get and possess, which depends on want and need.	*Agape* is freedom in giving, which depends on wealth and plenty.
Eros is primarily *man's* love; God is the *object* of *Eros*. Even when it is attributed to God, *Eros* is patterned on human love.	*Agape* is primarily *God's* love; God *is Agape*. Even when it is attributed to man, *Agape* is patterned on divine love.
Eros is determined by the quality, the beauty and worth, of its object; it is not spontaneous, but "evoked," and "motivated."	*Agape* is sovereign in relation to its object and is directed to both "the evil and the good"; it is spontaneous, "overflowing," and "unmotivated."
Eros recognizes value in its object—and loves it.	*Agape* loves—and *creates value* in its object.

The contrasts between *Eros* and *Agape* are profound. The fact that *Eros* is always acquisitive, desiring, and longing is the origin of the word *erotic*. *Agape* is born in the will, not in the beauty of the person. *Eros* always seeks to climb up in some illegal way (see John 10:1). This describes much of Christianity. *Agape* is the Kingdom of God coming down to us (see Rev. 21:2). The egocentric nature of *Eros* is sophisticated and refined, while *Agape* is unselfish love and gives itself away. *Eros* says if there is one piece of pie left, let's fight over it. *Agape* says that if my Father did not have it, He would gladly make it for you. There simply are no limits to God's Eternal Seed.

Thoughts and Questions

- In your view, why is this list representative of basic Christianity?
- Which comparison stands out to you the most? Why?
- How has *Agape* created value in you?

Endnote

1. From *Agape and Eros* by Anders Nygren. Louisville, KY: Westminster Press, p. 210

Governing Our Desire

And particularly those who walk after the flesh and indulge in the lust of polluting passion and scorn and despise authority. Presumptuous [and] daring [self-willed and self-loving creatures]! They scoff at and revile dignitaries (glorious ones) without trembling (2 Peter 2:10 AMP).

A T the original transgression, *Eros* entered in the form of ungoverned desire. The righteousness, peace, and joy of the Kingdom depend on how well we govern our desires. It seems to progress like this: Religion, apart from Christ, teaches that all *desire* must be denied and slain. Christ, however, says that *desire* is both good and bad; He can convert and govern it (see Rom. 8:5; Gal. 5:16; Phil. 2:13). What governs our *desire* determines our conduct.

Agape controls us. The *governing* factor of *Agape* is the freedom that He promised. Until and unless we begin to *govern our desires*, including the wild ones, we cannot understand or walk in Kingdom freedom. Peter's denial of our Lord came out of ungoverned desire.

We are created in God's image, which includes the human emotion of desire in its intense form: passion. There was, in the creation, the liberation or release of some innate and created human energy or force that has been, up to the moment of the original temptation, *directed and docile.* When desire is awakened by whatever cause, its energy or sheer force has the strength to cause the *intentions* of the human will to bend. This yielding of the will meets the demands of desire and passion, good or bad. Jesus, as *Agape* Incarnate, is the embodiment of God's Own desire. Christ's desire was totally centered on God as His Father. In life, as in temptation and in other crises, Jesus held His love for God and doing Father's will as His governing desire. In this consistency, we can see His sinlessness; tempted in all manner, He was without sin.

We must consider the fact that even when human desire can be turned to earthiness, sensuality, and animal-like behavior, or its radical opposite as fanatical religious zeal, it still retains the *quintessence* of the highest mystery of human existence. Man's desire, even when distorted and misused, is the seal of God's creation, His image in man. Passion, then, cannot and must not be killed or eliminated; it must be redeemed and redirected by having been taken through the cross. Remember, the alternative to passion is to find ourselves *without passion*, or more commonly known as apathy. Oswald Chambers says that "the bedrock of Christianity is personal, *passionate* devotion to the Lord Jesus."[1] Passion is one of the most pivotal issues in the Christian experience.

"Now those who belong to Christ Jesus have crucified the flesh with its **passions** *and* **desires**" (Gal. 5:24). It is important to see the flesh as the *Eros* aspect of self-will. Desire and passion follow what is governing us—either *Agape* or *Eros*.

Thoughts and Questions

- Why do you think righteousness, peace, and joy depend on how well we govern our desires?

- Read Romans 8:5, Galatians 5:16, and Philippians 2:13. How can God convert and govern our desire and thus affect our behavior?

- Desire and passion follow what is governing us. Identify some of the things you are passionate about.

ENDNOTE

1. Chambers, Oswald. *My Utmost*, December 23.

READING 30

Sitting in Darkness

People sitting out their lives in the dark saw a huge light; sitting in that dark, dark country of death, they watched the sun come up
(Matthew 4:16 TM).

EROS is darkness. Iis spiritual, but it has been grossly misunderstood and misapplied. Most people think they are living in the light while people at a biker bar are living in darkness because the bar is dark, their motorcycle is dark, and they wear dark clothes. Darkness can be defined as: *every living individual has one consuming interest—one's self as a living individual.* When we start turning in on ourselves, there is a form of darkness, which is exceedingly subtle and very spiritual, becoming the one consuming thing in our lives. For example, when you got your high school yearbook, whose picture did you try to find first? Yourself, of course! That happened to us in the fall—we turned in on ourselves, and darkness became something we love.

One time I was in the depths of a cavern way down in the earth. When they shut the lights off for a few moments, you could actually *feel* the darkness. Darkness is spiritual insensitivity to light (i.e., blind, deaf, obtuse, and resistant). It is an unrestrained animal impulse that includes compulsive and addictive behavior, including addiction to food. The DNA of darkness is a desire to possess, acquire, and control. We want to possess our children, control our home and work, and acquire a safe future. This all sounds "normal," but that is not the Kingdom; our motivation is often born out of *Eros.*

Stubbornness is probably the earliest symptom of darkness. Many of us could acknowledge that we are more stubborn than we intend or desire. Jesus said, *"We love [Agape] darkness rather than light because our deeds are evil"* (John 3:19). For years, I thought that meant we love alcohol, shooting heroin, or prostitution. That is not the darkness we are talking about; spiritual darkness is something every one of us loves. The prophet Isaiah warned the Israelites about light being turned into darkness: *"Woe to those who call evil good, and good evil; who substitute darkness for light and light for darkness; who substitute bitter for sweet, and sweet for bitter!"* (Isa. 5:20).

"God is Light, and in Him there is no darkness at all" (1 John 1:5). This is how far light is separated from darkness. In our day, a lot of gray prevails. Light becomes increasingly lighter, while darkness becomes increasingly darker. You may have faith and say, "I don't live in darkness; I'm a Christian!" That, however, is making the issue doctrinal; Jesus made it *behavioral* by demonstrating the Father's nature and giving Himself to betrayal. Father is asking us to make *Agape* behavioral as well, saying if we walk in the Light as He Himself is in the Light, we have fellowship with one another (see 1 John 1:7). The issue is not whether you have light in your mind but whether you have light in your behavior, which produces good fruit.

Thoughts and Questions

- How would you define darkness?
- In what ways is the desire to possess, acquire, and control a form of darkness?
- Why is walking in light (*Agape*) considered behavioral?

Reading 31

Insights into Darkness

Then watch out that the light in you is not darkness (Luke 11:35).

THE DNA of darkness begins with the seed of *Eros*, and it has a phenomenal ability to transform every law into its own agenda. It captures Christ, the Gospel, and His Kingdom and uses it for its own advantage. Religion is outer darkness and strangely enough, includes many forms of Christianity. Over the next two sessions, we will study a list of 12 points of darkness, along with my own comments. This list is from George MacDonald,[1] the man who discipled C. S. Lewis, and it describes spiritual and behavioral darkness. It is important that we understand these principles of darkness because we all act upon them without even being aware of it. You will notice that darkness does not include substance abuse, beating up grandmothers, or robbing banks, but it is still behavioral. I am asking you not to run or hide from this list because I am about to show you how much darkness we continue to embrace. When I saw this in my own life, I had no idea how deep it went, and I am confident that you don't either. I have divided the 12 points into two sessions because the strength and magnitude of spiritual darkness disallows us from absorbing all of these in one session.

1. *I am my own. I am my own king and my own subject.* This is a direct, unadulterated declaration of self-sufficiency, contradicting the clear instruction that we should not live unto ourselves (see 2 Cor. 5:15). This is an *Eros* prison.

2. *I am the center from which go out my thoughts.* Centering upon ourselves is in direct contrast to our new center, which is Christ

and His Kingdom. Our ego-centered thought process breaks spirit control.

3. *I am the object and the end of my thoughts; back upon me as the alpha and omega of life, my thoughts return.* Darkness causes our heart and emotions to completely turn in upon ourselves in an unavoidable and inexorable way, leaving us without hope of finding our way out of our own self-made prison with bars stronger than iron.

4. *My own glory is and ought to be my chief care.* Glory as the motivation of life becomes distorted and perverted when our own glory is the intended goal.

5. *My ambition is to gather the regards of men to the one center.* The false center of number 2 reappears, demanding and commanding that we be the center of attention. Personality cults reveal consummate darkness.

6. *My pleasure is my pleasure.* Pleasure (Greek: *hedonism*) turns us in upon ourselves, effectively destroying permanent pleasure and joy by the law of diminishing returns. Darkness reasserts itself with an increased vengeance and tyranny.

Take some time and allow these to sink in. Understanding how much darkness we are actually in is the first step to walking in light.

Thoughts and Questions

- Explain why darkness is usually considered external behavior.
- Why would being the object and end of our own thoughts be a prison?
- In what ways have you lived a lifestyle of hedonism?

ENDNOTE

1. *Creation in Christ*, Geo. MacDonald, Kingship, pg 140. Creation in Christ by George MacDonald edited by Rolland Hein © 1976. Harold Shaw Publishers, Wheaton, IL.

Reading 32

Further Insights into Darkness

Then watch out that the light in you is not darkness (Luke 11:35).

FOLLOWING is the continuation of the list of 12 points of spiritual and behavioral darkness by George MacDonald.[1] It is important that we really grasp these because we all act upon them without even being aware of it. Understanding how much darkness we are actually in is the first step to walking in light.

7. *My kingdom is as many as I can bring to acknowledge my greatness over them.* Every small country dictator who rises to power illustrates this form of spiritual darkness. The small country may be a family, local church, or a denomination, but the principles are the same—illegal extension of authority. The moment a personality is illegally extended for the purpose of controlling others, it robs what belongs to Jesus Christ. Darkness creates and maintains the smallest kingdom possible—me, myself, and I. Jesus said failure to die to ourselves would cause us to be alone—all alone.

8. *My judgment is the faultless rule of things.* One of the more complex and difficult problems in society today is instantaneous experts. While people may be gifted, many are unqualified, untested, erratic, and self-centered, with arrogant, non-negotiable, and subjective opinions. Self-deception reveals itself as a most frightening form of personal darkness.

9. *My rights are what I desire.* Being right is the most obvious basis for serious offense and relational breakdowns. Marriages are

destroyed by both partners' determination to be right. Defense, extension, and projection of our rights reveal the hidden darkness—being right, being recognized, and being first. This darkness is more than ugly; it is relationally destructive.

10. *The more I am all in all to myself, the greater I am.* Someone said that originality is unrecognized plagiarism. We often take the credit for something that was given to us. We are all far more dependent upon each other than we recognize or acknowledge. Darkness exhibited as self-deception requires massive, impenetrable defense mechanisms.

11. *The less I acknowledge debt or obligation to another, the more I close my eyes to the fact that I did not make myself; the more self-sufficing I feel or imagine myself, the greater I am.* This is self-deception and consummate darkness. To think that we are right within our own sphere when we are very deceived is most frightening. We cannot help someone who is self-deceived. The overwhelming purpose of darkness is to convince us of our own self-sufficiency. Acknowledging our debt or dependence upon others is belittling and diminishing.

12. *I will be free with the freedom that consists in doing whatever I am inclined to do, from whatever quarter may come the inclination. To do my own will so long as I feel anything to be my will is to be free, to live.* Rampant individualism, anarchy, and determination to go our own way and do our own thing are not new to human experience. However, when this phenomenon of personal freedom is latent with Bible verses and borrowed authority ("God said…"), the bright light of the Gospel is transformed into spiritual darkness that has both an imprisoning effect and one that distorts and twists the idea of freedom.

We cannot know the bright light of the Gospel without seeing how these affect our lives.

Thoughts and Questions

- ❦ Why are instantaneous experts a problem?
- ❦ Why are our rights a basis for serious offense and relational breakdowns?
- ❦ Explain why self-deception is like consummate darkness.

ENDNOTE

1. George MacDonald, *Creation in Christ, Kingship* (Harold Shaw Publishers, Wheaton, Il.) p. 140.

READING 33

Acting Against Myself

For Christ Agaped us and gave Himself for us (Ephesians 5:2 paraphrased).

WE are now able to recognize light and darkness. This may be far less complicated if we reduce light to desire for God and His Kingdom and darkness to desire for the right to ourselves. Darkness entered in the form of desire; Eve desired what had been prohibited. Acting against ourselves involves recognizing that our desires are often ungoverned. Paul stated, *"The love of Christ controls and urges and impels us"* (2 Cor. 5:1 AMP). Only *Agape* has the capacity and strength to enable us to govern our strong and unruly desires.

Christ acted against Himself by leaving His Father's throne, putting aside His resident splendor, taking on human form, suffering, and dying in our behalf. *Father acted against Himself* when He sent His Son, knowing that we would resist, reject, abuse, and mistreat Him. *God acted against Himself* so He could reveal His love for us. Paul, writing like a papa in Ephesians, is encouraging us to love as Christ loved by teaching us *how to act against ourselves.*

The divorce rate for Christians is the same as non-Christians because the church is nursed on the consummate idea that God's ultimate goal for us is to be happy, and if you are not happy, you should do something about it. When discipled in *Eros*, we are simply incapable of coming out of darkness. *Agape* alone expects and requires us to learn to act against ourselves, maturing to the point of being able to give ourselves away. We were buried in water so we are dead to the world and the world system; we are not our own, and we are not the center of the universe.

I am appealing for an *Agape* reformation that begins by learning to act against ourselves (see Matt. 16:24-25). In spite of all the people coming to Christ in these days, it is entirely possible that apart from a resurgence of a reformational release of *Agape* imparted and released in the larger church, we could possibly enter a new Dark Ages. Another 80 million believers just like the first 80 million will not make much difference if we do not know how to act against ourselves.

In order to act against ourselves, we must make a preferential choice. We have to choose to go through the cross in order to continue to do what God asks of us. When we are ignorant of, misled about, or refuse God's rule in our lives, His Kingdom suffers. This is described as coming short of God's glory. We must abandon our competitive franchise mentality and learn how to act against ourselves so we can love, accept, and receive one another.

Acting against ourselves is a radical way to live the Christian life. It involves dying (see Rom. 6–8) to selfishness and intentionally choosing the welfare of others in everyday situations. This is termed: living for another. Like an eternal rain cycle that waters the mysterious Seed, we love because He first loved us. We cultivate and learn to walk in *Agape,* esteeming and delighting in one another. When we learn to act against ourselves, we walk out of the darkness that has controlled and dominated us into the freedom of light.

Thoughts and Questions

- In what ways have you been nursed on an *Eros/Agape* mixture?

- What does acting against yourself mean to you?

- Why is an *Agape* reformation of acting against ourselves needed in the Church today?

READING 34

Mouthful of Splinters

He has weakened my strength in the way; He has shortened my days
(Psalm 102:23).

M Y understanding of God's anointing has always approximated the idea of His imparting His strength, only to discover God's power is perfected in weakness (see 2 Cor. 12:9-10). Our own strength most often comes out of self-confidence, functioning as one of the more subtle and insidious enemies of God's purpose. We think that because we did something twice, we can now do it any time. "I started two churches; now I can start one anywhere."

The Lord has a way of shortening our days. This could be interpreted two ways. It could be that He shortened your work day and you can't do as much as you used to or He shortened the number of your days on earth, which is a veiled threat. A premature death would, of course, prevent us from Father's intended inheritance.

Jesus told us to beware when all men speak well of us (see Matt. 5:11). Jesus identified the inherent danger of a comfortable lifestyle as the cares of this age. This is darkness in another form. Father asks us to kiss the cross with joy even when it is painful because it is part of the process of being conformed to Christ's image. Kissing the cross is walking the *Agape* road where we are not on the right or on the left. We cannot identify completely with either side, so everybody seems dissatisfied with us. Having taken the third choice of following Jesus on the *Agape* road, we discover the Lord requiring that we act against ourselves. Kissing the cross with eagerness and affection causes us to wind up with a mouthful of splinters.

When we kiss the cross, we discover ourselves unable to take refuge in a single system of past truth that is based on any denomination. Truth is continually emphasized, clarified, and transformed; we just keep collecting it. Hopefully we have more truth today than we had last year. Because truth continues to come to the Church, we have to collect it and move on in God without rejecting or becoming imprisoned by our past or heritage. Our commitment is to His Person. Sometimes we have to trade our pearls—what we thought of as valuable—for truth. That process can be painful as we embrace it.

Seeing more clearly, loving more inclusively, and refusing to be captured by unwritten denominational rules will demand kissing the cross and ending up with a mouthful of splinters. When truth is foremost, we find ourselves loving, ministering, strengthening, and teaching the whole body of Christ. Only by kissing the cross and getting a mouthful of splinters can we find the answers for a hurting world.

Thoughts and Questions

- Explain what kissing the cross means to you.
- In what ways have you had to embrace the cross with eagerness and affection?
- Why would our search for truth require us to kiss the cross?

PART IV

Cup and Cross

Drinking the Cup

The cup that I drink you will drink (Mark 10:39 AMP).

A LL of us have embraced the redemptive act of Jesus, yet we remain ignorant of the *content* of His message. The cup represents the Father's wishes. His cross gives us the freedom from ourselves to be able to drink His cup. We must know how to act against ourselves in order to intentionally choose to do His will rather than our own.

As Jesus faced the crucifixion, His single purpose was to drink the entire cup the Father had given Him (see John 18:11) because His preferential choice and intentional purpose was to do the Father's will. Jesus *chose* to drink all of it because of His love for the Father. On the cross, He could have called twelve legions of angels who were waiting at His command, but He surrendered Himself into the hands of the Roman soldiers. No man could take His life, but He did have the authority and power to lay it down. He did so as an absolutely free, moral person who chose *Agape* as a lifestyle. Jesus was not a fatalist, nor a determinist; He believed in divine providence—*nothing could touch His life that had not passed through the Father's purpose.*

This principle is equally true in our own lives. When we are faced with circumstances of life, it requires our preferential choice of an *Agape* lifestyle. This is what it means to drink the cup, and sometimes it is almost more than we can bear. Drinking the cup is never coercive or forced upon us—it is the result of our *decision* to live an *Agape* lifestyle. Jesus' choosing to drink the whole cup was not for religious merit, asceticism, or stoic austerity. His only motive was His *Agape* for the Father: *"not My will, but [always] Yours be done"* (Luke 22:42 AMP).

The disciples thought they could drink the same cup, but Jesus said, *"Where I am going, you cannot come"* (John 13:33). At that point, they had developed neither the ability nor the capacity to drink the cup. Following Jesus means that His convictions, behavior, and choices must become our own. It was through this process of *Agape* being perfected in them that Jesus was able to say to His disciples, *"The cup that I drink you shall drink; and you shall be baptized with the baptism with which I am baptized."*

The early church displayed great acts of courage because they were living an *Agape* lifestyle. They, too, chose to drink the whole cup. Jesus never explains, defends, or justifies the Father's cup, He just says, "Drink it!" The cup is different for each of us, but most people out of immaturity and fear assume that by drinking the cup He is asking us to die of some horrible disease or to be martyred in Iraq. If we learn to be lead by *Agape*, we lose the fear of the Father's cup, knowing it is His pleasure. The result will be *Agape* perfected in us. Our confidence is in His nature—who He is. If we allow Him, Jesus will birth in us a desire to please the Father in such a way that we grow in our capacity and ability to drink the whole cup, take up our cross, and follow Him.

Thoughts and Questions

- Describe what the Father's cup means to you.
- Describe a time Father required you to drink the whole cup.
- In what ways can you see your capacity increasing to choose the cup?

Reading 36

Seven Giants

The land through which we went to spy it out is a land that devours its inhabitants. And all the people that we saw in it are men of great size (Numbers 13:32).

THERE were seven nations in the Old Testament who kept Israel out of the Promised Land (see Num. 13:28-29). They were literal giants to the people of Israel. Today, the shadow or type of internal and spiritual giants that oppose us from entering our own land of promises of righteousness, peace, and joy are what I call the Seven Giants:

- Look Good
- Feel Good
- Be Right
- Stay in Control
- Hidden Agenda
- Personal Advantage
- Remain Undisturbed[1]

These Seven Giants are able to confuse, hinder, put us to flight, and create desires and urges that cause conflict and injury within our marriages, families, friendships, and church relationships. After 50 years of ministry, I have seen more than my share of strife, discord, feuds, conflicts, quarrels, fighting, jealousy, coveting, envy, anger, etc. The source was not primarily demonic but the result of the effect of the Seven Giants. They are very efficient in keeping us from entering and enjoying the milk and honey of the Land of Promises.

Each of these Seven Giants is *really* bad. They are exceedingly effective, especially when we are forced to face them in various combinations. The Seven Giants are pure *Eros*. They are the instruments by which the *Eros* shift is implemented in a life, family, church, and an entire nation, eventually destroying an entire civilization.

These Seven Giants can exist quietly and appear subdued, but they are nonetheless very resilient, invasive, and dominant. Each of the Seven Giants functions in a synergistic manner, one adding strength and synergy to the next. They are illusive and increasingly insidious in their various groupings. The kingpin, *Stay in Control*, however, is the most dominant of all. The first three giants are motivations to possess and intimidate. When effectively exposed, the giant of control will begin to lose its strength. The last three giants are manifestations of the need to acquire or manipulate someone or something. As we set our love upon God, His love fills our entire person. As a result, we will find that each giant, with its synergistic companions, begins to lose its grip, freeing us to love God and one another. This is the meaning of *Agape* perfected.

QUESTIONS AND THOUGHTS

🕯 In what ways have you felt something holding you back from living a life of righteousness, peace, and joy?

🕯 Have you ever had to deal with a manipulative person? What was the outcome?

In what ways have you seen acquiring and manipulation in yourself?

ENDNOTE

1. The first four giants were discovered in a personal conversation with My Friend Daniel Tocchini. More information about the Seven Giants is included in *Agape Road*.

READING 37

The Cross Defeats the Giants

He stripped all the spiritual tyrants in the universe of their sham authority
at the cross and marched them naked through the streets
(Colossians 2:15 TM).

THE Seven Giants are a constant source of conflict. Listen to them one more time: Look Good, Feel Good, Be Right, Stay in Control, Personal Advantage, Hidden Agenda, and Remain Undisturbed. Every one of us has engaged these Seven Giants and been harassed and plagued by this *Eros*-driven personality. It is only by abiding in *Agape* that the cross can expose and defeat them. The cross is our preferential choice to act against ourselves; it is never imposed, coerced, or forced.

The complete fulfillment of God's purpose in our lives depends on our developing the skill of abiding. If we can consistently and without strain learn to abide in *Agape* in the presence of personal loss or personal gain (temptation comes both ways), God's purposes will begin to unfold in our lives. Embracing the cross means choosing Father's will and way rather than our own in a particular circumstance. This preferential choice results in brokenness, humility, and Christ-likeness. The effectiveness of the cross is revealed in our refusing to switch chairs when circumstances pressure us to satisfy one of the Giants. When we do switch chairs, it personally costs us, but the Church and the Kingdom also suffer. Christ paid the price for our *freedom* to live an *Agape* lifestyle.

The cross establishes Christ's government over our desires and releases *Agape* in our character. Apart from and in the absence of the cross, *Eros* simply reappears in religious forms and uses the Scriptures themselves to justify selfish behavior. *Eros* borrows the authority of God's name to satisfy one of the Seven Giants. When the giants are alive and well in us and everything in our mind tells us to do something, it requires faith to embrace the cross and act against ourselves. Without faith, it is impossible to please the Father. Unless God meets us and delivers us from *Eros* by means of the cup and the cross, we have both the potential and the capacity to be very *religious*. *Eros promises* freedom even while it holds us in total bondage (see 2 Peter 2:19). Only through following Jesus, embracing the cross, and drinking the cup of circumstances when it is offered can the struggle with the Seven Giants cease. It is Father's intent to bring the Eternal Seed in each of us to maturity, for where His Kingdom reigns, there is peace.

Thoughts and Questions

- How would you define the cross?
- What are three results of embracing the cross?
- What three factors are involved in defeating the giants?

READING 38

Offense of the Cross

"And blessed is he who does not take offense at Me" (Matthew 11:6).

MANY people think this verse refers to being persecuted for our biblical values or perhaps trying to walk straight in an ungodly world. The offense of the cross, however, goes two ways. Man is *offended that Father would dare make a person righteous by simply believing.* Father did this at the expense of His Son who became our righteousness. Christ's sacrifice is a gift. When we attempt to earn our righteousness, we dismiss Christ's sacrifice, which is an offense to God. When Paul says, *"I am not ashamed of the gospel"* (Rom. 1:16), he is saying that however religious we think we are, Father has made righteousness available through Christ. I, for one, believe that! It is the power of God.

Going Back Over the Line

Old Covenant · New Covenant

Birth of Jesus Christ · Destruction of Jerusalem

At the very moment when Jesus died on the cross, a new creation and a new race began. The Old Covenant ended, and the New Covenant began. Everything on the Old Covenant side of the kairos moment involved *works of the law to earn our righteousness,* but at that moment when Jesus took His last breath, righteousness suddenly became a gift. To many, this is an offense. If we had been orthodox Jews laboring our whole lives at being good and carefully keeping all the feasts, commandments, and food laws just as our forefathers did and then suddenly *none of it mattered* because it was all now a gift, we would be bent too! But, from the moment Jesus died, everything that was kept in obedience to the law was given as a gift. When we dismiss the New Covenant and what Christ did for us as not being enough righteousness and revert to the Old Covenant laws, we offend God.

Can you imagine the offense of orthodox Jews struggling for righteousness, hearing a Gentile say, "I am God's beloved son"? They would be more than offended; they would have killed for that because Gentiles were seen as heathen dogs. No wonder the Jews stoned Paul. We really are God's beloved sons and daughters! Some people have been waiting 40 years to get perfect enough to enjoy the Father. Their consciences tell them that they haven't quite fasted, prayed, read, or believed enough, but their consciences are contaminated and their confidence is off-center. Paul said, *"I do not nullify the grace of God, for if righteousness comes through the Law, then Christ died needlessly"* (Gal. 2:21). Refusing to believe that Christ's gift was enough to cover our contaminated conscience and make us completely clean and holy is an offense to God because He paid for that with His Son's death on the cross. Each of us must understand that it is Christ plus nothing.

Thoughts and Questions

- ❦ How would you explain the offense of the cross to someone?

- ❦ Can you say, "I am God's beloved son/daughter"? If you struggle with this statement, keep saying it aloud until you start believing it!

- ❦ In what way is your belief system nullifying your own supply of the grace of God?

Crossless Christianity

For many walk, of whom I often told you, and now tell you even weeping, that they are enemies of the cross of Christ (Philippians 3:18).

IT is possible to be an enemy of the cross but not be an enemy of Jesus Christ. Jesus is welcomed, loved, and exalted by many, for with Him comes *all of the benefits.* Why He insists on bringing His cross with Him is beyond their imagination. But the refusal to embrace His cross is an attempt to divide that which is indivisible—His cross and His Person.

"Keep your eye on those who cause dissensions and hindrances contrary to the teaching which you learned, and turn away from them" (Rom. 16:17). Paul said that men who create dissensions, difficulties, and divisions are slaves not of our Lord Jesus Christ but are captive in the *Eros* prison. With insidious progress, Christian believers become *enemies* of the cross and slaves of their own appetites, finding themselves serving their own interests and not the things of Jesus Christ (see Phil. 2:21).

Thus, we have arrived at a strange place—Crossless Christianity: *Believers who are not following Jesus.* In the absence of the cross, ungoverned passions and desires have regained their hold in the person's life. Crossless Christianity is not losing our salvation. It involves messing up the Gospel message by our self-willed determination to live this life and make this journey on our own terms and according to our own standards. Paul considers these people as enemies of the cross because they have no intention of ruling their own appetites, and neither is their intention to set their mind on the things of the Kingdom. Their goal is their sensual appetites, and their glory is their shame because they side with earthly things. It is like Jesus' words to Peter, "*Get behind me Satan! You are a stumbling block to me; for you are not setting your mind on God's interests, but man's*" (Matt. 16:23).

Crossless Christianity is a hybrid, misnomer, or distortion; it is something that should never have appeared on the scene. Paul says their loss is real, both in this life and in the age to come. However, like Peter, through the *Agape* conversion we become Kingdom citizens by following Jesus, drinking His cup, and embracing His cross. By waiting earnestly for Jesus, we can be formed and transformed into His image and glory. This is why there must be an *Agape* reformation to restore us to all that is biblically sound.

Thoughts and Questions

- Describe an enemy of the cross.
- In the absence of the cross, what do we experience?
- Describe a Kingdom citizen.

Adding to the Cross

For the story and message of the cross is sheer absurdity and folly to those who are perishing…, but to us who are being saved it is the [manifestation of] the power of God (1 Corinthians 1:18 AMP).

WHILE Crossless Christianity involves removing the cross, the other extreme is adding to it. Both modifications remove the power of the cross. Adding to the cross is to pack it with religious accoutrements for the purpose of watering down or releasing us from the demands of the cross rather than learning to act against ourselves. This is like implementing our own agenda by packing additional members on the Supreme Court, weakening the authority of the ruling administration and diluting its effectiveness.

The entire book of Hebrews addresses one basic problem: *adding something to Christ in order to fulfill the works of the law and be more perfect.* The Hebrew believers were grown adults in the church who still needed milk and to be taught the elementary principles of God when they should have been teachers (see Heb. 5:12-13). Likewise, the message of Galatians is not only about leaving or falling from Christ but the unspoken desire that to be righteous they needed Christ plus Moses. We make the Cross of Christ of no effect when we feel we have to keep the Law of Moses rather than rely on what Christ already did for us. Paul reprimanded the Galatians for this by saying, *"Are you foolish? Having begun by the Spirit, are you now being perfected by the flesh?"* (Gal. 3:3). It is the acts of adding to Christ which caused the apostle to say, *"…you have fallen from grace"* (Gal. 5:4).

Paul talks about *another Christ*, not the one he presents to them. This is the effect or the confusion of adding to the cross, diluting its message, and compromising its authority. He is jealous for the community to belong exclusively to the Lord Jesus Christ and His Kingdom. Abiding requires embracing a personal cross that is taken up daily.

Like the repeated failures recorded in Scripture, we are *incurable* at wanting to do things our own way. We start in the Spirit and then say, "Now I've got it. Thank You, Lord, I'll take it from here." What we are wrestling with is a mixture of two covenants—the Old and the New. We start off believing that everything Christ did was enough to make us holy and acceptable and our faith in Christ alone is adequate. Then religion worms its way back into our mind, pressing and demanding that we do something more than simply believe. Like the Galatian believers, we seek to absolutize everything that is external and become bewitched, responding to the religious expectations as if they had validity.

The cross of Christ is our redemption. When we add *anything* external to it, we have injured and compromised our journey. There is one absolute for the believer: it is Christ plus nothing.

Thoughts and Questions

- ❦ What is the basic theme in the book of Hebrews and Galatians?
- ❦ Why is the mixture of two covenants a problem?
- ❦ Explain how you have mixed the two covenants in your own life.

The Other Side of the Cross

You have been severed from Christ, you who are seeking to be justified by law; you have fallen from grace (Galatians 5:4).

IT is rather simplistic but extremely effective to see the cross as that which releases us from compulsive, controlling desire. Its release comes by bringing death to unruly desires. When we see *real ashes* as the result of the cross of Christ at work in our lives, we are beginning to see and live on the other side of the cross. The cross, as Father's instrument, does not disappear. It does, however, require that we take it off the chain around our neck and spiritually internalize it. When the cross of Christ is overly emphasized, it is strangely transformed into a religious weapon that is used to lacerate ourselves and oppress others. Through history, the Church has used the cross in a very manipulating manner. *Nothing* in all of human history, philosophy, religion, or psychology has the power and capacity to reveal hidden personal interests like the *internalized cross of Christ*. This is the hope of the world.

Even within the inner circle of Jesus' own disciples, *Eros* activities were manifested that would have destroyed His Kingdom intentions and Father's revealed purpose had they been left hidden and untouched. *Eros* uses personal interests that seem so innocent (see Phil. 2:21) to gain entrance. Controlling self-interest is revealed by His saying, "I go up to Jerusalem to die!" Like barbed wire, pride, malice, envy, competition, self-assertiveness, and self-confidence entangled themselves on those 12 unsuspecting disciples. We are misled if we think there is less of this going on in the Church now than was prevalent and manifested in that small, foundational, and carefully chosen group of men. The religious politics, human pride, and hidden but carefully planned agendas that rule our culture are just as powerful now as they were then. With what weapons do we engage and defeat these not-so-subtle enemies?

Jesus' cross is a *kairos* moment in time when everything that was darkness stopped and everything that is light began. When the earthly Jesus embraced death and resurrection, He gave us *the other side of the cross as reconciliation for the entire universe*. The other side of the cross seeks to point us to the completed purpose of God in the mystery of the incarnation.

Martin Luther could see the other side of the cross in his time. He observed that the cross was more than the individual person becoming justified but that in the cross, God as Creator would regain His rights over creation. In the cross and the resurrection there is "the juridical realization of God's rights to Lordship."[1] The internalized cross is the essence of the Kingdom of God whose nature is being displayed in us. His glory is in the cross. The cross is the testimony of Jesus, the spirit of prophecy. The Kingdom cannot appear until and unless we learn to act against ourselves as the direct result of having embraced the cross of Christ. One of the Church fathers said that the cross is to me what wings are to a bird. It is the essence of the Christian life.

Thoughts and Questions

- What happens when the cross is over emphasized?
- Why did Paul resolve to know nothing but the cross?
- Explain why apart from the cross people are capable of anything.

ENDNOTE

1. Jurgen Moltmann, *Theology of Hope: On the Ground and the Implications of a Christian Eschatology* (Harper and Row, New York, NY. 1967) p. 207

Water Baptism: A Kairos Moment

The Father has delivered and drawn us to Himself out of the control and the dominion of darkness and has transferred us into the kingdom of the Son of His love (Colossians 1:13 AMP).

ONE of the Greek words used for time is *kairos,* a particular time period that begins with an extremely important event. In this crucial historical event, God unveiled a dimension of His eternal purposes for us—He sent Christ to save us. The *kairos* moment came when Jesus died. It was a moment when something old died and something new began. Our kairos moment

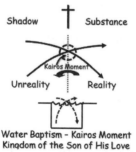

Water Baptism - Kairos Moment
Kingdom of the Son of His Love

first happens in water baptism as we take the journey from the kingdom of darkness to the Kingdom of the Son of God's Love. We do this in the prophetic perfect; Father declaring as *finished* that which has now been proclaimed and acted upon. At that moment, our old life dies and our new life in Christ begins. Jesus said, "follow Me" because He wanted to take us somewhere—from shadow or type of His intention to the very reality or substance of His intention so we could find ultimate reality, which is God as Father. Reality is *Agape,* the incarnate Christ being perfected in our internal human spirit. It is in that Kingdom reality that Christ is able to take us to His Father. Anything less than Christ is simply unable to do so.

It is this water of death (type of Noah's flood) that releases within and without the circumstantial events of the new birth. This is what takes us through the natural (that which is born of flesh is flesh) into the spiritual dimension (that which is born of the Spirit is Spirit), opening the natural eyes to see the Kingdom so it can be entered. The Kingdom dimension is where men and women seek to do God's will here on earth as it is in Heaven irrespective of the personal cost.

Only John teaches us the actual meaning of water baptism. He does so in Jesus' discourse with Nicodemus, whose faith was just being formed but not yet strong enough to allow him to make his leap of faith into the chaos of a public confession of Christ. Jesus explains the necessity of an *inward* new birth that produces the desire and motivation for us to move toward an *outward* and public identification with Jesus Christ and His Kingdom in the earth.

Water baptism is an act against ourselves. We are asking God to bury every personal desire that prevents us from identification with Christ so we can live in a new place of light and life. The preferential choice of water baptism is asking to be taken out of *Eros* and its darkness and brought into the Kingdom of His *Agape*. Light involves the ability *to act against ourselves* and results in freedom, which is our inheritance.

Thoughts and Questions

- Explain why water baptism is a kairos moment for each of us.
- When Jesus says "follow Me," where does He intend to take us?
- What is the purpose of water baptism?

Water Baptism—Changing Governments

I have been crucified with Christ; and it is no longer I who live, but Christ lives in me; and the life which I now live in the flesh I live by faith in the Son of God, who loved me and gave Himself up for me (Galatians 2:20).

THE first time I was water baptized, I was a sweaty little 10-year-old kid running the streets with a friend who was just as scrappy and scrawny as me. We happened upon a Baptist church having a baptismal service, and I said to my friend, "Wait here for me; I've got to go in and get baptized." I didn't really understand what I was doing because I didn't even know the Lord then. I was baptized fully clothed and ran out of the church soaking wet. I finally met the Lord two years later but was so unsure of my relationship with God that I would go forward for every call for salvation or water baptism just in case I may have missed something. I must have been saved and baptized three or four times just to make sure. Even at 12 years old, I had a deep desire for God to bury the internal contradictions that were going on in me.

In water baptism He takes us out of *Eros*, the kingdom of this world, and brings us into *Agape*, the government or Kingdom of His Son. These are two different kingdoms and two different forms of authority, each with totally different demands and expectations. Water baptism is moving from one government or kingdom to another, and the process changes at least five things for us:

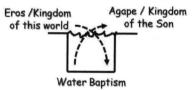

1. *Water baptism changes our yoke.* Jesus said, *"Take My yoke upon you and learn from Me, for I am gentle and humble in heart, and you will find rest for your souls. For My yoke is easy and My burden is light"* (Matt. 11:29-30). In water baptism we exchange the burden or yoke of *Eros* for the light and easy burden of *Agape*. The yoke of *Agape* is a custom made fit for each one of us.

2. *Water baptism changes our government.* We leave the government and control of darkness where we are taught to get, claim, and demand and begin to live under a government that insists on reality and God's love and where we are taught to give, believe, and receive.

3. *Water baptism changes the focus and object of our life* as we set our affection on the things above. When our affections are continually toward the Lord, we want to understand what He is doing.

4. *Water baptism changes the goal and purpose of our life.* Our purpose is not waiting to be raptured; it is God perfecting His *Agape* in us so we can love as He loves.

5. *Water baptism officially proclaims the beginning of our journey of following Him.*

If you have not been water baptized, I encourage you to make it a priority to find a place to do so. The act of transferring governments through water baptism is significant.

Thoughts and Questions

- What is the basic transaction that happens to us in water baptism?

- Describe the characteristics of the two different kingdoms.

- In what way does water baptism change the goal and purpose of our life?

Faith and Water Baptism

Giving thanks to the Father, who has qualified us to share in the inheritance of the saints in light. For He delivered us from the domain of darkness, and transferred us to the kingdom of His beloved Son (Colossians 1:12-13).

THIS sovereign King asks for two things: faith and water baptism. Faith is intellectual sacrifice in that we consciously choose to surrender to truth even when it does not make logical sense at the time. Faith is so constructed that it allows God's truth to remain just out of our reach so it cannot be manipulated or controlled. Faith is the coin of the Kingdom, and the Kingdom keeps on coming whether we like it or not. The sovereign King puts the Kingdom just out of our control and asks us to believe Him for it when we want to see it and hold it.

The sovereign King also asks for water baptism. Under certain circumstances, He seems to suspend this requirement, as seen in the thief on the cross. Water baptism is our personal permission, energized by the act of our will as a fallen sovereign, for God to de-create and re-create our inner person. It is the biblical route to preserve our childlikeness. Everything we are is buried in water, and we are recreated with His incorruptible Seed planted in us. Paul calls this the new creation emerging out of chaos because the old things have passed away and new things have come in the form of the Kingdom (see 2 Cor. 5:17). Nothing less than a complete death and resurrection can take us to the Kingdom of God. Our help must come from someone who understands who we are, what we have lost, and where we need to go. Through water baptism, we give God the freedom to take us where He wants us to go. He is our needed guide who we are to follow (see Heb. 4:14-16). Water baptism is the first step in our journey toward the perfection or maturity of *Agape* in us.

When God's DNA comes into our heart by faith as a result of the new birth and is followed by water baptism, we are inseminated with the incorruptible Kingdom Seed and we begin to see, taste, and smell the Kingdom. Water baptism is God's loving kiss of death. There is no other possible route to bring us out of the sheer strength of original sin, the *Eros* prison, and unreality. Father gives us Himself in the new birth, follows it with a request to bury all that is unreal, and then seals the entire transaction by an impartation of the Holy Spirit or what He identified as the promise of the Father so we could know Him.

Thoughts and Questions

- Why is faith a form of intellectual sacrifice?
- Describe your understanding of water baptism.
- Why is death and resurrection through water baptism necessary to enter the Kingdom?

Enemies of the Cross

For there are many, of whom I have often told you and now tell you even with tears, who walk (live) as enemies of the cross of Christ (the Anointed One) (Philippians 3:18 AMP).

PAUL was addressing Philippian believers who were probably very good and sincere Christians, but their goodness was based on religious performance rather than upon Christ's righteousness. It has always amazed me how we can receive the goodness of Christ and then, for whatever reason, become *enemies of the cross of Christ.* The Philippian believers relied on their own righteousness, which put them in direct opposition to the cross of Christ. Paul considered this a serious deviation because ultimately it harms both themselves and others. *Eros* rules in religion, and apart from a full and biblical application of the cross, the human person, saved or unsaved, is capable of the most horrendous deeds and actions. Church history bears witness to this ugly fact.

Paul said, *"For I resolved to know nothing (to be acquainted with nothing, to make a display of the knowledge of nothing, and to be conscious of nothing) among you except Jesus Christ (the Messiah) and Him crucified"* (1 Cor. 2:2 AMP). Paul was not seeking to abbreviate or minimize the Kingdom Gospel. He was saying that the cross of Christ must never be eliminated or neglected because all men, *apart from the cross,* are capable of anything and are determined to accomplish their own program "for God." Jesus, in a most subtle and almost unnoticed observation warned us about this: *"an hour is coming when whoever kills you will think and claim that he has offered service to God. And they will do this because they have not known the Father or Me"* (John 16:2-3 AMP). Very simply, apart from the restraint and expectations of the cross, men are capable of any act, including murder, for religious purposes!

When we do not know the Father or the principles of His Kingdom, we cannot understand what Christ did for us on the cross. In our ignorance, we proceed in self-will and arrogance, often in the name of God. Only when we embrace and internalize the cross of Christ can we expose and ultimately slay the seven *Eros* giants.

The evidence of the Kingdom is righteousness, peace, and joy, the presence of which produces the fruit of the Spirit. Embracing the expectation of the Kingdom by kissing the cross is the only known antidote to the venom of Satan. God, as Father, has given us this eternal and effective antidote in the person of Christ. When we find ourselves *fearing* to embrace the cross, *resisting*, or *acting* as enemies of the cross, remember how Moses lifted up the serpent in the wilderness. Paul said *"I have been crucified with Christ [in Him I have shared His crucifixion]; it is no longer I who live, but Christ (the Messiah) lives in me; and the life I now live in the body I live by faith in (by adherence to and reliance on and complete trust in) the Son of God, Who loved me and gave Himself up for me"* (Gal. 2:20 AMP). Only Christ can release healing and life to all who receive Him.

Thoughts and Questions

- What was the issue Paul was addressing with the Philippian believers? Why was it significant?
- What was Jesus warning us about in John 16?
- What kind of conduct are we capable of apart from the cross?

READING 46

Transition to Kissing the Cross

I have glorified You on the earth, having accomplished the work which You have given Me to do (John 17:4).

FOR years I interpreted Christ's completed or accomplished work as His suffering on the cross. However, what He accomplished was effectively taking what the Father had given Him and imparting it to the 11 disciples so they came to know the Father (see John 17:8). This impartation is called *generational transfer*.

Jesus was the transitional Man. His transition involved warfare with the systems of His day and required that He kiss the cross. He wrestled with His Father in the garden and in that wrestling became the transitional man on which all of life and history shifted; He brought about the ultimate transition from the Law of Moses to the *Agape* law of the Kingdom. Jesus personally walked each of the disciples through their own needed transitions so they could allow God to take hold of them in such a manner that their lives would affect society in real and meaningful ways. The moment we choose to follow Jesus with any degree of intentionality, the pressures mount, warfare increases, and unexpected things occur for which we did not bargain. This is all part of our transition into being conformed to the image of Christ. It is not possible to be transitional people without a mouthful of splinters.

There are many transitional people in history, including Adam, Abraham, Jacob, Moses, and Christ. Jacob, for example, wrestled with the angel, and a marvelous shift in the purposes of God happened in his life and in future generations. We must be a transitional people, or we will continue to think new and act old. Real discipleship must be done one on one so Kingdom vision and life can be relationally *imparted* from one person to another. This transition is existentially authentic when spoken through lips that have experienced a mouthful of splinters. Jesus taught that ministry means death in you and life in others. When the going gets rough, we must kiss the cross, fully embracing the process of being conformed to Christ's image so we can transition from individualism to people who impart life to future generations.

Thoughts and Questions

- 🌱 In what ways are you participating in Kingdom generational transfer?
- 🌱 Explain why Jesus was the transitional Man.
- 🌱 Why does transition involve a mouthful of splinters?

READING 47

Seven Areas of Transition

Let this be recorded for the generation yet unborn, that a people yet to be created shall praise the Lord (Psalm 102:18).

FOLLOWING are seven areas of needed transition that will require us to kiss the cross!

1. *The call to preach must be transformed into a call to follow Jesus.* This requires that we internalize the cross, which reveals any personal idols we call ministry. Many people are more committed to ministry than to the Person of Jesus. We were called to follow Jesus and sometimes that requires that we embrace a mouthful of splinters.

2. *The success syndrome must be transformed into impartation.* Impartation means changing a perfect meeting to a perfecting one. It is in weakness that Father chose to dwell. In a climate of weakness, imperfect people who are experiencing weakness have opportunity and occasion to mature.

3. *Individual human strength must be transformed into dependence on the body of Christ.* God's power is revealed in weakness. Failure to reveal our weakness leaves us in the realm of personal success rather than interdependence on others. A giant Sequoia can live for several hundred years but must die in order for new Sequoia trees to have sufficient sunlight to grow. There is a difference

between personal success and the need to impart to the coming generation.

4. *The perfect image must be transformed into the wounded healer.* People are looking for reality, vulnerability, and authenticity. While human weakness is real, so is the anointing. The world waits for leaders to acknowledge that this treasure really is in earthen vessels.

5. *What we can do must be transformed into what we can impart to others to do.* When Jesus said, *"Greater things shall you do"* (John 14:12), He was giving us the transitional pattern. The primary key to growth and success in the Church is impartation so others can learn to move in the power of the Holy Spirit.

6. *Crusades to bring in the Kingdom must be transformed into openness to receive the Kingdom.* Church history is littered with man's counterproductive attempts to bring in the Kingdom, but Jesus said, *"it is your Father's good pleasure to give you the kingdom"* (Luke 12:32 AMP). The Kingdom of God is righteousness, peace, and joy in the Holy Spirit. It is the creative work of God toward man, never man's attempt to climb up to God (see John 10:1).

7. *Personal gain must be transformed into gain for Jesus Christ.* "Whatever things were gain to me, those things I have counted as loss for the sake of Christ" (Phil. 3:7). Whatever promotes a personality or personal fame is a direct loss to the person of Christ. It is hard for a wounded healer to promote a personality cult. God's grace really is perfected in weakness, so we must guard ourselves from being scandalized that God could actually use a person so wounded.

Unless we begin to intentionally impart to others what God has given us, we will be unable to be a transitional person.

Thoughts and Questions

- Why must the success syndrome be changed to impartation?
- Explain the significance of the giant Sequoia needing to die.
- Why is it important to impart to others what God has given us?

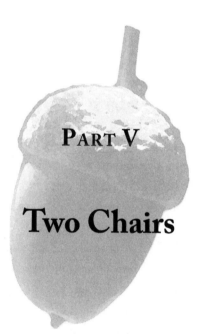

PART V

Two Chairs

Reading 48

Black Chair

For they all seek after their own interests, not those of Christ Jesus
(Philippians 2:21).

WE have learned that believers who rely on their own righteousness are in direct opposition to the cross of Christ and are considered enemies of the cross. Only when we embrace and internalize the cross can we expose and ultimately slay the seven *Eros* giants. This process involves some transition, however. Jesus won this battle for us. His statement, *"It is finished"* (John 19:30) reveals that the conflict has already been settled. This process involves some transition, however. In His own sacrifice as the Lamb of God, He brought about the ultimate transition from the Law of Moses to the *Agape* law of the Kingdom. We often discover some type of spiritual duplicity in that our *intention* is to follow Jesus; nevertheless, we keep going back to the Law of Moses, relying on and placing our dependence upon our own righteousness. We seem to fluctuate from being seated with Christ to being seated in *Eros*. In this section, we will look at this subject in light of what I am identifying as two chairs: the black chair and the white chair.

Eros is pictured as the black chair, which represents original sin and the inherent corruption in the nature of every one of us due to the fall of Adam. Sin is what made us all become takers. *Eros* is seeking after our own interests, not those of Jesus Christ who, as Father's first born, is the first giver.

We were born sitting in the black chair, so it is in our innate, self-referential nature to possess, acquire, and control. It is not what we do; it is who we are. If we are sitting in the black chair, the motivational forces for our life are the Seven Giants—Look Good, Feel Good, Be Right, Stay in Control, Hidden Agenda, Take Advantage, and Remain Undisturbed. Sin twisted us, causing the entire universe to be bent.[1] At the beginning of our encounter with Christ, we seem to be overwhelmed with our own bent and are incapable of being concerned about others in need, let alone about the needs of the world. If we sit in the black chair long enough, we become predators. These are described as "predators who use charm, manipulation, intimidation, and violence to control others and to satisfy their own selfish needs. Lacking in conscience and in feelings for others, they cold-bloodedly take what they want and do as they please, violating social norms and expectations without the slightest sense of guilt or regret."[2]

The black chair represents original sin. It involves keeping the external laws out of a self-willed determination to be holy rather than living under the love and freedom given to us in the righteousness Christ. Jesus told us that the scribes and the Pharisees did this when they seated themselves in the chair of Moses and that we should *not do according to their deeds; for they say things and do not do them* (Matt. 23:2-3). When we sit in the black chair, resentment and hypocrisy result, causing us to *run, hide, and shift blame.* God asks us to sit in a different chair and love Him without reservation and with complete spontaneity.

Thoughts and Questions

- ❦ What is the inherent nature of sitting in the black chair?
- ❦ What are our seven motivational forces when sitting in the black chair?
- ❦ What did the Pharisees do that Jesus tell us not to do?

ENDNOTES

1. Imagination and the Spirit: Essays in Literature and the Christian Faith Presented to Clyde S. Kilby, ed. By Charles A. Huttar. (William B. Eerdmans Publishing Company. Grand Rapids, Michigan. 1971) Pg 200-201

2. Oakley, Barbara. *Evil Genes*. Prometheus Books: Amherst, NY, 2007, 29.

White Chair

And raised us up with Him, and seated us with Him in the heavenly places in Christ Jesus (Ephesians 2:6).

I like to picture *Agape* as the white chair. When we are seated there, we are seated with Christ, and the motivation for our life is God's DNA: compassion, grace, slow to anger, mercy, truth, faithful, and forgiving. The white chair was created by Christ's incarnation when God came to us in human form. Christ was the first human since Adam who came for the single purpose of doing the Father's wishes. Pleasing the Father was the ruling force of His life. Christ purchased our privilege of sitting in the white chair with His blood.

Paul told us that every believer has been raised up with Christ and is seated with Him in heavenly places. Christ paid the price so we could be permitted to be where He is—seated at the right hand of God the Father. This is the realm where decisions are made that influence and direct the purposes of God in the earth. Sitting in the white chair is an aspect of the Kingdom of God and results in righteousness, peace, and joy. When we are seated with Christ, we enter into rest. Once we are seated in the white chair rather than the black one, our behavior and attitudes begin to change. Our conduct is affected because God's DNA—His seven attributes—are birthed, nourished, and cultivated within us while resting in the white chair.

The white chair is a birthright and *inheritance* in Christ given to us and our children. When we see *Agape* as our inheritance, we can remain seated with Christ in heavenly places and enjoy an intimate relationship with Him. It is vital that we understand that remaining in the white chair involves suffering because it requires us to act against ourselves. This is the reason few people want to abide in Christ and remain seated in the white chair.

The Kingdom of God is a very powerful force with strong influence. However, like public opinion or the wind, both of which are strong and influential, they are invisible—we can only see their effect. If, for whatever reason, we lose our *inheritance* in the Kingdom, we lose our ability to remain (abide) in the white chair and discover the loss or diminution of our ability to walk in the light. Remember, it is a behavioral issue, not a doctrinal one. The Kingdom is relational, showing up as *Agape* behavior in every human relationship. This spiritual Kingdom of light is so different that we need to be born again to even see it.

The Kingdom is not only *of* the Holy Spirit; it is *in* the Holy Spirit. If we entered and are now abiding in the Kingdom, we are seated in the white chair of *Agape*.

Thoughts and Questions

- Describe one of the aspects of our Kingdom inheritance.
- Why does remaining in the white chair involve suffering?
- If we lose our inheritance in the Kingdom, what have we really lost?

READING 50

Switching Chairs for Reward or Gain

For the flesh sets its desire against the Spirit, and the Spirit against the flesh;
for these are in opposition to one another, so that you may not
do the things that you please (Galatians 5:17).

NO one ever told me it was possible to switch chairs. I thought that once you were saved, you were in the white chair forever. Then I realized that we often switch back and forth. Sometimes we are in the white chair, and sometimes we are in the black one. It makes sense that we cannot (unable as contrasted to being prohibited) sit in both chairs at the same time. *We are forced to choose.*

There are always two motivations to switch chairs: to avoid loss or to gain something. The essence of all temptation is to switch chairs; we can do so and still be a Christian. In any crisis, we are faced with a choice. Jesus and Paul both chose the white chair, but to think we can choose the white chair and stay in it forever without switching for personal advantage is living in denial and making the Gospel to be some sort of magic. The reality is that we live in a fallen world and must work out our salvation daily. It is on this basis that John says, *"If we say that we have no sin, we are deceiving ourselves"* (1 John 1:8).

The nature of Jesus' three temptations was to switch chairs. In the white *Agape* chair, He was a giver and a Father-pleaser; the temptation of the black *Eros* chair was to become a taker and manifest ownership and control. Satan sought to awaken in Him the desire to acquire, possess, and control: acquire the bread, control the world, and possess success in the temple (see Matt. 4:1-11). Few people understand how strong the temptation was for success in the temple, especially in that day. However, Jesus knew those were not His Father's wishes. In the presence of both reward and threat, He never switched chairs. He repeatedly declined the black chair for personal advantage and remained in the white chair. Remaining in the white chair required Him to forgive the religious and political systems who betrayed Him and the two soldiers who crucified Him. He forgave over and over again because He knew that you and I could not be seated with Him and abide in a Kingdom lifestyle of righteousness, peace, and joy without learning how to freely forgive even at great personal cost.

Thoughts and Questions

- ❦ What are the motivations for switching chairs?
- ❦ In what ways is working out our salvation daily remaining in the white chair?
- ❦ Why is forgiveness necessary to remain in the white chair?

God's Ways and Means Committee

Whoever does not carry his own cross and come after Me
cannot be My disciple (Luke 14:27).

HAVE you ever wondered why God always seems to be dealing with you? Here you are trying to be a good Christian, and the pressures of life never seem to cease. When we do not especially want to move, God uses His own Ways and Means Committee to help move us from the black chair to the white one. He doesn't force us; He just uses circumstances to make us *want* to move. The Lord starts dealing with our finances, our social life, our goals and plans, as well as our speech and attitudes until He unwinds us out of our narcissistic knot. God's committee uses the needs in our life to get us in the white chair because He wants to reveal Himself to us. As long as our needs are met and we have no desire to go any farther, we are inclined to stay where we think we are comfortable.

The Greek word *cannot* in Luke 14:27 is *dunamai* meaning "to be able, have power whether by virtue of one's own ability and resources, or of a state of mind, or through favourable circumstances."[1] *Cannot* does not mean prohibitive; it means we do not have the ability. We cannot be Christ's disciples and follow Him unless we deny ourselves. God never coerces, but this does not mean He cannot get us where He wants us to go. God does know how to sovereignly move on our behalf, and His Ways and Means committee is quite effective.

Pressure from the Seven Giants plays a significant role in our switching chairs. We want to look good, feel good, be right, or stay in control, so we move from chair to chair. These giants are the embodiment of ungoverned desires. A good illustration of mixture and repeatedly switching chairs can be seen in *Treasure Island's* Long John Silver. He repeatedly switched sides for personal advantage.

It is possible to switch chairs mentally but not do so literally. Today I am in the white chair; tomorrow I am in the black one. Paul expressed this same frustration when he said, "What I want to do, I don't do"—this is a rather normal Christian conflict because the flesh really does set its desire against the Spirit. This mixture intensifies when we are acting contrary to the DNA or *Agape* nature that God our Father planted in us. Paul gave us the essence of the Christian life when he said, *"make my joy complete by being of the same mind, maintaining the same love [stay in the white chair], united in spirit, intent on one purpose. Do nothing from selfishness or empty conceit [do not switch chairs]"* (Phil. 2:2-3). As we learn to abide, *Agape* is worked into us and as our desires start to change, the mixture and conflict begin to decrease. We see things from the perspective of being seated with Christ and begin finding ourselves engaged in the needs of others. We discover that Father really does have a purpose for this hurting earth and wants us to be a participant.

Thoughts and Questions

- Describe some examples of God's Ways and Means committee in your own life.
- In what ways do the Seven Giants contribute to you switching chairs?
- Explain why *Agape* can be worked into us when we remain in the white chair.

ENDNOTE

1. James Strong, The Exhaustive Concordance of the Bible. (Woodside Bible Fellowship, 1996) G1410.

READING 52

Recognizing When We Switch Chairs

For they all seek after their own interests, not those of Christ Jesus
(Philippians 2:21).

I was teaching in Australia with another man from America, and every time he got up to preach, he would use the subtle *Eros* technique that *faith without hints is dead*. At some point during the service, he would say in whining and religious tones, "If the Lord would ever bless me while I was in Australia, it would be to go black Marlin fishing." By the third day, someone put his hand up and said, "I'm a charter fisherman and I fish off the reef. I'd be glad to take you fishing." Everyone clapped at what was perceived to be answered prayer. It made me nauseous. The lesson was a set up for me, and I said, "I see him switching chairs, Lord—You don't have to rub my nose in it anymore!" Using the pulpit for personal advantage is no small transgression.

For the purpose of illustration, suppose we are injured by someone sitting in the black chair. They may not even know they have hurt us, but if resentment starts and we find ourselves wanting to *acquire, possess,* and *control,* we know we have switched chairs. Our conduct shows which chair we are sitting in, but it is possible to switch chairs and not have anyone but ourselves know it for a long, long time. Because we want to abide in the white chair, we can posture ourselves in spiritual maturity by not reacting and immediately forgiving them. One of the reasons I personally forgive so freely is because if I don't, I know that I will not be forgiven (see Matt. 6:15) and the pressure increases to move to the black chair. There is a security, identity, and belonging in the white chair that keeps us from getting mad, defending, or protecting ourselves. Christ imparts to us the ability to respond as He would respond.

Often what we think of as Christian giving is highly motivated from the black chair, reaching for an obvious payoff or reward that did not originate in the Father. Givers who are seated in the black chair often become enablers and have a hard time saying no to anyone. But when we begin to see things from the *Agape* chair, we can discern if our giving is motivated by one of the Seven Giants. If we are more concerned for the reward than the person to whom we are ministering, something is amiss because *Agape* does no injury to his neighbor. A good question to ask myself is, "Am I doing this for the sheep or for the wool?"

Staying in the white chair can get us in trouble with everyone. The moment we make a heart decision to remain in the white chair, we find ourselves in conflict with all kinds of things going on around us because it is in the fallen human nature to seek after our own interests rather than those of Christ Jesus. When this happens in our own sphere, we can know we have switched chairs.

Thoughts and Questions

- How can you tell when you have switched chairs?
- What does forgiving have to do with switching chairs?
- If you are concerned for reward, what chair are you in?

READING 53

Peter Switched Chairs

And the rest of the Jews along with him also concealed their true convictions
and acted insincerely, with the result that even Barnabas was carried away
by their hypocrisy (their example of insincerity and pretense)
(Galatians 2:13 AMP).

PETER had been hanging out with the Gentiles and enjoying himself. In spite of personal preparation by Jesus, when he heard that the Jewish elders were coming to Jerusalem, Peter panicked and switched chairs for personal advantage. His single purpose was to avoid conflict and to look good (see Gal. 2:11-14). Even though he had become the lead apostle, denominational pressure of what others would think was extremely severe. He went back to the black chair in order to please the elders. Instead of eating with the Gentiles as Jesus did, he put on his yarmulke and his prayer shawl and began to pray in Hebrew. Even Barnabas and a few other Jews were carried away by Peter's hypocrisy. It may have cost Peter a bundle to stay in the white chair when the brothers came, but the Kingdom suffered by his shift because the lead apostle and a good man switched chairs. The result was mixture, confusion, and diminution of the glory of God.

It is tough to be a Democrat at a Republican convention. During times like this, it is tempting to sit in both chairs at the same time. I have personally switched chairs under these circumstances, so I know exactly how Peter felt, and as long as God gives me breath, I will never do it again. When Paul came, he opposed Peter to his face. It was the action of switching chairs that was condemned, not the person because Jesus paid the price for our freedom.

Peter switched chairs again when he opposed Jesus. Although he loved Him, Peter was *overly concerned for his own agenda*. When Peter said to Jesus that He could not go up to Jerusalem and suffer, he was worried that the whole deal was going to collapse and he had just made it to vice president. He was not concerned for the things of God but for the things of man.

Peter also switched chairs for personal advantage when he denied Jesus three times. Jesus intentionally restored Peter when He asked him, *"Do you love Me?"* (John 21:17). His whole restoration was carefully orchestrated and based on a play of the words for love—*phileo* (brotherly love) and *Agape*. The pain of his failure was replaced by *Agape*. During Peter's *Agape* conversion, his *Eros* giants were being crushed, and he developed a greater capacity to remain in the white chair. Jesus effectively eliminated human affection as being sufficient to feed His sheep and tend His lambs. Feeding others demands *Agape* behavior and the capacity to remain in the white chair.

Thoughts and Questions

- What external pressures make you want to sit in both chairs at the same time?
- How does *Agape* restore us to the white chair?
- What *Eros* giants do you think Peter was struggling with when he switched chairs?

Switching Chairs Involves Mixture

Out of the same mouth come forth blessing and cursing
(James 3:10 AMP).

LIKE givers and takers, switching chairs involves mixture. Martin Luther, father of the Reformation from Catholicism to Christianity, had a lot of mixture in his personal life and character. However, he was amazingly consistent in his exegesis of Scripture and his love for God. While he brought in the Reformation, he was also known as an anti-Semitic because the common thinking at the time was that the Jews had killed Jesus. The fact that he never compromised when it came to a scriptural injunction no matter what it cost him seems to be all the more supernatural. He was sitting in the white chair when he ushered in the Reformation but was in the black chair in regard to his behavior toward the Jews. He did what Peter did—shifted chairs when it appeared to be advantageous. This deep and conflicting contradiction in Luther's own person caused the Kingdom to suffer. His grievous anti-Semitic stand was the basis of Hitler later executing millions of Jews. In this case, Luther's influence and failure were catastrophic. We are free to make our own decisions, but we are not free to determine the consequences of those decisions.

Abraham manifested mixture by switching chairs on several occasions. He was heading toward Canaan but had to pass through Egypt and feared he would be killed so his beautiful wife could be taken as part of the royal harem. Under the pressure, he told Sarai to say she was his sister. God had just told him about his immense inheritance, but the fear of man overruled his trust in God, causing him to be deceitful and cowardly (see Gen. 12:10-20). Abraham was still dealing with mixture because he repeated this mistake a short while later when they came into the land of Gerar and met king Abimelech (see Gen. 20:1-14). Abraham's son Isaac did the same with his wife, Rebecca.

The prophet Micah saw this mixture when he wrote, *"Her leaders pronounce judgment for a bribe, her priests instruct for a price and her prophets divine for money. Yet they lean on the Lord, saying, 'Is not the Lord in our midst? Calamity will not come upon us'"* (Mic. 3:11). This kind of mixture has increased in our day.

Some years ago, a young woman came to me for some advice, and when I attempted to redirect her back to her own pastor, she said in pain and desperation, "I would talk to him, but he has more problems than I do." Unfortunately, the woman's pastor was full of mixture. The chair we are sitting in will determine what we have to say to someone. We need to discern a man's heart—whether he is seated in the white chair or the black one. *Agape* seeks to know what is motivating the other person and then makes allowances for the mixture and conflicts that are going on. *Agape covers a multitude of sins.* By doing so, we would have increased motivation to change our own behavior and have grace for the behavior of others.

Thoughts and Questions

- What caused Luther to have so much mixture in him?
- What caused Abraham to switch chairs?
- In what ways can you see mixture in yourself?

READING 55

Switching Chairs Damages Trust

Keep praying for us, for we are convinced that we have a good (clear) conscience, that we want to walk uprightly and live a noble life, acting honorably and in complete honesty in all things (Hebrews 13:18 AMP).

WHEN the majority of people, including believers, are sitting in the black chair, we experience an *Eros* shift (see diagram in the appendix). Christians can do some very ungodly things! Because lawlessness is increased, most people's *love for each other* (not for God) will grow cold (see Matt. 24:12 Moffatt). When everything shifts toward *Eros*, lawlessness abounds and hope is deferred, which results in heart sickness. Repeated breaches of trust cause us to become street-smart and defensive survivors. We can see it in political, economic, and religious leaders.

Song of Solomon tells us that love is stronger than death, but trust has a different consistency than love. *Trust is comparable to a very delicate flower.* When you break the bridge of trust, most often it is directly due to switching chairs. Repairing the bridge of trust is tedious and difficult. Many people's trust factor has been repeatedly traumatized or injured to the point of them being unable, perhaps even paralyzed, to risk another disappointment. This *risk avoidance* is rather common in the church. Heartsickness means we are despondent from grief or loss of love; we become incapable of *trusting* but not incapable of *loving*. It means we expected *Agape* but found *Eros* until we want to say with David that all men are liars (see Ps. 116:11).

The breakdown of trust in any relationship is a sign of mixture. I was counseling an outwardly successful pastor and his wife. He was telling me how wonderful the church was, but I knew something was wrong. When he was finally done talking, my instincts caused me to turn to his wife and ask, "Do you love him?" She said, "With all my heart." Then I said, "*Do you trust him?*" Her lip started to quiver, and she hung her head as the tears flowed; she did not even have the courage or the strength to answer. She had seen such mixture of the two chairs in his life that her trust in him was devastated and she was on the brink of being scandalized.

Switching chairs has become the modern method of self-fulfillment. Instead of the Church teaching us how to *abide* in the white chair, even if it gets us in trouble, we are taught how to succeed, give a positive confession, and believe that God only wants to bless and prosper us. Christ showed us that He did not please Himself. We have wandered so far from the Kingdom dimension that we are now being taught the skill of switching chairs according to our need—the very opposite of the Gospel. We are encouraged to switch because circumstances, spouses, or people no longer please us. Once we develop the *Eros* skill of switching chairs without anyone knowing it, we are now free to switch churches, jobs, wives or husbands, friends, and geographical locations in a heartbeat—all because we are not being served. By doing so, we seriously injure any trust that has been built in our relationships. Abiding and faithfulness in the midst of difficulty is becoming a lost art.

Thoughts and Questions

- ❦ Explain why switching chairs injures trust in relationships.
- ❦ Briefly describe an experience when you saw someone switching chairs.
- ❦ How is switching chairs the opposite of the Gospel?

Switching Chairs for Loss or Gain

For to me, to live is Christ and to die is gain (Philippians 1:21).
But godliness with contentment is great gain (1 Timothy 6:6 KJV).

WHEN we develop the skill of switching chairs without anyone knowing it, we sit in the black chair but change the upholstery to make it look like the white chair. Unfortunately, many in the larger church are preaching about the white chair while seated in the black one, though no one moves and nothing changes. What matters is where we are seated because it shows up in our behavior. Jesus said, *"We played the flute for you, and you did not dance; we sang a dirge, and you did not mourn"* (Matt. 11:17). When paralysis sets in, trust factors are broken, making us unable or perhaps more tragically, unwilling to respond. Switching chairs is intensified by desire for gain or by threat of loss. The Christian church has entered a season theologians are calling post-doctrinal, a season when it doesn't matter what people believe or what doctrine is taught as long as they can *gain* something from attending church. This is not relational but utilitarian.

Have you ever walked into a store to buy a jacket and the sales clerk comes up and asks, "May I help you?" and you immediately can feel that he doesn't care what jacket you buy, he just wants to make a sale. Another salesperson can say the exact same words, but you feel he really does want to help you find the right jacket.

A friend of mine was planting a new church, which involved everything from starting a childcare program to a worship team. One day in came five talented musicians with all their instruments who said, "We just left the church down the street, and we want to help you get your worship team started." My friend could see that they were motivated by gaining something and were trying to change the upholstery of the black chair. He knew that if they switched from one church, they would switch again, so he said, "No thanks, we don't need any more musicians." In sending them back to their home church in faithfulness and relational integrity, he directed them into a Kingdom dimension and in my opinion, prevented a future church split in his own congregation.

Sitting in the black chair determines whether a pastor, parent, or counselor is being utilitarian, seeking to *use* you in some manner that would directly or indirectly benefit them. This is what the Pharisees did when they devoured widows' houses and then covered it up with long prayers (see Matt. 23:14). Switching chairs when something is to our advantage is *Crossless Christianity* and is far from what the Father of our Lord Jesus intended. If we are sitting in the black chair, the very source of our counsel to others has been seriously contaminated with mixture.

Thoughts and Questions

- Describe a situation where you tried to change the upholstery on the black chair.
- Why is switching chairs intensified by desire for gain or threat of loss?
- Explain why our counsel has serious mixture if we are sitting in the black chair.

Capacity for Inner Restraint

For this very reason, adding your diligence [to the divine promises], employ
every effort in exercising your faith to develop virtue (excellence, resolution,
Christian energy), and in [exercising] virtue [develop]
knowledge (intelligence) (2 Peter 1:5 AMP).

CHARACTER is moral excellence and firmness or what we may call the capacity for inner restraint. Carefully examined, we can see clearly that it is another aspect of acting against ourselves. Character involves breaking the power of *Eros* as personal advantage and gain and making a conscious choice to sit in the white chair. When Christ is fully formed in us, God's *character* (fruit of the Spirit) shows up in our behavior. Unfortunately, many Christians are lacking character even after they have experienced enormous forgiveness or supernatural anointing.

It is possible to be a Spirit-filled and water-baptized Christian who sits in the black chair using Scripture with an *Eros* motivation. In a city with one of the largest seminaries in America, I read a sign on the counter of an auto parts store that said, *"Make a profit; don't deal with Christians."* The store owner said students would get a part for their car and promise to come back with the money, but he never saw them again. Evidently, the students had a sense of entitlement that the parts should be free since they were in seminary and "doing God's work." Even though they were Christians, their capacity for inner restraint was limited. Their behavior stemmed from the black chair.

It is common in the church to raise money by putting an *Eros* spin on the Scripture *"it is more blessed to give than receive"* (Acts 20:35). That is not the intent of that verse; it used out of the black chair and unfortunately, frequently taught in churches. A friend of mine called me and said, "Bob, my wife has cancer. Is it possible that she got cancer because I wasn't faithful in my tithing?" He did not get that idea from the Bible but from someone with a lack of restraint using Scripture out of the black chair.

Without inner restraint, it is possible to switch chairs five times in three seconds, but the moment we do, any conduct is possible. The list of *"works of the flesh"* in Galatians 5:19-21 describes people who have known Jesus as their personal Savior. Godly character is the restoration of the image of God in us and is formed by our being trained to sit in the white chair, particularly at the time of disadvantage and personal loss. When we break the power of sin and *Eros*, we increase our capacity for inner restraint and are able to subdue sexual desires, impulses, and anger. *Agape* covers a multitude of sins.

Remaining seated in the white chair continuously and without interruption even at personal cost involves our preferential choice. Abiding in the white chair is what breaks the power of temptation and affects our conduct. As we make our preferential choice of the white chair over the black one, God's DNA is worked into us and replicated, releasing compassion, grace, forgiveness, and the ability to be slow to anger. Having a capacity for inner restraint is part of walking in the Kingdom.

Thoughts and Questions

- Why does developing moral excellence call for a capacity for inner restraint?
- Explain why Christians can sit in the black chair and use Scripture with an *Eros* motivation.
- How is the image of God restored in our person?

READING 58

Loyalty and Faithfulness

You [are like] unfaithful wives [having illicit love affairs with the world and breaking your marriage vow to God]! Do you not know that being the world's friend is being God's enemy? So whoever chooses to be a friend of the world takes his stand as an enemy of God (James 4:4 AMP).

FAITHFULNESS is one of the seven hidden attributes of God the Father, and He wants that attribute replicated in each of us. Faithfulness signifies the ability to remain steadfast no matter what shifts the winds may bring so that we can have undistracted and undivided devotion to the Lord (see 1 Cor. 7:35). Unfaithfulness is changing chairs for the purpose of gain or advantage.

In the original language, the word *loyalty* is lovingkindness or faithfulness. God does not ask for loyalty in the unqualified sense of the word. Human loyalty can become a prison with bars stronger than iron. Loyalty is included in faithfulness but is more than that. We need more than a loyal friend; we need a faithful one. Sometimes our friends can be faithful in ways we don't really like. "Yes men" on a corporate board may be loyal in a way that is detrimental. Loyalty is a strong feeling of support or allegiance that can be used against us and often carries tremendous bondage. When the threat of being *disloyal* is hung over us, we are quite likely being coerced into a relational circumstance because we have something either to gain or something to lose. Relationships based on human loyalty easily become a serious snare. False loyalty is the stuff cults and fanaticism generates; it is the fuel upon which most false systems run. It requires strength and character to be faithful.

Relationships based on *faithfulness* are evidenced by freedom. A faithful person has the freedom to speak the truth in love and tell the emperor (politician, pastor, expert) he or she does not have any clothes on. *"Speaking the truth in love"* (Eph. 4:15) is more accurately translated "truthing in *Agape*," which requires solemn faithfulness. This faithfulness means that we are genuinely concerned about the overall welfare of another person. Faithfulness implies that we cannot use, acquire, possess, or control others in any illegal way. Tough love is faithfulness from the white chair—the ability to express Kingdom expectations in sheer *Agape* apart from legalism or control. We must speak the truth in love whether it makes others happy or not. Strangely, *Agape* faithfulness is often mistaken for being disloyal. Many times, Kingdom faithfulness can become very expensive. Being faithful does not allow us to get someone off our back, put him down, or win an argument. Out of our love for them, we are trying to see the given situation from a Kingdom perspective. Their welfare and good is the ultimate issue.

In the parable of investing, Jesus commended two of the men, saying, *"Well done, good and faithful [worthy of trust] servant"* (Matt. 25:21 AMP) and made both men His partner. God's faithfulness can be seen, felt, embraced, and relied upon when He said, *"I will never desert you, nor will I ever forsake you"* (Heb. 13:5). God remains faithful even when we are unfaithful.

Thoughts and Questions

- ❦ What primary skill do we need for God's DNA to be fully formed in us? Why?
- ❦ Describe some of the characteristics of a relationship you have that is based on faithfulness.
- ❦ Explain why faithfulness requires us to speak the truth in love.

Reading 59

Faithlessness and Faithfulness

Well done, good and faithful slave. You were faithful with a few things,
I will put you in charge of many things; enter into the joy of your master
(Matthew 25:23).

FAITHLESSNESS is switching chairs for personal advantage. When we are faithless in our marriage, home, relationships, or job, we switch chairs to satisfy whatever is most convenient for us at the time. With a group of Mike's friends, we say, "Oh, me and Mike are really good friends." But in the company of his enemies, we say, "Mike who?" Peter did this when he denied Jesus. There have been several occasions when I have been faithless and switched chairs in a relationship for personal convenience. When the hostile Indians were bearing down on them, the Lone Ranger turned to Tonto and said, "What are *we* going to do, Tonto?" Tonto replied, "What do you mean 'we,' white man?" Even Tonto switched chairs when it was to his personal advantage.

Faithlessness and switching chairs is a result of *Crossless Christianity*. The answer is abiding and faithfulness—both are characteristics of the cross. When we abide, the cross is at work in our life and we learn to be faithful to one another. In spite of the mess we might make in learning to be faithful, God knows how to make it come out right at the end. Amazingly, the evangelist can frequently switch chairs for personal advantage, but people still get saved in their meetings. The reason is simple: God uses "all things." Christ is preached, and His Kingdom inexorably goes on. The Kingdom issue is faithfulness.

Abiding is the biblical basis for answered prayer: *"If you abide in Me, and My words abide in you, ask whatever you wish, and it will be done for you"* (John 15:7). Faithlessness leaves our prayers unanswered. A friend of mine saw how abiding was the issue and taught it to his birddog! He said, "If the birddog doesn't *abide* on point, he's not worth anything." With training, we, too, can learn to abide faithfully in the white chair.

The strength, viral nature, and deceptive power of the black chair in both sensual and religious forms clouds our ability to see ourselves in reality. Robert Burns wrote, "Oh, that God the gift would give us to see ourselves as others see us." This is faithfulness. We have this gift in our brothers and sisters in Christ, but unless we choose to abide in faithfulness, we can miss or refuse it. When we are faithful, we are literally full of faith, trusting God's promises that we *"will be like a tree planted by the water, that extends its roots by a stream and will not fear when the heat comes; but its leaves will be green, and it will not be anxious in a year of drought nor cease to yield fruit"* (Jer. 17:8).

Thoughts and Questions

- Explain why switching chairs for personal advantage is faithlessness.
- In what ways have you had to embrace the cross through someone's faithfulness?
- What is the route to getting our prayers answered? Why?

Wounds of a Friend

Faithful are the wounds of a friend (Proverbs 27:5-6).

*A*GAPE faithfulness is expected of us while seated in the white chair even to the point of wounding someone. *Agape* that fails or refuses to function is useless, and our love becomes hypocritical. The *Agape* character traits needing to be replicated in us then lose their purity and effectiveness. Mixture and confusion follow.

Faithfulness is maturing to the point of discovering the balance between not intentionally offending and refusing to compromise by switching chairs. It is a skill we have to learn. We may not even know we're switching chairs until our wife says, "Honey, that's not what you said last week." And of course, we love hearing the truth!

Christ's faithfulness to wound can be seen in His words, *"If it were not so, I would have told you"* (John 14:2). The unadulterated truth is necessary for us to make this journey, but there are some things that God knows we are not able to accept right now. Abiding and faithfulness teach us the value of taking admonition, adjustment, and correction by faith. It is God's faithfulness that allows us to be able to incrementally see truth. Paul explained this when he said, *"From whom the whole body, being fitted and held together by what every joint supplies, according to the proper working of each individual part, causes the growth of the body for the building up of itself in love"* (Eph. 4:16). Our faithfulness to each other should facilitate normal spiritual progress so we can grow up personally and relationally.

*"A man of **too many** friends **comes** to ruin, but there is a friend who sticks closer than a brother"* (Prov. 18:24). This friend is always Jesus, but we also need a friend with skin on, and that is the Body of Christ. He or she could be your next door neighbor or someone in your fellowship group. Carefully preserve the words and exhortations from those you know to be in the white chair, even if you do not agree with them at the time. The prodigal gathered to himself false friends who used him until his money was gone and then left him in his time of need.

The Book of Acts describes a church that had found its first love. They shared all their possessions with one another depending on who had a need. If you try to replicate the community they had without understanding these two chairs, you will understand another form of religious suicide. You can just imagine the excitement if you have $10,000 and someone else has $2 and it all goes into one purse. While sitting in the black chair, our actions are revealed irrespective of our words. Most often, the primary reason we are unable to *receive the wounds of a friend* is because we are driven by personal preservation and determined to remain undisturbed. Choosing to abide in the white chair releases us from this. Our primary concern should be others' well being so the Kingdom can come through us to a hurting world. Only *Agape* can enable us to make the tough decisions and provide the grace to embrace others' reactions (positive or negative) so God can meet each of us.

Thoughts and Questions

- Have you ever experienced *Agape* faithfulness to the point of wounding? Explain.
- Why would *Agape* that fails or refuses to function be useless?
- What is one of the reasons we cannot/do not receive a friend's *Agape* faithfulness?

PART VI

Intentionality

Accidental or Intentional

God causes all things to work together for good to those who love God
(Romans 8:28 KJV).

QUINCY Magoo, the 1960s cartoon character, found himself in all kinds of problems because he stubbornly refused to admit he was nearsighted, and neither would he agree to correct the problem by wearing glasses. His friends were concerned for his safety, especially when speeding cars barely missed him or when he nearly walked off a bridge. Although Mr. Magoo lived in the *accidental*, everything usually worked out for him.

There is a difference between the properties of accidental and intentional. A trivial but helpful example is that it is the intentional property of a bachelor to remain unmarried. The accidental property of a bachelor is that he has brown hair. God's *providence* works in a similar manner in our own lives—He has the ability to use "all things," both the accidental and the intentional, to conform us to Christ's image. That which is accidental occurs with an apparent cause.

In the parable of the treasure in the field (see Matt. 13:44), a man accidentally found a treasure and speedily sold everything he had to buy the field; this was an intentional act. God, as Father uses that which is accidental to preserve His own Sovereignty; He does not allow us to control or possess Him. He uses unexpected, unintentional, and seemingly coincidental events in our journey for His purposes. Our perception that God is involved in the events causes us to become alert so we can become *intentional:* we want what God wants in the mysterious manner in which He has chosen to approach and reveal Himself to us.

God, as Father, wants us to worship Him in Spirit and in truth. He approaches us both *accidentally* through circumstances and events over which we have no control or understanding and *intentionally* through His Word or by means of the gifts of the Holy Spirit. Irrespective of the manner in which the Father chooses to reveal Himself, He is asking us to develop the skill of recognizing Him in the accidental.

One of the Church Fathers said that *the providence of God works on a narrow, dangerous margin.* There are events and catastrophes in life that no one can predict or prevent. Being a believer in no way guarantees us immunity from the difficult or the unexpected. The one thing we *can* do when accidental circumstances and events become confusing and difficult is to *abide* in the white chair. Only here can we understand and interpret the circumstances and properly respond to them in an intentional manner. We must know and believe that nothing touches our life that does not come through Father's hand. That is providence. We all can testify of the times He overruled the foolish things we did. He provides for every accidental contingency and has the sovereign and providential ability to take the whole mess—including our sin and failure—and cause them to serve His purpose. In God's initiative of grace, He can and will override our ignorance and mistakes.

Thoughts and Questions

🦌 Describe a situation where God worked accidental circumstances in your life for good.

🦌 How did the circumstances serve His purposes?

🦌 In what ways were you nearsighted and missed what God was doing in a situation?

Intentionality

Your intention is [when you get what you desire] to spend it in sensual
pleasures (James 4:3 AMP).

MY first experience with *intentionality* occurred when I spent time with the Roman Catholics in the early days of the Charismatic outpouring of the Holy Spirit. When I innocently asked the Mother Superior for prayer, she very directly asked, "And what are your intentions?" As a rather superficial protestant, understanding intentions was quite new to me. *Stanford Encyclopedia of Philosophy*[1] defines intentionality as having to do with the directedness or aboutness of mental states—the fact that, for example, one's thinking is *of* or *about* something. Intentionality includes, and is sometimes taken to be equivalent to, what is called mental representation.

In both the Old and the New Testaments, becoming intentional has to do with freedom without coercion or compulsion. It is much deeper than our idea of will or desire. Somehow, it is a basement concept that originates somewhere down in the depths of one's person. Hebrews compares the thoughts and intentions of the heart with dividing of the soul and spirit or joints and marrow (see Heb. 4:12). The intentions of our heart can be evil and need to be forgiven (see Acts 8:22).

When young men began dating my two daughters, I would ask them, "What are your intentions?" If they had not given the question much thought, it usually stunned them. That which is intentional is purely inward, deeply subjective, and very difficult to assess or determine. This can be seen in court cases when a first-degree murder charge is hanging on proof beyond doubt of predetermined *intention*.

Intention has to do with seeing through, not looking at. When Jesus laid hands on the blind man's eyes, he looked intently, was restored, and began to see everything clearly (see Mark 8:25). When Stephen was being stoned, *"he gazed intently into heaven and saw the glory of God"* (Acts 7:55).

While God rules over all accidental events in a providential manner, there must be a route that allows us as disciples and followers of Jesus to move from accidental to mature intentionality. His own intentionality is expressed in His words, *"I come to do Thy will, O God"* (Heb. 10:9). This was a course set by the Father. Our course would be moving from living by the accidental to cultivating the intentional, which involves preferential choice. We *choose* to abide in the white chair irrespective of the cost. The route cannot be based on a self-willed determination to be holy. The process involves response-ability—the ability to respond properly without religious striving.

Most of us have been taught that the accidental is the normal Christian life, but intentionally choosing the white chair is the Kingdom standard that has to do with *"being of the same mind, maintaining the same love, united in spirit, intent on one purpose"* (Phil. 2:2). We can only lead Mr. Magoo-style lives for so long; at some point, we need to correct our nearsightedness so we can live intentionally for the glory of God.

Thoughts and Questions

- Describe a situation where you chose to respond properly to an adverse circumstance.
- How were your intentional actions a reflection of God's glory in your life?
- What aspects of God's DNA did people see?

ENDNOTE

1. Malpas, J., "Donald Davidson", *The Stanford Encyclopedia of Philosophy* (Winter 2003 Edition), Edward N. Zalta (ed.), URL = <http://plato.stanford.edu/archives/win2003/entries/davidson/>.

Intentional Discipleship

Staying right at the center of God's love, keeping your arms open and
outstretched, ready for the mercy of our Master, Jesus Christ! (Jude 21 TM)

SIX things are repeatedly asked of a disciple: to deny one's self, to take up one's own cross, to lose one's life, to be last and least, to drink the cup that Jesus drank, and to be baptized with His baptism (see Matt. 16:24-25; 20:16; Mark 10:39). Each of these requires an *intentional* act and is what Jesus meant when He said "Follow Me." Intentional discipleship is designed to arrest the *Eros* shift and cultivate the *Agape* lifestyle, which is the source of Kingdom freedom. In order for Christ's DNA to be imputed and imparted into our person, we must intentionally abide in an unbroken relationship with Him. When we intentionally choose to allow God to guide our lives, we bring glory to the Father. Intentional discipleship embraces the accidental as necessary yet refuses to live there.

A disciple knows that when someone who is hurting or seriously in need crosses our path, it is not really an accident—it is an opportunity for an intentional act. Father is using this accidental event to reveal His Kingdom in the situation. When we live intentionally, our whole life begins to take on purpose. Before I left for a hunting trip, my wife said, "I know why you're going hunting. You just want to get out there in the woods, sit on a log, and open up the concepts of the Kingdom to those guys." My goal is to live intentionally; I really do live and breathe the Kingdom of God.

By choosing to abide and keep ourselves in the exact center of God's *Agape* regardless of the cost, we can lessen our unprofitable experiences. Intentional disciples say, "Lord, here I am in this situation and I know You placed me here. I am not running, changing jobs, churches, or friends; I am asking You to redeem this situation." Christ made hard decisions. He can strengthen and enforce His intentionality within us when we resist the mold of modernity and live as one who has discovered purpose and meaning. Our intentions then become actions, and actions become the fruit of the Kingdom. When God's *Agape* Seed has been received, cultivated, nourished, and defended, the Eternal Seed begins to bring forth fruit after its kind in our lives, marriages, and businesses. When we choose to be increasingly intentional, the Kingdom of God opens, confusing issues become clear, and Father's love comes *to* us and then through us. By intentionally choosing to stay right at the center of God's love, we move from depending upon the accidental to an increasing maturity. It is not works of merit but response-ability—a proper response to grace.

Father God is willing to expose Himself to the risk of rejection and misunderstanding. Father's future promise is pulled into the present by the strength of His *Agape*. Accepting the challenge to become more intentional disciples requires that we take the same risk.

Thoughts and Questions

- Why do each of the six requirements of a disciple require an intentional act?
- In what ways have you seen God use accidental events to extend His Kingdom?
- Why do you think living intentionally requires risk?

Peter's Intentional journey

Peter remembered Jesus' words… (Matthew 26:75 AMP).

JESUS knew Peter in a way that Peter could not know himself and pur-
posely led him to certain discoveries about himself. Jesus, in His love for
this man, even understood his inner intentions, predicting Peter's triple denial
before the rooster crowed. What Peter was not expecting was the intense circumstances of Jesus' arrest in which this all happened, and he wept bitterly in
response to his shameful failure.

About a week later, Peter, with six of the other disciples, assumed it was all
over and decided to go back to being fishermen. Having fished all night, they
did not catch anything. In the morning, Jesus was waiting for them on the
beach with fish laid on a charcoal fire and bread. Although the disciples did
not recognize Him at first, from the shore Jesus called out, *"Boys (children), you
do not have any meat (fish), do you? They answered Him, No!"* (John 21:5 AMP).
Jesus used this "accidental" event to reveal Peter's (and the others') intentions
toward Himself. After telling them to cast their net on the right side of the
boat and they would find a catch, He invited them to come and have breakfast.
He then took the bread and the fish He had cooked and gave it to them. As an
epilogue to the resurrection, this account gives us some valuable insights into
our theme of intentionality. One commentary opens it beautifully:

> The Lord appears to His disciples busied about their occupation
> for their daily bread…when we know that by their toiling long
> and taking nothing, but at His word enclosing a multitude of
> fishes, was set forth what should befall them as fishers of men.…

Besides, He graciously provides for their present wants, and invites them to be His guests: why but to show them that in their work hereafter they should never want but He would provide?[1]

God, as Father, watches each of our responses from a Romans 8:28 perspective and says, without coercion or control, "I must give Bob the needed insight so that he can continue this journey without getting lost." The accidental, however wonderful and exciting, is to be received with joy and alacrity. The unexpected and unearned displays of His nature are designed to lead us toward greater confidence in Him. When Father's communicable attributes are replicated in the individual believer, *intentionality* emerges. Our Kingdom mission statement is *Agape* perfected and brought to the full intention of Father's pleasure. *Agape*, however spontaneous and risky, *cannot* be premeditated. We must learn what God wants from us, which involves moving from an accidental lifestyle to an intentional one.

Thoughts and Questions

❦ What did Jesus see in Peter that Peter wasn't aware of himself?

❦ Explain how Jesus used the disciples' accidental fishing trip as a teachable moment.

❦ At what point does intentionality begin to emerge from our person?

ENDNOTE

1. Lange, John Peter and Schaff, Philip. *A Commentary on the Holy Scriptures: John.* (Bellingham, WA: Logos Research Systems, Inc., 2008.) p. 632

READING 65

Peter's Intention to Follow Jesus

Simon, son of John, do you love Me more than these [others do—with reasoning, intentional, spiritual devotion, as one loves the Father]?
(John 21:15 AMP)

JESUS asked Peter the same question three times: *"Simon, do you love Me?"* In this same verse, Peter's first two answers were, *"Yes, Lord, You know that I love You [that I have deep, instinctive, personal affection for You, as for a close friend]."* In response, Jesus said *"Feed (tend) My lambs...and shepherd My sheep"* (John 21:16 AMP). The third time Jesus asked the same question, Peter was grieved and hurt, saying, "Lord, You know everything; You know that I love You." When Jesus told Peter to "Feed My sheep," He knew what Peter would face in his journey of leading people to the Kingdom and was preparing him to make *continual intentional choices* to walk in *Agape*. A commentary sets this out most clearly:

> The nice, and yet important gradations in the distinction between *lambs* and full-grown *sheep*...which are, nevertheless, to be treated tenderly like lambs; and the distinction between *to lead to pasture, to provide with food,* and to *guide* and *govern as a shepherd.* The first and most necessary thing (intellectually it is also the easiest, though it presents peculiar difficulties to an imperious, high-soaring mind) is this: to provide for the lambs, *i.e.,* those of tender age in the faith, with spiritual sustenance, to lead them to the spiritual pasture. It is *more difficult to guard and guide the full-grown sheep,*—mature

Christians,—to make them seek the right pasture, find the true spiritual food; *most difficult of all: to offer to these full aged members appropriate spiritual food.*[1]

After Jesus' first open rebuke when He told Peter that he was a stumbling block to Him (see Matt. 16:23), Peter began to see how he was living in the accidental. When Jesus was telling Peter about how He would soon suffer and die, Peter strongly contradicted Him. Peter's response to his Master was nothing less than pure *Eros.* Jesus, without condemnation or rejection said, *"you are not setting your mind on God's interests, but man's"* (Mark 8:33). When Peter denied the Lord Jesus three times, his education regarding the accidental had come quite clear. He simply did not want to go that way again and sought to move toward a more intentional lifestyle. Peter had now experienced both the easy way and the hard way to walk with the Lord and knew what it meant to make promises he could not keep. *Intentionality* sets its priority on the King and the Kingdom. Perhaps Peter was considered the lead apostle because he was forgiven for more failures than the other 11!

Intentionality can be summarized in two words: Follow Me. "This, in a wider sense, is the sum and substance, the beginning and end of Christian life, as an imitation of the life of Christ in its sinless perfection, its divine-human character, its prophetic, priestly, and kingly office, and in its states of humiliation and exaltation from the cross to the crown."[2]

Thoughts and Questions

- ❦ Explain Jesus' statement: *"Feed (tend) My lambs...and shepherd My sheep."*
- ❦ In what ways have you walked the easy way and the hard way with the Lord?
- ❦ What does "Follow Me" mean to you?

ENDNOTES

1. Lange, J. P., and Schaff, P. (2008). *A commentary on the Holy Scriptures: John* (Logos Research Systems, Inc., Bellingham, WA) p. 638.

2. Ibid. p. 641.

Living Intentionally in a Fix

...add to your faith... (2 Peter 1:5 KJV).

PETER'S *Agape* conversion clearly explains the more intentional path from the black chair to the white chair so we don't have to make the same mistakes he did. The answer to the intentional route does not rely on human effort or willpower but on accepting the grace and peace God grants us so we can be conformed to His nature. All of the aspects of Kingdom transformation begin and end with a faith operation; we can only *believe* our way from one chair to the other. Peter goes on to show us that we start with faith and add virtue. To virtue we add knowledge, then self-control, perseverance, godliness, brotherly kindness, and finally *Agape*. This sequence is not accidental; each of these consists of *intentional* choices we make in our life. It is a progressive journey that is neither boring nor dependent upon human wisdom. God's purpose is that we will be *"neither barren nor unfruitful in the knowledge of our Lord Jesus Christ"* (2 Peter 1:5-8). This is *Agape* being brought to maturity—the fruit of the eternal, incorruptible Seed coming to fruition.

If we interpret what Peter is saying as taking up our self-willed determination to be holy and here are eight things you must do to get started, *we are on the religious road and are missing his heart and intent*. If someone adds another eight things to us, we are likely to collapse! Peter is explaining the process of transition from living accidentally into a mature lifestyle gained from never departing from the white chair.

Virtue is a Greek word for character—the ability to give your word and stand by it or to stay in the white chair. God uses the spontaneous, accidental events that happen in our lives in an *Agape* manner, enabling us to develop response-ability—an ability to properly respond. We cannot plan the Kingdom—it just emerges in front of us—but we can advance the Kingdom by responding to the events in an intentional manner.

Imagine reeling from some mega-saga in our life, one with some serious negative consequences. The tendency is to move into self-pity, which is one of the more damaging responses in all of life. With spiritual integrity, we can face it with a degree of intentionality, knowing that Christ uses "all things" to bring the Eternal Seed to maturity in us. Even if it takes a long time to see and embrace the lesson, we can learn to recognize and deal with our own *Eros* reactors and do so without condemnation. This is the lifestyle of faithfulness, and it is in these circumstances that we learn to function in *Agape*. When we miss the proper intentional response, God can and does redeem the circumstance in some providential way and puts us in another similar fix until we get it right. *If God fixes a fix to fix you and you fix the fix before you're fixed, He has to fix another fix to fix you!* God wants us to live intentionally with a maturity derived from Christ being formed in us. We can meet every crisis—financial, relational, or physical—from an *Agape* posture by intentionally choosing to sit in the white chair. And God always provides just the right environment for us to do so.

Thoughts and Questions

- How do we intentionally move from the black chair to the white one?

- In what ways have you intentionally developed response-ability?

- Describe a fix that God put you in. What was the outcome?

READING 67

The Rubber Room

For the grace of God has appeared, bringing salvation to all men, instructing
us to deny ungodliness and worldly desires and to live sensibly, righteously
and godly in the present age (Titus 2:11-12).

THE rubber room is my term for Paul's summary of how grace works in the Kingdom of God. It is a safely padded room where we can make mistakes and learn lessons as we grow up. We enter the rubber room with self-confidence and full of promises to God, ourselves, and others, which we have neither the courage nor the ability to fulfill. Failure, disappointment, and self-revelation follow as we bounce under the pressure of the accidental as Father uses "all things." Grace enlightens, teaches, and trains us to become increasingly intentional. When grace (*Agape* incarnate) is formed in us, it becomes part of our own nature, and we take on the attributes of our Father that were given to us in the person of Christ.

Grace of God appeared. If grace appeared, then it is more than doctrine or unmerited favor; grace, like truth, is a person—*Agape* incarnate. Grace is Christ functioning in His priestly office toward Father's own with whom He has been entrusted.

Grace trained us. Because we are trained by grace (God's own person), we are as safe on our journey as we are when we get there. Grace functions by Christ putting us into Himself—in Christ who *is* the rubber room. When we are in Christ, He becomes the safety padding on the walls of the room in which we are being trained. Hebrews 12 says something similar with the metaphor of a gymnasium, which we will open in another session.

Grace has an end product. Within the safety of the padding, we are free to bounce, rebel, question, or pout until we learn the lesson. There is grace for all our reactions in the process.

Grace is the sovereign purpose of God made incarnate. If God is for me, who can be against me? Grace cannot be presumed upon in the rubber room because we do not come out of the process until we have learned the lessons. We all enter without understanding how far we are from the principles and presence of the Kingdom. Christ is both the lesson and the teacher.

Grace is the only dynamic that can train us. The law is not capable of bringing us to any degree of internal, spiritual transformation; neither can it increase our love for God and others.

Paul shows us 12 amazingly complete *fruits* that begin to grow as a result of our time in the rubber room. Some of these include deliverance from sin, rejection of all ungodliness, refusal of all worldly desires, living discreetly and upright in this present world, and purified so that we can be His very own (see Titus 2:11-15). Grace knows when fruit is beginning to appear and we have ceased living in the accidental. Grace knows when we have moved toward the intentional and shows us the exit from the rubber room. God provides many rubber rooms in our lives as He teaches and cultivates the mysterious Seed within each of us.

Thoughts and Questions

- Describe a situation when you needed God's rubber room of grace.
- How does grace instruct us?
- Why does God continually cover us with grace?

Quitting Is Not an Option

If you abide in Me...My Father is glorified by this (John 15:7-8).

THE Lord provides us with a room carefully padded with the grace of God so we can learn our lessons without getting seriously hurt, being taken down by undue despondency, or becoming hardened in the deceitfulness of *Eros*. While we are in this rubber room, Christ literally wraps us in His grace and holds us while we bounce. Once we recognize the rubber room in our own life, we more readily perceive when others are in it themselves. Some of us live in there for longer periods of time than others until we get through a particular lesson, but grace is always sufficient. When we enter the rubber room of grace, we do so with some part of our life in an ungodly state (out of conformity to Father's pleasure), but when we finish bouncing, having learned the lesson, we exit a little more godly. Remember, grace trains us to reject *and* renounce all ungodliness and worldly (passionate) desires (the root causes of wanting to change chairs), and to live temperate, self-controlled, upright, devout, spiritually whole lives in this present world.

Going to heaven has been so emphasized in the evangelical world that grace working in *this present age* seems almost foreign. But Paul uses the term again in Galatians: *"who gave Himself for our sins so that He might rescue us from this present evil age"* (Gal. 1:4). The Greek verb for *rescue* means *root us out of this present age*, making the redemptive process very much a present reality. As grace roots us out of this age, we begin to take on the fruit of the Kingdom. As the lessons are learned, we stop bouncing and walk out a different person.

When we stop bouncing and come out the other side, we know we have matured. The lessons are designed to grow us up.

Quitting is not an option. Father is determined to see His fruit grow in our lives and simply waits for another opportunity to teach us the lesson. Most of you have heard me say, *"I will never desert you, nor will I ever forsake you"* (Heb. 13:5) is not a promise; it is a threat. His faithfulness and tenacity to His Promise and our well-being are supernatural. Time is on His side because He has already calculated into our journey aspects of failure and learning in the rubber room. When we come out the other side, the Lord says, "I've been waiting for you to grow up in this area." If we will abide in the rubber room, God will reveal His glory within us.

Most of us experience many rubber rooms in our lifetime. There are rubber rooms for individuals, families, congregations, cities, and nations. There is even one for the entire creation (see Rom. 8:19-21). Judith and I have watched God bring each of our children and grandchildren into His purposes, sometimes by a painful route. Our whole family has been in the rubber room more times than I can count. I have known congregations over a 20-year span and could almost pick out the times when the entire body was in a rubber room. To know this and plan accordingly is a great advance in our journey toward intimacy with the Father.

There is a hurting world out there waiting for us to come through the rubber room. Embrace the circumstances, allow grace to work in your life, and let Jesus show you how He intends to prepare each of us to represent the Father to those around us.

Thoughts and Questions

- What is the purpose of the rubber room?
- Describe a rubber room that God specifically designed for you.
- When you exit the rubber room, what is different about you?

Aspects of Grace

Because of the hope laid up for you in heaven…, as in all the world also it is constantly bearing fruit and increasing, even as it has been doing in you also since the day you heard of it and understood the grace of God in truth (Colossians 1:5-6).

THIS is a revolutionary text that will help us understand different aspects of grace. Paul breaks it down into two actions.

Bearing fruit and increasing. Grace and truth came to us in Jesus. The more we begin to look and act like Him, the more we are prepared to extend grace to a hurting world. Just as we grow physically, grace should also increase and bear fruit in our lives, and this growth is revealed in relationships. We grow in grace as we learn to properly relate to our spouse, siblings, friends, and others God has put in our lives. Relationships are the soil where the fruit grows and the pruning happens. The Kingdom is purely relational. It comes without observation for the simple reason that we cannot objectively see godly, mature, and fruit-bearing relationships until some fruit begins to appear. This is similar to not realizing how much your kids have grown until none of their clothes fit them any longer.

Hearing and understanding. First, we must hear the good news, and then we must understand it. Kingdom fruitfulness involves both experiencing God's grace as well as the intellectual apprehension of His outreaching generosity (grace) as transforming power. This is the fertile soil needed for grace to grow and it can do so without fail in any climate. Unfortunately, grace is usually either too loose or too tight. If we do not properly understand grace and interpret it in the light of the rubber room, we either become religiously legalistic or justify our worldly actions. These are the two alternative roads that we sought to make clear in the book *The Agape Road*.

A man who had once walked with the Lord called and asked me to meet him in a bar later that night. When I showed up, he was drowning his pain with alcohol. He asked, "Aren't you afraid to come in this bar?" I said, "Certainly not!" My job description includes being a messenger of grace, willing to travel to find one of God's stray kids wherever they are. As it turned out, the man had been an elder at a church and for whatever reason, rebelled while in the rubber room. He had gone up both the religious and worldly roads and needed a new understanding of grace. God the Father desired for him to hear and understand that grace was still working in his life. With a graduate degree in the rubber room, my job was to be that vehicle.

So, grace is that which causes the Gospel to bear fruit and increase in our lives through the soil of relationships. When we hear and understand grace, we both experience it circumstantially and understand it intellectually. Abiding in the white chair when all of our circumstances would dictate the necessity to change is what bears fruit.

Thoughts and Questions

- What does the Gospel look like when it is growing in your life?
- What is involved in hearing and understanding the Gospel?
- Have you ever misapplied grace? What was the result?

Walking in Grace

My grace is sufficient for you (2 Corinthians 12:9).

WHATEVER your situation and no matter how complicated, back-slidden, or messed up you are, God's message is the same: My grace is sufficient for *you*! We must learn to call on the grace of God rather than get ambushed by walking in our own strength. In spite of understanding grace, we often rely on works and merit to be accepted by God. Many of us say, "God, help me over this one, and I'll handle the next one myself." Paul addressed this heresy by asking, "*Are you so foolish? Having begun by the Spirit, are you now being perfected by the flesh?*" (Gal. 3:3). This is the curse of the Church even today. We start with an anointing and a freedom, but before long, we move into religious works and doing things in our own strength.

Most of us were taught that grace is *unmerited favor*. If so, why does God withhold it from the proud and give it to the humble? (See 1 Peter 5:5). If it is unmerited favor, how can we fall from grace? Finally, if it's unmerited favor, why was Jesus full of grace and truth? Allow us to address these questions individually.

Grace is a person. His first appearance was at the incarnation. Grace is often withheld from the proud as part of the lessons in the rubber room. We can fall from grace when we injure or spurn our reception of grace as a person by actions and attitudes that declare that His grace is not sufficient for us. We have not rejected the free gift of salvation but have done injury to the person who is grace. Finally, Jesus was full of grace and truth because all of Father's DNA was incarnate in Him so that glory could be seen and understood. It is an existential reality that He is truth and He is grace. It is His person with whom we are in relational interchange in the rubber room.

When I was a seminary student, I was a poor and physically out of shape book worm. Someone hired me to drive a big Ford truck for a road construction crew, and I needed the money, so I took the job. Not only was it a complete change of pace, but many of the guys were asking about Christ. One day, one of the men failed to show up, so I had to do his job—shovel 250-degree asphalt from the back of the truck so it could be spread while it was still hot. The temperature outside was over 100 degrees. I felt weak and dizzy and thought I was going to fall off the truck. The other guys were used to the labor and were watching me closely. Suddenly this prayer rose up inside me, and I silently cried out, "Lord Jesus, don't let my testimony come into reproach. Give me Your strength!" The grace of God came over my person, and the strength to continue shoveling filled my being. I kept going—they thought Samson had arrived! I was not worried about my being personally embarrassed; I just did not want God's reputation to be ruined and risk those guys rejecting Him. So, I shoveled asphalt for the rest of the day with the best of them. When the day was over, the anointing left, and the next morning I was so sore, I could hardly get out of bed. The empowering presence of Jesus Christ came to the situation, and I was able to walk in grace.

Thoughts and Questions

- In what situations do you need God's grace to be sufficient for you?
- In what ways do you rely on God's grace and then resort to your own strength?
- How do religious works circumvent grace?

READING 71

Allowing Grace to Teach

For the grace of God has appeared…instructing us… (Titus 2:11-12).

THE Greek root word for "grace" comes from *charis* meaning favor, good will and lovingkindness. According to Strong's concordance, grace is favor expressed as *merciful kindness* by which God, exerting His holy influence upon souls, turns them to Christ, who keeps, strengthens, and builds them up in Christian faith, knowledge, and affection. It is His person who kindles in us the insatiable desire toward exercising the Christian virtues. God's affectionate nature inclines or leans toward us just because He decides to do so, not because there is something in us that forces Him to do so. Jesus is God's grace, which He sent to us to *train* us to live sensibly, righteously, and godly in this present age. Grace has very little to do with eternity and heaven because we will not be in need of grace there.

The first testing ground for grace is in the home. Years ago an elder of my church was coaching a baseball team of which my 5-year-old son was a member. My son continually swung and missed the ball, yet this man was very patient with him. When his own son came up to bat, the first time he missed, the father yelled, "What's the matter with you, stupid?" At that moment, I realized that what he possessed was not adequate for life. He was able to teach my son with grace (maybe because I was the pastor) but was unable to do so with his own child. We must rely on the grace of God to teach us how to deny ungodliness and worldly lust and bring us into the confines of God's Word. This enables us to be patient not only with others but also with ourselves. If we are going to fellowship together as brothers and sisters in the body of Christ, we must understand that others may be on the wrong road and give them grace. Grace responds to Christ within us, covering all that is *Eros*. If we are looking for *Eros* in others, it is not difficult to find.

Grace *instructs* (the Greek word is to train or chastise). Our model for this is Jesus, a truly spiritual Man who loved people, including sinners. He patiently *trained* the disciples. Father is doing the training, and grace is what He uses to train us. We know that if we make a mistake by responding poorly in a situation, He gives us another chance at it until we finally learn the lesson. We change internally as He deals with our desires and intents from the inside out.

Without grace, we cannot be instructed or saved. Grace is God's free act, which excludes merit and is not hindered by guilt. Grace, like love, is a virtue coming from God. Most of us struggle with being loved in a manner that we feel is undeserved, yet there is nothing we can do to earn or deserve God's favor. The absence of condemnation in the rubber room is designed to release us to the joy of learning so we have the freedom and motivation to become who we were created to be. Grace is the foundation to receive more grace. The more we understand grace, the more we're able to receive it, enjoy it, live in it, and walk in it. In other words, *"grace upon grace"* (John 1:16).

Thoughts and Questions

- ❦ What does grace mean?
- ❦ What does grace teach us?
- ❦ Why is it important in our learning process?

What Keeps Us from Grace?

Clothe yourselves with humility… for God is opposed to the proud, but gives grace to the humble (1 Peter 5:5).

WHILE God's grace is no more hindered by sin than it is conditioned by works, our own responses can keep us from enjoying God's grace.

Unforgiveness. While teaching in a maximum-security prison, I was speaking about the grace of God when I saw it suddenly dawned on a 19-year old boy, just old enough to get life without parole for murder one, the realization that God had truly forgiven him. No matter what the prison or anyone else did, he saw it by illumination, and we both knew he was free. He declared several times, "I'm free, I'm really forgiven!" Grace came to him by illumination, and he chose to accept it. It is possible, however, to refuse, reject, or wrestle with God's forgiveness. In addition to accepting forgiveness, we must choose to give it. Forgiveness is a very serious issue with God because if we do not forgive others, then our Father will not forgive us (see Matt. 6:15). If we want to be instructed by grace so we can grow up in the Lord, we must first learn the lesson of forgiveness.

Ungratefulness. God is not so much troubled by external sin as by unthankfulness. Paul listed ungratefulness along with 19 other problems, such as unholiness, malicious gossiping, and treachery. He tells Timothy to avoid such men as these (see 2 Tim. 3:2-5). In the Sermon on the Mount, Jesus groups ungrateful and evil men together (see Luke 6:35). A major hindrance to the grace of God in our life is the loss of gratitude. He is seeking a grateful heart, and when He finds it, grace upon grace abounds.

Pride. God is opposed to the proud but gives grace to the humble (see 1 Peter 5:5). One night in a house group meeting, I could feel the warm love and power of God while praying for people—until I approached a certain man. The climate surrounding him was like a freezer. I blurted out, "Are you a preacher?" He responded, "Yes, how did you know?" My answer was based on the resistance I felt God exerting toward this person, "You're mad at God because He didn't heal you, and you think that after so many years in the ministry, you *deserve* healing." Tears began to flow. Even as inadequate humans, we are inclined toward the humble and reject the proud because that is the nature of God in us.

Self-Impeachment. When we refuse to accept God's grace because we do not feel we deserve it, we impeach ourselves. A man needed to cross a frozen river but was afraid that his weight was too much and the ice would crack, so he got two big boards in his hands to evenly distribute his weight and began to shuffle across the ice on his hands and knees. Then he heard horse bells ringing. He looked up to see a farmer driving a sleigh with a load of logs pulled by two horses going down the frozen river. Suddenly, he realized how foolish he had been. Most of us believe in the grace of God, *but we are unsure whether it will hold us because we know how rebellious and sinful we really are.* However, the grace of God is like ice 20 feet thick, and it *will* hold us. Grace is a person who is sufficient for *you.*

Thoughts and Questions

- Which of these issues keep you from walking in grace? Why?
- Why is unforgiveness such a serious issue with God?
- In what ways have you been self-impeached?

Running Out of Grace

If you abide in Me, and My words abide in you, ask whatever you wish,
and it will be done for you. My Father is glorified by this, that
you bear much fruit (John 15:7-8).

HAVE you ever really enjoyed something for a period of time but then the grace seems to run out? What used to be so wonderful and enjoyable now becomes wearying, boring, and even oppressive. This is the puzzling process of death. Running out of grace means to continue to do something after the blessing or favor of God no longer rests on it.

Suppose your pastor calls a prayer meeting every day from 5:00 a.m. to 6:00 a.m. and there is grace and the presence of God on it. At some point, however, the grace of God may cease to be in the meeting. At that point we typically just keep it going with or without God because having a prayer meeting in the morning is the right thing to do. There is nothing worse than getting up at 4:30 a.m. to go to a dead prayer meeting, just as there is nothing better than to get up at 4:30 A.M. to go to one that is living. *Running out of grace is a tremendous form of guidance.* Abiding involves learning to watch what the grace of God is or is not resting on and choosing to stay where His grace is present, knowing that grace is a Person. If you are a serious follower of Jesus, you will find yourself acutely aware of what His grace rests upon and what is dead and smelly.

The song "Amazing Grace" has always had the grace of God on it. It does not matter if it is sung in a cathedral or the army barracks, the presence of God shows up. Other songs have had the grace of God on them and for whatever reason, His grace lifted, but we still kept singing the same songs and preaching the same messages. God's grace lifting from something is a method of Father's pruning and is His privilege. Grace as a means of guidance serves to keep us moving in the right direction.

Walking in the Spirit requires sensitivity to the presence and grace of God in a given situation. It means being responsive if the Lord says, "No Bible study today; go down to the mission and work with the homeless." If we do that on the day He speaks to us, we can be assured that the grace of God will be on it and there will be fruit. Going to the mission to get brownie points may be tough if there is no grace on it. When things are done out of human effort, there is something counterproductive or *fruitless* about it. It is possible to do many things, including studying the Bible beyond normal limits, but we need to find out what God's grace is on for us. There are times when there is grace to tell someone what Jesus did for you and times when there isn't. There may be grace for prison ministry or pro-life support while others may have no grace for this. We need to learn to recognize, interpret, and walk in the grace God gives us. This is fertile soil for the Eternal Seed to produce after its kind in our own life as well as in others.

Running out of grace does not suggest that we are no longer abiding in the white chair. In fact, learning to move into the sphere of being led by the Holy Spirit is the end result of developing the skill that allows us to become aware when the grace of God is no longer on that which we knew was alive on previous occasions.

Thoughts and Questions

- Describe a situation in which you ran out of grace. How did you respond?
- Why is grace a form of guidance?
- List some things in your life that have grace on them. List some things that do not.

PART VII

Fallen King

Difficulty of Being a Fallen King

Behold, the man has become like one of Us…so He drove the man out
(Genesis 3:22, 24).

WHEN God created man, He created him in His image as a king or vice-regent, one who rules on His behalf. God is the One who actually created our personal sovereignty; we were created to rule. When we were in proper relationship with God, we were abiding and at rest, enjoying God and allowing Him to enjoy us. However, at the original transgression, Adam and Eve, the original pair, attempted to enter God's space, requiring Him to force them out. They became a *fallen* king and queen, and the struggle down through time began. Kings who were created to rule in *Agape* were infected with *Eros* and they then desired to be owners, not stewards.

A fallen king is not gender specific; both males and females are considered sons of God. No wonder some of us are so difficult—we are fallen kings and queens created with genes that were designed by God to rule! This sovereignty can be seen in our own children because they learned from the very best how to insist on their own way. If we were not a fallen king, we could submit to Jesus in a heartbeat, but we have to deal with a sovereignty of our own—we have rights, goals, and purposes for our own life. I have counseled people who have shaken their fists and cursed in God's face because as a fallen king they felt their sovereignty had been violated. The strength of the human will is a phenomenon.

God created us to rule. Therefore, we do have a destiny! We may not even know what that destiny is, but it is present somewhere in our DNA. As kings, part of our destiny is that we are going to judge the world (see 1 Cor. 6:2). When the incorruptible Seed attempts to grow in us, we may not understand the internal upheaval, but what we are experiencing is the Holy Spirit moving us forward in the destiny of God. The degree and intensity of the conflict can be measured by the purpose of God, which is being restored and made operative. The internal conflict we experience, defined as spiritual warfare, has been designed to reveal the presence and function of the Seven Giants. Paul's concept of "all things" now enters the stage, for we have engaged the eternal purpose of the Living God, which He had for you before the foundation of the world (see Phil. 3:12).

Thoughts and Questions

- What is one reason man was created in God's image?
- What caused us to become fallen kings and queens?
- Have you ever experienced what felt like God violating your personal sovereignty? Explain.

Fallen King and the Five I Wills

But you said in your heart… (Isaiah 14:13).

D ARKNESS makes its appeal by means of the five I Wills which, as fallen kings, is how we express our *perverted* sovereignty. Fallen creation crowding into God's space began in Genesis, continues through Revelation, and includes angels and man. Isaiah 14 describes Satan's spiritual pride:

> *How you have fallen from heaven, O star of the morning, son of the dawn! You have been cut down to the earth, you who have weakened the nations! But you said in your heart, 'I will ascend to heaven; I will raise my throne above the stars of God, and I will sit on the mount of assembly in the recesses of the north. I will ascend above the heights of the clouds; I will make myself like the Most High.' Nevertheless you will be thrust down to Sheol, to the recesses of the pit* (Isaiah 14:12-15).

Exaggeration is far more serious than most of us realize. It undermines trust because it is an issue of keeping your word. People *exaggerate* everything from the size of a fish they caught to the size and influence of their church.

Selfish ambition is the source of *"disorder and every evil thing"* (James 3:16). It is a primary source of failure and confusion in business and personal relationships and is prevalent in the larger body of Christ.

Domination and control. The most workable description of this in the New Testament is called the "Diotrephes disease" because he loved to be first (3 John 9). Like the Greek word *Nike*, which means to conquer, the doctrine of the Nicolaitans (see Rev. 2:15) promoted leadership that sought to conqueror or dominate the people. This is a major issue in our time both in business and in the Church.

Position and titles have to do with reputations. It seems the church is dying by degrees—PhDs, DDs., etc. There is nothing wrong with titles and degrees; the problem lies in people trying to impress others with them. Jesus always draws us to His face in intimacy and to His person in accountability. We, however, erroneously seek security, identity, and belonging from our status, title, office, or some *created* reputation rather than from His Person. We need to transfer our confidence from the title or the degree to the Person of Christ.

Imitation or simulation. Imitation can be used in a positive sense (i.e., be imitators of God), but when used in a negative sense, it has to do with creating an image that is not authentic. This is sometimes referred to as posing. Efforts to simulate the real thing are plentiful. Leather is real, but imitation leather is not so great. The problem is that the real thing sometimes costs us more than we are willing to pay. To get leather costs the death of an animal.

Spiritual pride is nothing less than an attempt to enter God's space. Most often, religion seeks to substitute itself for the nature of God. Entering God's space is a form of arrogance and is dangerous. Demonic forces use the Seven Giants in these five realms as leverage against us; this is spiritual warfare. They look innocent but carry such deadly force!

Thoughts and Questions

- Which one of the five I Wills do you struggle with the most?
- Think of someone you know who loved to be first. How do you feel about this person?
- Explain why spiritual warfare would be in these five realms.

The Bent-Knee Society

Creation itself also will be set free from its slavery to corruption into the freedom of the glory of the children of God (Romans 8:21).

CHRIST surrendered His personal sovereignty when He came to earth. Although Jesus existed in the form of God, He *"did not regard equality with God a thing to be grasped"* (Phil. 2:6). I call this the Bent-Knee Society. God is perfectly free, but He sometimes chooses to limit His own freedom. God limited His own freedom when He said that He would never again destroy the earth with water. Because we are being conformed to His image, we must eventually and by choice surrender our sovereignty, whether by illumination or by subjection. Illumination involves some maturity in understanding the reasons and necessity for bending our knee and surrendering our sovereignty. When we surrender by subjection, it is usually because events in life have forced us there and we are *required* to change, adjust, and bend our knee.

Conflict is the result of God challenging our fallen personal sovereignty with His own Sovereignty. God entering our space often comes in the form of one of His kids—another fallen king. Some of the worst marriage fights are over personal sovereignty—you are not telling *me* what to do!

Jesus was sent as a light both to Israel and to the nations, but Israel's leaders were unable to receive this intervention into their space; it displaced their own imagined *sovereignty,* and they wanted Him out. They said, *"If we let Him go on like this, all men will believe in Him, and the Romans will come and take away both our place and our nation"* (John 11:48), so they rejected and crucified

Him. They were more concerned with their titles, offices, and reputation than the Kingdom of God. When God enters our space, our personal sovereignty is challenged in the form of one of the "I Wills," and we are required to make a conscious, preferential choice to surrender. That choice begins with water baptism, the ultimate bending of the knee.

To truly love one another, we must surrender our personal sovereignty. This requires that we develop the ability to *renounce, refuse,* and *retract.* The 3 Rs of personal surrender are often neglected or intentionally overlooked due to the price tag involved. For instance, we can exercise our sovereign rights to *not* forgive someone, but we will suffer the consequences. Rebellion makes us unable to renounce, restrain, or retract. The three Rs involve spiritual warfare because one or more of the Seven Giants are involved on a whole new level. We *choose to renounce* selfish ambition and hidden agendas. We *refuse* to look good and impress others with our title and education. We *choose to retract* our personal sovereignty and give up control by exaggeration or domination. By renouncing, refusing, and retracting, we allow Christ to reveal Himself through us. When His Kingdom comes, our kingdom goes. Humility and repentance result in the recognition of the five I Wills, allowing us to limit our own freedom. Jesus said that He would never leave us nor forsake us. He is willing to limit His own freedom to walk us through our changes because He is covenantally faithful.

Thoughts and Questions

- Have you ever had another fallen king get in your space? How did you respond?

- What three actions are needed to surrender our personal sovereignty?

- What makes us incapable of or unable to renounce, restrain, or retract?

Restoring Our Sovereignty

You crowned him with glory and honor (Hebrews 2:7).

JESUS is the root, the Eternal Seed, that contains all the DNA for the fulfillment of our destiny. Just as the acorn contains the full-grown oak tree, so Christ gives us all that is needed for the purpose of God to be fulfilled in our lives. He was crowned with glory and honor, not for Himself but in our behalf—He intention is to restore the crown and Father's glory to His people. To receive His crown, we must allow Jesus Christ, the Sovereign King, to enter our space, de-create and transform our personal sovereignty, and replicate His own Kingship within us. Salvation is an invasion of God's purpose and presence entering man's sphere. It is not man seeking God but God's redemptive act initiated toward us. The distinction is critical.

When we *renounce, refuse,* and *retract* our fallen, personal sovereignty in the form of the Seven Giants and the five I Wills, we are presenting ourselves to be re-created or to become a new creation. Once this happens, we can begin the process of having our sovereignty restored. Restoration of our sovereignty is a process of the Kingdom coming to us in several steps:

Preferential Choice. When we choose or prefer Christ's will, knowing it displaces the Five I Wills, it results in our being able to seek first the Kingdom of God (see Matt. 6:10).

Change of Focus and Object. When Christ's will effectively displaces the five I Wills, our focus (seek first the Kingdom) is on God's own nature. The *Shema*—loving God with all our heart, soul, mind, and strength—becomes a reality in our lives. As our focus is restored and the object of our affection becomes God's own nature, Christ, as He promised, can take us to the Father.

Capacity to Love Others. When we choose to love God, our capacity to love others increases. The Eternal Seed within us begins to mature; Christ is being formed in us, and our capacity for God in the form of *Agape* grows. All of this is precipitated by the new birth. We literally and existentially begin to love others *as* the Father loves them. This is God's intent and is the route to the supernatural. The Kingdom is Father's love being replicated.

Cultivate the Seed in Others. As we invite and make room for the Kingdom to come to us and our own personal sovereignty is restored, we begin "looking on the things of others," seeking to cultivate the Eternal Seed that has been planted in them. We can speak to our fellow *Eros*-infected and distorted fallen kings as a farmer rather than a sheriff, cultivating that Eternal Seed that has not yet produced normal Kingdom fruit.

Paul summarized these four points when he said:

> *Him we preach and proclaim, warning and admonishing everyone and instructing everyone in all wisdom (comprehensive insight into the ways and purposes of God), that we may present every person mature (full-grown, fully initiated, complete, and perfect) in Christ (the Anointed One)* (Colossians 1:28 AMP).

Thoughts and Questions

- Why was Jesus crowned with glory and honor?
- How can we receive the crown?
- Explain how our personal sovereignty is restored.

Crown of Life

Be faithful until death, and I will give you the crown of life
(Revelation 2:10).

THE crown of life has to do with ruling and reigning, not in the millennium, or in heaven, but now, in this time-space *"present wicked age"* (Gal. 1:4 AMP). When Adam failed, the earth was cursed, and death rather than life reigned in us. If you do not believe this, just try planting a garden. You have to continually fertilize and cultivate just to get a tomato to grow, but weeds will grow without water or nourishment! If we can understand the curse, we can understand the crown.

Reigning in life is living life as God intended it when He created us. It is the Kingdom agenda that the Church essentially lost by neglect and *Eros* agendas. However, through grace and the gift of righteousness in Christ we can *"reign as kings in life"* (Rom. 5:17 AMP). When we grasp the fact that God actually *wants* us to reign, we are forced to realize that: a) We have not been provided the crown needed; b) we are ignorant that we have one; or c) it has fallen into disuse. We are forced by our own intellectual honesty and integrity to grapple with God and the issues of life because we know that we are not reigning.

Jesus bought our crown by wearing His own crown of five-inch thorns made from the acacia tree at His crucifixion. It was God's testimony to what He needed to do because of our failure. Paul saw every person with whom he shared the Lord as an opportunity to give insight into the curse and into Christ's suffering as part of his crown (see Phil. 4:1). Paul also talked about fighting the good fight and faithfully finishing the course because of the crown of righteousness that was waiting for him in heaven (see 2 Tim. 4:7-8). This righteousness is not only imputed; it is also *imparted*. When we stand before the Lord, we will be part of the crown of Christ.

Many Scriptures describe our being crowned and made to rule. God told Adam and Eve to be fruitful and multiply, and fill the earth, *subdue* it, and *rule* over it (see Gen. 1:28). God crowned us with glory and majesty when He made us. He put all things under our feet and made us to rule over them (see Ps. 8:5-6; Heb. 2:6-9). However far the present Church may be from Father's ultimate intention or reigning, it is still a necessity.

David understood the weight our crown carries when he said of the Lord:

> *Who pardons all your iniquities, Who heals all your diseases; Who redeems your life from the pit, Who crowns you with lovingkindness and compassion; Who satisfies your years with good things, so that your youth is renewed like the eagle* (Psalm 103:3-5).

The crown of life literally means the ability to rule or reign victoriously and triumphantly in life. This is God's glory being revealed in the earth.

Thoughts and Questions

- What does God expect us to do with our crown?
- At what cost were we provided a crown?
- In what ways can you see God crowning you with lovingkindness and compassion?

Dominion Mandate

Be fruitful, multiply, and fill the earth, and subdue it [using all its vast resources in the service of God and man]; and have dominion over the fish of the sea, the birds of the air, and over every living creature that moves upon the earth (Genesis 1:28).

THE crown consists of four intimate and functional parts called the dominion mandate: the urge to rule, the sexual drive, dignity or usefulness, and the need to belong.

Urge to rule. When God created man from a pile of dust, He breathed into it, and man stood up on his feet *with the urge to rule*. Externally he was to rule God's creation; internally, he was to rule himself. The urge to rule is deep in every person; when off-center or perverted by *Eros*, this desire reverts to illegal control and becomes detrimental and destructive. The urge to rule often shows itself in the ungoverned desire to get ahead of others, causing people to step on each other for the privilege and expectation of getting 18 inches closer to their undefined goal.

Sexual drive. Few forces are as powerful as the sexual drive. At creation, God gave us the mandate to subdue and replenish the earth, which involves all sexual activity, particularly in marriage. Sexuality may be one of the strongest urges of all creation. The necessity to reproduce to guarantee the longevity of the species is inherent and powerful. At the same time, nothing has been more distorted, altered, or perverted than the sexual drive. The necessity of Scripture having to forbid sexual activity with animals shows us the urgency of ruling ourselves when it touches the sexual dimension.

Dignity or usefulness. The drive to be useful is dominant. Failure to experience usefulness causes us to want to die. Studies have revealed this as a hidden source of suicide. It is possible not only to fail to rule, but in consequence, to become ruled by passions and ungoverned desires. We are then more than *not* useful but become useless. Obsessive-compulsive actions and fears deplete our very will to live. Welfare systems tend to destroy one's usefulness.

Need to belong. This is an unmitigated, un-erasable *urge to know security, identity, and belonging.* The cry for belonging is primal and innate in each of us, but many people have never found a safe place where they can belong. Security, identity, and belonging involve knowing who we are, to whom we belong, and where we are going.

God speaks of things that are not as though they are. This, we have learned, is the prophetic perfect. Soon after the Lord prophetically speaks our name, places the crown on us, and declares us righteous, strange and unexpected things begin to manifest—actions and attitudes that are not in agreement with the crown! We soon discover ourselves in the mystery of the Christian life *seeking to understand how to become what He declared us to be.* The ambiguity of the Christian life is becoming who He said (in the prophetic perfect) we were to Him. When we acknowledge and receive the crown of life, we accept Jesus' Lordship, and our internal drives, motives, and intentions begin to come under His Kingdom principles and expectations. When we embrace the crown of life, His Kingdom laws are written on our heart.

Thoughts and Questions

- Explain the importance of our dominion mandate.
- Which of the four parts of the dominion mandate do you struggle with the most?
- Why is our need to belong so strong?

Idolatry and the Dominion Mandate

No person practicing sexual vice or impurity in thought or in life, or one who is covetous [who has lustful desire for the property of others and is greedy for gain]—for he [in effect] is an idolater—has any inheritance in the kingdom of Christ and of God (Ephesians 5:5 AMP).

THE images of idolatry have changed since the New Testament, but idolatry itself has not passed away in the slightest; it is perhaps more concealed and subtle, but major idols still function powerfully in our own age. The dominion mandate summarized is the desire to rule, the desire to procreate, the desire to be useful, and the desire to know security, identity, and belonging. Man has made many attempts to substitute these basic urges; the end result has been idolatry leading to oppression, sexual deviance, performance, unreality, creation of false personalities, and attempts to drown our damaged dreams in materialism or substance abuse.

While there were many gods in biblical times, three of the most well-known still function in our own time/space world. They demonstrated totally different characteristics than *Jehovah*. Baal/Ashtoreth are the fertility gods; they represent *unrestrained sexuality*. Moloch is the god of *unrestrained cruelty*; Israel sacrificed their own children to this god. *Mammon*, the only god who dared compared itself with the God of Creation, rules our present culture in the form of *unrestrained materialism*.

Idolatry involves spiritual warfare with the purpose of preventing the four Kingdom mandates from appearing in our personal life and journey. The Lord, who brought Israel out of Egypt with a strong arm and who cared for her like a compassionate mother, faced competitors for His affections. Israel had as many gods as they had towns and as many idolatrous altars as Jerusalem had streets (see Jer. 11:13). In the language of the Bible, Yahweh is the God of gods, *"For the Lord your God is God of gods and Lord of lords, the great God, mighty and awesome, who shows no partiality and accepts no bribes"* (Deut. 10:17 NIV). The real enemy of the true knowledge of God is not atheism but rival gods. The defining challenge is *"choose for yourselves this day whom you will serve"* (Josh. 24:15 NIV).

Paul told us that idolatry will cause us to lose our *Kingdom inheritance*. We do not lose our basic salvation, which is God's gift to us in the person of His Son, but we can lose our Kingdom *purpose of that gift*, which is the Kingdom dominion mandate. When we seek the Kingdom first, we will, without question, find ourselves in conflict with one or more of these idols.

Thoughts and Questions

- In what ways have you encountered the idols of unrestrained sexuality or cruelty?
- How has the subtle god of Mammon affected those you know and love?
- Why would idolatry cause us to lose our Kingdom inheritance?

Losing Our Crown

I am coming quickly; hold fast what you have, in order that no one take your crown (Revelation 3:11).

JESUS was victorious in every sphere of His life, and on His head are many kingly crowns (see Rev. 19:12). Some may possibly be those that other saints have laid before His throne (see Rev. 4:10). Suppose we could look into the future and see ourselves arriving at Jesus' coronation without a crown of our own to lay at His feet because we allowed someone to take it from us.

The possibility is real that someone could take our crown. The most common reason is being scandalized. Taking offense or becoming offended involves unusual and extreme reactions to situations that defy our human understanding, and it costs us. One man told me that when he found out that his trusted pastor was a homosexual, he was so angry that he decided he couldn't walk with the Lord any more. Because of his offense, he allowed the pastor's actions to take his own crown. When we are bent out of shape because of someone else's conduct, we need to exercise caution in our responses. Our ability to respond properly—response-ability—in the midst of mysterious, uncalled for, and unexpected circumstances is what determines whether we will allow someone to take our crown.

Another way we can lose our crown is to assume that we do not have any victories in our life. Many people live as defeated Christians—defeated spiritually, financially, sexually, mentally, and emotionally. Our crown is part of our inheritance, but we have to stand firm and persevere (see James 1:12). Paul referred to us as his *"delight and crown (wreath of victory), thus stand firm in the Lord, my beloved"* (Phil. 4:1 AMP). There are multitudes of defeated people who need a Kingdom priest, but we cannot be priests if we have lost our crown. We cannot be a priest if we act like the sheriff or attempt to make God do what we think He should. Christ crowns our life with lovingkindness and compassion so we can have personal and corporate victories.

Because Paul kept the faith, he knew there was a crown waiting for him. He also knew it was only through Christ that he could be faithful. Without Jesus' strength, none of us could live a Kingdom lifestyle; it certainly is not because of self-righteousness or religious effort. The casting down of the crown is an act of humility, a sense of absolute adoration and full recognition of Christ as our source and strength. It is God who brought us to a place where we could even live life. Increasingly, we are eager to give our crown to the One to whom it *actually* belongs; He is the one who earned the victory and carried us through. The crown is God's call for us to subdue ourselves (internally) and the earth (externally). What will we lay at His feet? We can only give the fruit and triumph of the repeated victories that He wrought in our own life. Our victories truly do belong to Him. He has allowed us to steward them for Him in *Agape*.

Thoughts and Questions

- ♔ What are some of the ways we can lose our crown?
- ♔ Why are we crowned with lovingkindness and compassion?
- ♔ What does casting down our crown signify?

Internalizing Our Crown

And the effect of righteousness will be peace [internal and external], and the result of righteousness will be quietness and confident trust forever
(Isaiah 32:17 AMP).

IF we want to be Father-pleasers, we must recognize the necessity of reigning in life and becoming more intentional about our existence counting for God's Kingdom. Therefore, we must embrace the ongoing and costly process to *internalize* the crown in several key areas:

1. *Joy and personal freedom.* We can't fake joy; it is something we either do or do not have. Fake joy is nothing less than a hidden agenda. Joy involves freedom from fears, habits, and all kind of unhealthy attachments. If it is missing, do something about it.

2. *Contentment without strain.* Living in contentment means resting in a state of peace, happiness, and satisfaction regardless of our circumstances, and it brings great gain. Contentment can be misunderstood for passivity. Do not be afraid of the process.

3. *Increase in prosperity.* This includes spiritual, intellectual, financial, and social prosperity. There are seeds that never grow; we call them wallflowers. There are also seeds that sleep in hope knowing that spring is coming. The opium of the people is TV, media, and multitudes of distractions, so people are increasingly intellectually and socially underdeveloped. God wants us to develop our ability to think, reason, and act. When we *internalize* the crown, we grow

spiritually and socially. We think. We plan. We prosper. We grow in every area of our lives, and the culture changes.

4. *Fulfillment.* God satisfies our life. Like joy, we can't fake being fulfilled. It involves living a satisfied life in our personal relationships, jobs, and communities. Being satisfied with God as Father needs to be verbalized; He waits for our words. Secular or religious voices can disrupt our satisfaction, so we must learn to abide.

5. *Generosity.* We find ourselves *wanting* to give rather than receive. We become the lenders rather than the borrowers and part of the answer, not part of the problem. Sometimes it is harder to give of ourselves and our time than to give money. Reciprocal generosity is vital. Jesus said that it is better to give than receive.

6. *Relational maturity.* This involves every kind of relationship but especially marriage. Most of us can weep with others, but rejoicing when someone is blessed is another issue. Lids on a crab buckets are unnecessary because if one crab starts to crawl out of the bucket, the other crabs grab him and pull him back. Internalizing the crown delivers us from the crab-bucket mentality.

7. *Proclamation, evangelism.* An internalized crown of life teaches us how to rule. We discover an increasing desire to share what we have found with others. People become important, not just souls to be won or a church to be filled.

Our crown is designed to permeate our entire person. The Lord insists that we be just as interested in cultivating and nourishing another's crown as we are of our own. May our crowns not only be in place but also internalized in such a way that we could measure the reality of our transformation by the presence of the fruit of the Kingdom.

Thoughts and Questions

🌱 Why is it important to internalize the crown?

- Which of the seven guidelines do you struggle with the most?
- In what ways are you cultivating your crown?

PART VIII

Pride and Rage

God's Sphere and the Death Line

But from the tree of the knowledge of good and evil you shall not eat, for in the day that you eat from it you will surely die (Genesis 2:17).

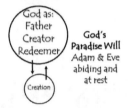

GOD—AS Father, Creator, and Redeemer—created the world separate from or out from Himself. He is different from yet an intricate part of His Creation. In His paradise, Adam and Eve were abiding and at rest in the world as God created it.

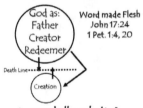

Because of the original transgression, death entered and we were separated from God, who is life. God was very clear about life and death when He told Adam and Eve not to eat from a certain tree. *We can be dead even while we live* (see 1 Tim. 5:6) in the same manner that we are dead in our trespasses and sins when separated from God. When Adam and Eve disobeyed, a death line emerged between man and God; we were separated from the Father, and the Father was separated from us.

Jesus came out from the Father to reconcile the world, heal the death line, and redeem His creation. Because we come to the Father by means of the Son, creation was able to touch the Father, and the Father was able to touch His creation through Christ (see John 17:24; 1 Peter 1:4, 20). Even though creation rebelled, God received it back into Himself by means of the person of Christ. We can only imagine what was in the heart of the Father that caused Him to reach for creation that had separated itself from Him.

When Israel entered God's sphere, she did so to follow her own purpose. In a manner similar to the Church today, Israel mishandled and misapplied miracles, mystery, and authority as well as seized titles and ownership in an attempt to enter God's space. Unable to see Christ as the manifestation of the I AM who was sent, Israel sought to acquire, possess, and control God. Eventually, as a nation, she became irredeemable and needed to be removed from God's own sphere, thus the destruction of Jerusalem, devastation of the Temple, and the necessity of implementing a New Covenant through the crucifixion of the Messiah (see Matt. 27:18; 21:43). Father had to force Israel out of His space in order to reveal His love for the whole created universe, including every tribe, people, nation, and tongue. The Kingdom was taken from Israel and given to another—those who would bring forth the fruit of that Kingdom. In order to stay in right relationship with God, we must refuse to enter His realm. When we remain in a place of abiding and rest, we can bring forth the fruit of the Kingdom—the compassion and healing nature of God.

Thoughts and Questions

- ꙮ Explain Paradise Will.
- ꙮ Have you ever experienced being dead while you still lived? Explain.
- ꙮ Why was Israel forced out of God's space?

READING 84

Cosmic Court Case

*Listen, O heavens…sons I have reared and brought up, but they have
revolted against Me. …Alas, sinful nation, people weighed down with
iniquity, offspring of evildoers, sons who act corruptly! They have
abandoned the Lord, they have despised the Holy One of Israel,
they have turned away from Him* (Isaiah 1:2-4).

THINK of it—God and fallen man in a cosmic face off! This universal
court case is clearly stated in Isaiah 1. God, as Father, is experiencing
relational injury, family disruption, and Fatherly grief and sorrow. The case
continues until Isaiah 53 when Father, Himself, intervenes. Choosing to act,
He laid on Jesus the iniquity of us all.

God is both Judge and Creator; man is the accused. As the Creator, He
has need of adjudication with all that He created. As the created, man stands
in the position of having God bring a lawsuit against him. Although this is a
court case, the Judge is not angry; He is a brokenhearted, injured Father who
is grieving over His children. God is experiencing the relational Fatherly grief
and sorrow that goes on until in Isaiah 53 when He laid on Jesus the iniquity
of us all. Someone once told me that because God is God, He does not feel
pain, but Paul writes, *"do not grieve the Holy Spirit of God"* (Eph. 4:30). God
grieves deeply about injured or broken relationships.

The redemptive process was God in Christ reconciling the world to Himself (see 2 Cor. 5:19). Taking the initiative and making the provision was
all settled before the foundation of the created universe. Once discovered,
understood, and embraced, we can see why Jesus would say the Kingdom is

like a treasure buried in a field. Once you find it, sell everything you have and buy the field. It is so much more than escaping hell or making heaven our home. We are responding to an injured Father who was rejected by His own family and is now offering you and me a once-in-a-lifetime deal: As many as received Him, Father gave the authority for us to become His own children. God brought a cosmic court case against us, found us guilty, and sentenced His Own Son on our behalf.

Thoughts and Questions

- What other aspects of the case against us can you see in Isaiah?

- Why do you think God is grieved rather than angry?

- In ways is the Kingdom a treasure to you? What have you sold to buy the field?

READING 85

Ravines and Valleys

*Every **ravine** will be filled, and every **mountain** and hill will be brought low; the **crooked** will become straight, and the **rough** roads smooth; and all flesh will see the salvation of God* (Luke 3:5-6).

IN Luke's prophecy, he is saying that this New Covenant is going to change everything! Father's stated goal as the result of our having been born from above is the comprehensive reformation of man into the image of Christ. This is Paul's picture of what he meant by, *"If any man be in Christ, he is a new creation..."* (2 Cor. 5:17).

The direct effect of *Eros* and the fall of man is stated blatantly and without religious modification in the following problems.

The *ravine* has to do with going down in depression or anger. Depression is probably the number-one problem in America. Valleys of depression and rage result in our inability or incapacity to rise to normal joy and relational maturity.

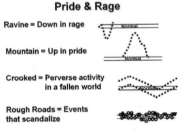

Pride & Rage

Ravine = Down in rage

Mountain = Up in pride

Crooked = Perverse activity in a fallen world

Rough Roads = Events that scandalize

(c) 2002 Lifechangers, Inc.   45

Mountains of pride are manifestations of self-sufficiency and illusion that cause us to attempt to enter God's sphere and literally, play God.

The *crooked* has to do with all that is perverse and distorted in human behavior (see Phil. 2:15). It is unrefined and raw. Although we live in a fallen world, it is shocking when a teacher, doctor, or police officer does something really bad.

The *rough roads* are human behavior or events that precipitate injury or betrayal and result in our being scandalized. We have *"a job to do among nations and governments—a red-letter day! Your job is to pull up and tear down, take apart and demolish, and then start over, building and planting"* (Jer. 1:10 TM). The ground must be level in preparation to build and plant. These four problems can only be solved by the Eternal Seed of *Agape* growing in our lives.

Thoughts and Questions

- Describe an experience you've had with ravines, mountains, crooked, or rough roads.

- How would you describe God's lawsuit with creation to someone?

- What are some of the things that cause the Holy Spirit pain?

READING 86

Up, Down or Abiding

The heavens are the heavens of the Lord, but the earth He has given to the sons of men (Psalm 115:16).

T HE entire Christian life can be summarized by moving up, moving down, or abiding. Movement up into God's sphere is very simply called pride. *"And the Lord God said, Behold, the man has become like one of Us [the Father, Son, and Holy Spirit], to know [how to distinguish between] good and evil and blessing and calamity; and now, lest he put forth his hand and take also from the tree of life and eat, and live forever...so **He drove the man out**"* (Gen. 3:22, 24 AMP). In the original language, this is an imperative statement requiring an emergency response. That which was created is now seeking to enter God's space, and something had to be done. God is required to drive man out of the Garden and out of His space back into a place where He could relate to us separate from Himself.

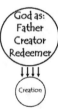

Moving up and down can be seen in Paul's statement, "Do not say in your heart, *'Who will ascend into heaven?' (that is, to bring Christ down)*, or *'Who will descend into the abyss?' (that is, to bring Christ up from the dead)'*" (Rom. 10:6-7). Pride says, "I'm different; I am more than, other than you." It involves acquiring, possessing, and controlling God and others. Synonyms for pride are haughtiness, arrogance, conceit, vanity, lordiness, imperious, despotic, magisterial, domineering, cruel, dictatorial, tyrannical, autocratic, absolute, arbitrary, and oppressive. When we enter God's sphere, we attempt to think and act like we are the Creator. God must push us out of His sphere so we recognize that we are the created and not the Creator. Pride *requires* that we be cast down or humbled.

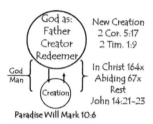

Movement down is rage and is also a clear transgression against the will and purpose of God. It is a biblical description of our human response to our powerlessness as fallen kings to acquire, possess, and control the plan of God in the earth. Synonyms for rage are fury, wrath, frenzy, vexation, resentment, and incensed.

The third choice is abiding. Christ came out from the Father to provide a place to rest for us. We rest in the completed work of Christ on our behalf. Abiding is the cessation of movement where God's grace is sufficient for us and His power is perfected in weakness (see 2 Cor. 12:9). It is a Kingdom gift that preserves peace. Synonyms for abide are remain, dwell, continue, endure, and stand. Enduring means to be left holding on to one's confidence after others have collapsed (see Heb. 10:35-39). The mystery of the Kingdom demands that we clearly understand and embrace the concept of abiding. We will go more into depth on these concepts in following sessions.

Thoughts and Questions

- Explain your interpretation of movement up and down.
- In what ways have you struggled to abide?
- Why do you think movement up and down is one of the enemy's tactics to discourage and wear out the saints?

READING 87

Pride

God is opposed to the proud, but gives grace to the humble. Humble yourselves, therefore, under the mighty hand of God, that He may exalt you at the proper time (1 Peter 5:5-6).

W HEN I was a new Christian just out of the Navy, I went to Bible college. On break, I went home and visited my home church, eager to be used by God. Without warning, a prophetic spirit came on me and I start to prophesy. I can still remember my bold and anointed prophecy: "Yea, the voice of the Lord of thunder...!" While I was still speaking, my head started to swell and I thought, *I am like Isaiah!* I quickly found out that the Lord has a cure for that. I got so caught up in my pride that I was distracted from hearing the prophetic word and stopped dead in the middle of it. Everyone in the church knew Isaiah was not there. I wish someone would have taught me about being pushed out of God's sphere when I was three weeks old in the Lord.

Pride is the ultimate refusal to embrace and display God's DNA. It is motivated by one of the Seven Giants. The quintessence of all spiritual warfare is crucifying the desires and passions of our *Eros*-ridden flesh. The formula goes something like this: Sin = *Eros* = my own lusts (not someone else's or Satan's) =

determination to acquire, possess, and control. Each of us is tempted when we are carried away and enticed by our *own* lusts. Unrestrained or broken loose desire takes us into God's own sphere. This is true whether one is a believer or not; it is a law of creation. In the Old Testament, Korah rose up in pride against Moses and Aaron asking, *"Why do you exalt yourselves above the assembly of the Lord?"* (Num. 16:3). Moses' response was one of humility—he fell on his face. Korah had to be pushed out of God's sphere and was violently swallowed up in an earthquake. Once pride has been engaged, it is like a vacuum that sucks us up into the consummate world of acquiring, possessing, and controlling.

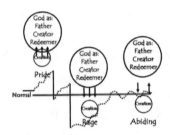

Pride requires that at some point we be cast down and that always involves humiliation. We cannot know humility without some degree of humiliation. However, after a humiliating experience, it usually is not long before we begin to climb back up into a sphere of pride and arrogance. We become hard and demanding of ourselves and others, and the Lord has to push us out of His sphere again. Then we humble ourselves and repent. If we can understand this, it will bring spiritual stability to our life because repeated breakings are not the normal Christian life.

Part of living in the Kingdom is developing self-control—the capacity to start and stop. God graciously provides a rubber room where we can learn to abide rather than go up into pride or down into rage. This rubber room of grace is passive righteousness, which allows us to be *addressable* and *accountable*. Only *Agape* gives us the ability to control and deny ourselves; it is our route to freedom so we can stand firm, free from enslavement to pride or rage.

Thoughts and Questions

- Describe an experience when you were full of pride and the Lord had to humble you.
- How would you explain pride to someone?
- Why are repeated trips up into pride and down into rage *not* the normal Christian life?

God Resists Pride

The arrogance of your heart has deceived you, you who live in the clefts of the rock, in the loftiness of your dwelling place... from there I will bring you down (Obadiah 3-4).

ONCE we yield to the upward surge of pride, the next time is easier. Entering God's sphere in pride can be conscious or unconscious, but the end result is a fatal form of self-deception. Pride is fed and nourished by a search for honor from man, which can come from titles, offices, religious labels, or external clothing. Personality cults are dangerous, especially when someone believes their own advertising. In the church, people tend to use the weapons of miracle, mystery, and authority to acquire, possess, and control. This is seen by people who repeatedly defend themselves and their conduct by the incorrect use of title and office: "I am the pastor/elder/prophet here!" or "...because I am the father/mother, that's why!"

Herod believed his own advertising and moved into God's sphere, intending to take His glory by allowing the people to call him a god. It was not long before an angel of the Lord struck him and he was eaten by worms and died (see Acts 12:23). He was trying to acquire, possess, and control God and consequently, needed to be pushed out of God's sphere. Although this is a serious issue with God, He does not respond in the New Testament like He did in the Old Testament; He gives us lots of grace.

God does not resist human frailty, but He does resist spiritual pride. When pride takes on religious connotation, it uses religious words, condescension, and superiority. God wants to be with us and wants us to reflect His *communicable* attributes such as compassion, grace, and mercy. However, when we attempt to appropriate His *non-communicable* attributes, such as omniscience and omnipotence, He must push us out of His sphere. These attributes are the nature of God, but they were not made available to humanity.

Communicable	Non-communicable
❖ Compassion	❖ Eternal
❖ Gracious	❖ Spirit
❖ Slow to anger	❖ Omniscient
❖ Mercy	❖ Omnipresent
❖ Truth	❖ Omnipotent
❖ Faithful	❖ Immutable
❖ Forgiving	

Christ had two natures—God and Man—unmixed. When He came to earth, He emptied Himself of His non-communicable attributes and imparted to us His communicable ones. This is the divine nature that Peter wrote about: *"For by these He has granted to us His precious and magnificent promises, so that by them you may become **partakers of the divine nature**, having escaped the corruption that is in the world by lust"* (2 Peter 1:4). This is the image of God in which we were created. We were given the communicable aspects of God's divine nature by His precious and magnificent promises, but He pushes us out of His sphere when we attempt to act like God in an illegal manner. We are forced, by pressure of circumstances, to retract our misapplied omnipotence. When our responses line up with His Own DNA, we are drawn into God. We are humans redeemed by the life of God, and in eternity, we are going to be in the *image* of God, but we will not be God. When we infringe on His non-communicable attributes, we are moving up in pride, and it is necessary that we be removed from His sphere.

Thoughts and Questions

❦ Why is entering God's sphere a fatal form of self-deception?

- Describe a situation in your life where pride took the form of religion.
- What is the difference between God's communicable and non-communicable attributes?

Movement Up and Down

So He drove the man out (Genesis 3:24).

THREE biblical examples of movement up and down will show us the importance of staying out of God's sphere. Pressure that seeks to bring us down out of God's sphere also tends to awaken the more animal instincts of sexuality, sensuality, and other degenerate behavior (see Rom. 1:18-32).

Nebuchadnezzar became very prideful and was bragging about what a great city and royal residence he built by the might of his power and for the glory of his majesty. While he was still speaking, a voice came from heaven telling him that his *sovereignty* had been removed and that he would be driven away from mankind to live with the beasts of the field and eat grass like cattle for seven years until he recognized that the Most High is ruler over the realm of mankind. This immediately came true, but at the end of that period, Nebuchadnezzar raised his eyes toward heaven and reason returned to him. His *sovereignty* was reestablished and he said, *"Now I praise, exalt and honor the King of heaven, for all His works are true and His ways just, and He is able to humble those who walk in pride"* (Dan. 4:37).

King David expressed pride and privilege by not going out to war. While he was abusing his office of king, David saw the UFO—Unclad Female Object—and misused his kingly privileges even more with the sequence of events with Bathsheba and Uriah (see 2 Sam. 11). What he did to Bathsheba was non-human, but what he did to Uriah was inhuman and this was our own King David. Pride, as ungoverned desire, releases murder, deception, and intrigue. But David came out of the deception into the reality of the fact that

God deals with us as *addressable and accountable* humans. David was sucked up into the vacuum of pride, and God had to push him out of His sphere. Humiliation is the downward movement necessary for God to bring us to Kingdom reality. David exhibited great insight and described an *Agape* conversion when he wrote, *"I was born in sin"* and then, *"create in me a clean heart, O God"* (Ps. 51:10).

The people to whom Jesus was ministering sought to force Jesus to be King, but He would not be moved up into pride, refused to accept false recognition, and remained unmoved and untempted. When He was forsaken by everyone, He was not in despair or cast down; He could abide in the providential care of His Father. Jesus taught us, both by precept and example, that like Himself, we are not subject nor are we ruled by that alien and hostile god called *fate*.

Movement downward is the source of humiliation and rage because God has to get us out of His sphere and return us to our human state. *Eros* always seeks to possess, acquire, and control. When *successful*, it results in the vacuum of pride. When it *fails*, it results in the vacuum of rage. When we are set in the Kingdom context of abiding, we are unmoved and unshakable.

Thoughts and Questions

- 🦌 What did Nebuchadnezzar come to understand through his difficult circumstances?

- 🦌 Have you ever experienced something that, like David, made you say, "Create in me a clean heart, O God"?

- 🦌 In what ways has Jesus set you free from the alien and hostile god called fate?

Rage

When they heard these things, all the people in the synagogue were filled with rage (Luke 4:28 AMP).

Move Downward – Satanic Vacuum

Creation

Alone
Robbed
Despair
Rage = the discovery
 that I am not God
 and cannot control
Shock
Reality
Ugly facts

RAGE may be an even more insidious problem than pride. Rage is violent, uncontrollable anger due to conflict. It is vehement desire or passion. It is movement downward into a satanic vacuum. Every one of us has experienced the extremes of both pride and rage at one time or another. These up and down movements are how Satan wears out the saints. Continually experiencing emotional highs and lows is mentally and spiritually exhausting. The moment we give ourselves to anger, we become temporarily insane, unable to think clearly or act rationally. The same is true of euphoria and/or spiritual highs.

Some years ago I was invited to Peru by a long-term missionary. By the time I arrived, his actions had caused him to have to suddenly and unexpectedly to leave the country. He had a 12-year-old Peruvian servant girl who, in spite of his repeated instructions, insisted on serving his meals from the right side after being told to serve him from the left side. Eventually, he became so enraged that one day he jumped up from the table and began to beat her with his fists. She later died of internal trauma. A few days later, he was recalled and permanently left the mission field. Pride and rage are most detrimental to the work and influence of the Kingdom of God.

Rage is a serious issue, and if left undealt with, murder is a clear possibility. The giants are not helpless, nor are they without power, but the Lord Jesus has already given us the weapons to deal with them. *Eros* seeks to acquire, possess, and control. When successful, it results in a vacuum of pride. When it fails, it results in a vacuum of rage. Responding in rage and animal-like behavior should be seen for the arrogance and danger that it really is. The result is obscuring, distorting, and injuring the image of God. However, when we re-gather our focus on the Kingdom, we recognize the early warning system that alerts us to the life-threatening danger in which we find ourselves. Pride and rage have a wide range of activity and significance, making it difficult to not play sheriff. Only in *Agape* can we discover and embrace what it means to be unmovable and unshakable and abide in the Father.

Thoughts and Questions

🐜 Why would rage be a more serious problem than pride?

🐜 How does Satan use these up and down movements?

🐜 What is the result of responding in rage?

Reading the Meter

*So I intend always to remind you about these things, although indeed you
know them and are firm in the truth that [you] now [hold]*
(2 Peter 1:12 AMP).

B EFORE idiot lights on the dashboard of our cars were invented, we
actually had gauges that told us exactly what was happening in the electrical system of our car. Each of us has an internal emotional gauge that func-

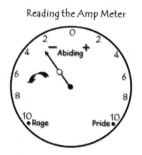

Reading the Amp Meter

tions something like an electrical amp meter. It drops to -4, then up to +6. We
can know something is wrong, even if we can't establish the cause. Abiding is
staying within the -2 / +2 range. Rage is -10 and pride is +10 on the meter.
Sometimes our meter goes to -10 or +10, but the little pegs keep the needle
from moving too far on the gauge. If an amp meter goes over to +6 and
remains there for a long time, it means the car is charging too much and
eventually the headlights, battery, or some other system will burn out. This is
equally as troublesome as if it were hanging around -6, causing our inability
to even start the car.

Trauma and emotional burnout can come from hitting the peg on either side too often. We get ourselves in trouble by going up into some euphoric place or by being cast down by some unexpected event, and then when we short out, we think something is wrong with the system. Reading the amp meter gives us an ability to abide in the normal zone. We cannot always be on top of the world, and it is okay to feel a little down or weird sometimes. That is the +2/-2 normal range where the life of the Lord Jesus can move in our person and our life is being conformed to His image. Latitude is most important, because being too rigid on ourselves is damaging.

Pride and rage are transgressions of fallen kings. They are expressions of the five I Wills of Satan, which are violation of a law, command, or duty. Violations can be doing something we should not have done or failure to do something we should have done. When we understand how the meter works in us, we are then able to more accurately read where others are on their meter to be able to *speak a word in season to him who is weary*" (Isa. 50:4 AMP). This is learning to give a proper word to someone no matter where he or she is on the meter.

One of my mentors taught me the Proverb about how eating too much honey makes one sick and afterward, he asked me, "Have you found honey?" I said, "I have. I don't read anything but the Bible!" He strongly suggested that I at least read the *Reader's Digest*! If you over-feed on spiritual things, there is a real possibility of getting sick of them, and it takes awhile to recover. Some of us have more capacity for honey than others. We can eat Scripture, pray, read, visit, and go to meetings for a long time. Others of us have a little less tolerance for these things. Once we leave reality and go into a religious realm, it is hard getting back. We end up bouncing back and forth from the positive to the negative sides of the meter. When we have had about all the honey we can eat, we need the wisdom to back off and discover balance. If we have had too little, we need the means of grace to help our needle come up out of the negative and into the positive.

Thoughts and Questions

- Describe an experience you had when your needle dropped out of the abiding zone.

- How does understanding the meter help us "speak a word in season to him who is weary"?

- In what ways have you eaten too much honey?

Jeremiah's Needle

Clean the slate, God, so we can start the day fresh! Keep me from stupid sins, from thinking I can take over your work; then I can start this day sun-washed, scrubbed clean of the grime of sin (Psalms 19:13 TM).

JEREMIAH, the weeping prophet, shows us how far a needle can go: *"Sing to the Lord, praise the Lord! For He has delivered the soul of the needy one from the hand of evildoers."* Then, in the next verse, he swings violently and says, *"Cursed be the day when I was born; let the day not be blessed when my mother bore me!"* (Jer. 20:13-14). At first Jeremiah's needle was way over in the positive

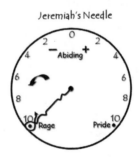

and he was rejoicing in God. Then some personal crisis suddenly caused him to be almost bi-polar or manic-depressive as his needle bounced back to other side and he cursed the day he was born. Jeremiah's needle didn't stop at nine or ten—it wrapped around the peg at the bottom. Jeremiah had a whole pile of these experiences in Scripture. One time he said to God, "You've deceived me!" I thought, *What courage for him to talk to God like that!* But he and God were getting to know one another. Jeremiah experienced the force fields of being sucked up in pride and being cast down in rage and depression. Father chose Jeremiah to speak to a people who needed a strong and unbalanced voice.

Others have wrapped the needle around the peg. Peter went +6 on the Amp meter when he said he would die for Jesus and then immediately wrapped the needle around -10 when he denied Him. But Jesus had been carefully watching Peter. His swing wasn't a surprise. He was being stabilized, instructed, and discipled to become the rock. Subjecting ourselves to events and happenings that seek to move us from the posture of abiding can be expensive and drastic. Sometimes when we're at -6, we are tempted to do something to gain attention; this is the nature of false or illegal attention. One child can disrupt an entire classroom because some attention is better than none. One young prisoner said, with all sincerity: "Mr. Mumford, sir, it is better to have the police looking for you than to know that no one cares."

Once we yield to pride or rage, it affects our relationships. If there are several people in the room and John walks in with a meter reading of -6, something happens to the whole group. Someone asks him, "How are you doing?" He responds, "Fine! I read my Scripture, did my praying, and I'm here. Anything else you want to know?" John needs someone to read his meter properly and not react to him. He doesn't need a sheriff; he needs a farmer who can nourish the Seed that is trying to grow.

Thoughts and Questions

- In what ways can you relate to Jeremiah's and Peter's needle movements?

- What has hitting the -10 / +10 pegs cost you personally?

- What happens in our relationships when we yield to pride or rage?

Reading 93

Retract, Restrain, Renounce

*There are many out there taking other paths, choosing other goals, and trying
to get you to go along with them. I've warned you of them many times; sadly,
I'm having to do it again. All they want is easy street. They hate Christ's
cross* (Philippians 3:18 TM).

DISTORTED, twisted, yet extremely powerful, personal sovereignty is
revealed as the Seven Giants. Every one of them, individually and corporately, signifies an attempt to move up into God's sphere. Each giant is
determined to preserve his/her rule in the face of conflict and failure. The
giants involve us in spiritual warfare, seeking to prevent our entrance into the
land of promise. When God breaks them, we are angry, crushed, hurt, injured,
and confused. The Seven Giants do not know the meanings of the words
retract, restrain, or renounce because they are the direct opposite in content
and direction of *acquire, possess, and control*. God's glory depends upon our
reception of the incorruptible Seed that imparts the ability for us to retract
and restrain the Seven Giants as well as renounce their hold over us. Death is
rebellion, a form of pride that *refuses* or perhaps is incapable (lacking capacity) of being able to retract, restrain, or renounce. Each of us must become
spiritually mature *"...lest he become conceited and fall into the condemnation
incurred by the devil"* (1 Tim. 3:6).

The Seven Giants represent *acquire, possess, and control*—the *"sin which so
easily entangles us"* (Heb. 12:1) in all their strength and complexity. Control
is the inability to admit or embrace the truth that we have been wrong; it is
quiet yet determined insistence that our way be implemented. The moment
we cease abiding, we either go up in pride or down in anger. The moment we

lose our ability to choose to act and respond properly, we are captured by the forces of the vacuum of either pride or rage. Essentially, we injure our Kingdom freedom in the form of our righteousness, peace, and joy. Creation must learn to abide with the Father because our freedom depends on it!

Paul said, *"These restrictions do indeed involve an assumption of religious enlightenment, with the self-imposed ceremonialism, their self-abasement and asceticism; but they have no real value even as checks to sensual self-indulgence"* (Col. 2:23 Way Translation). Religious activity cannot and does not check sensual self-indulgence. It does in fact feed and release religious *Eros*, turning the Seven Giants into a religious, socially acceptable form that is very difficult to identify and correct. Unless the retracting, restraining, and renouncing are applied to the Seven Giants and the essential *Eros* nature is broken, our real self remains trapped in a prison without bars.

Thoughts and Questions

- How is our personal sovereignty revealed?
- At what point are we captured by the forces of pride or rage? What is the end result?
- How do the Seven Giants become religiously and socially acceptable?

READING 94

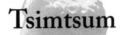

Tsimtsum

...but emptied Himself, taking the form of a bond-servant, and being made in the likeness of men (Philippians 2:7).

IN order to learn to abide, we must embrace the idea of *tsimtsum*, meaning a *contraction* after a previous expansion. This is what Christ did when He emptied Himself.

Years ago I ministered in several countries in South America and was moving in a rather strong apostolic anointing. I felt like the gifts of the Spirit were hanging off my fingers and was up on a spiritual level where oxygen was becoming scarce. I was increasingly moving into subtle unreality. On the journey home, I was physically exhausted and mentally confused and began to lose my compass and sense of spiritual direction. By the time I landed in the States, a kind of depression had set in. At baggage claim, I saw all the suitcases come off the luggage carrousel except mine. With some anger and resentment, I said to the Lord, "I'm a man of God, I have served You with all of my heart; can't You take care of one suitcase?" This was my moment of *tsimtsum*—God was *contracting* me so I did not remain in spheres that were not mine. Just because God uses us in certain spheres to meet a need does not mean that those spheres belong to us. God, as Father, saw the beginnings of pride and rage in my person and was required to bring the antidote, which is contraction.

There are six early signals of pride and rage. *First*, we can feel ourselves being scandalized and offended and nursing its source or cause. When rage progresses, we are resistant and refuse or are unable to renounce or release a particular issue, so it continues eating at us. The *second* signal is the loss of compassion. *Third*, we experience insidious feelings of superiority or condescension. *Fourth*, we become careless. Proud or angry people simply don't care what others think. *Fifth* is an emergence of the compulsive desire to control situations and tell people what to do. It is almost dictatorial. When we can't control things, frustration often turns to rage. *Finally*, we have the sense of a vacuum or force field that sucks us up into realms that are not based in reality. Denial of the first five has set us up. Most of us can feel the force field of anger in us long before it manifests. Pride, on the other hand, is a bit harder to discern. This force field seeks to remove us from the abiding position.

Simone Weil in her book *Waiting for God*[1] describes *tsimtsum* succinctly: "On God's part creation is not an act of self-expansion but of restraint and renunciation. God and all His creatures are less than God alone. God accepted this diminution. He emptied a part of His Being from Himself." God has already emptied Himself in this act of divinity. That is why St. John says that the Lamb of God was slain from the beginning of the world. God permitted the existence of things distinct from Himself and worth infinitely less than Himself. By this creative act, He denied Himself, as Christ has told us to deny ourselves for Him. This response, this echo, which it is in our power to refuse, is the only possible justification for the folly of love of the created act.

THOUGHT AND QUESTIONS

- Describe an example of *tsimtsum* in your own life.
- Which of the six early signs of pride and rage are you the least aware of in your life?
- What is being asked of us through Christ's creative act?

ENDNOTE

1. Weil, Simone. *Waiting for God.* (Harper Perenial, New York, NY, 1951) p 45.

The Deception of Unbroken Success

Think of yourselves the way Christ Jesus thought of himself
(Philippians 2:5 TM).

THERE is a real deception to uninterrupted success. In the business community, this is called a bubble. Disallowing or ignoring the absolute necessity of some clear and meaningful contraction or disruption allows the *Eros* contamination to increase without hindrance or interruption. The result of unbroken success is the emergence of the kind of pride that seeks to take us into God's realm. A stock market or real estate crash is not always bad; sometimes it is a needed correction. Nothing less can modify the bubble. If the stock or real estate market doesn't correct itself, we lose our sense of value and reality. Failure or refusal to retract, restrain, or renounce results in the loss of our life and inexorably leads to an *Eros* prison. This is not a threat or judgment, just an indisputable fact. I know people who have had so much success that they have gone straight up to where there is very little oxygen.

Unbroken success will inevitably and inexorably lead to an *Eros* prison. *Eros* as the strong man does not have the ability to retract; to do so would be a house divided. To always succeed and never retract means one cannot find balance and reality. Think of what would happen if every time we prayed we received what we asked for...or if we never received what we asked for. I've had a few prayers answered so dramatically that it scared me. As a brand new believer, I returned to my ship, anxious as to how I would be able to tell my buddies what had happened to me. I said, under my breath, "Lord, I will need an alarm clock to get up and seek Your face." Within 20 minutes a ship-mate knocked on the sick bay door where I worked. Opening it, I expected to see an injury or crisis, but the sailor said, rather meekly, "I have two alarm clocks and thought you could use one." My first thought was, "Now I have got a racket! All I have to do is ask and it happens!" If every prayer was answered in that manner, we would be in trouble.

The incorruptible Seed of *Agape* is our only hope to break the *deception* of success. The DNA of *Agape* alone has the ability and capacity to contract itself. God contracted Himself when He came in human form. It is not easy to contract things that appear to be successful; we must learn and be disciplined in the skill of contracting ourselves. We do this by eating humble pie and receiving God's grace, which is more than unmerited favor (see 1 Peter 5:5). We *must* pull in our know-it-all mentality and allow God's power to be perfected in our weakness (see 2 Cor. 12:9). We *must* understand the difference between governing things and people from our title, office, or reputation and not from our person. The more we move upward or downward, the more we're left on our own. The purpose, of course, is to discover the real me.

Deception of unbroken success provides the needed dimension to understanding abiding as the rest of God. We cannot abide until and unless we are willing to contract and/or deny the *Eros* forces that demand our response. *Agape* is essence of denying ourselves.

Thoughts and Questions

- Describe what unbroken success means to you.
- In what ways have you experienced the deception of unbroken success?
- What does contracting ourselves have to do with abiding?

The Fallen King's Reaction to Disappointed Expectations

So be done with every trace of wickedness (depravity, malignity) and all deceit and insincerity (pretense, hypocrisy) and grudges (envy, jealousy) and slander and evil speaking of every kind (1 Peter 2:1 AMP).

THESE five attitudes and actions—malice, deceit, hypocrisy, envy, and slander—are a special kind; they are *Christian* sins identifiable as the fallen king's reaction to disappointed expectations. They are indicative of his anger and reaction because he did not reach his imagined goal. Attempts to get to an imaginary goal are usually more intense than one within the range of normal. The following will give us insight into the righteousness, peace, and joy of the Kingdom lifestyle. Remember, we are diagnosing and not accusing:

- *Wickedness, depravity, malice*—all kinds of *Eros* conduct is evident in the Church. The way we speak to one another is one symptom. Malice is a result of the lack of compassion. Proverbs says, *"No matter how cunningly he conceals his malice, eventually his evil will be exposed in public. Malice backfires; spite boomerangs"* (Prov. 26:26-27 TM).

- *Guile/deceit*—is sly or cunning intelligence. It is crafty, tricks others, and creates impressions that are not based on reality. Hidden Agenda utilizes this tactic.

- *Hypocrisy*—is the practice of pretense or claiming to have higher standards or more laudable beliefs than is the case.[1] Young people identify this as a *poser.*

- *Envy*—discontented or resentful longing aroused by another's possessions or qualities.

- *Slander/evil speaking*—making a false spoken statement about others that damages their reputation or degrades them. This activity is most prevalent in social gatherings.

The idiosyncratic nature of the fallen king allows the probability of our embracing one or more of the Seven Giants as a distortion of our personality. Because of these distortions, any one of the Seven Giants can become predominant due to circumstances or pressures. The Seven Giants can't be cast out; they are not demons. The manifestation of the giants is complex because they appeal to something that is in our nature that requires our cooperation.

It is disturbing to observe the rapidity with which we can forsake our faith, cease abiding, and lose our freedom when our expectations have not been met. Paul addressed the Galatian believers regarding their loss of abiding in Christ: *"O, you poor **and** silly **and** thoughtless **and** unreflecting **and** senseless Galatians! Who has fascinated or bewitched or cast a spell over you...?"* (Gal. 3:1 AMP). This is why we are capable of such emotional swings of both pride and rage. The fallen king uses the freedom God gave us in ways Father never intended. Repentance is surrendering our fallen personal sovereignty even when we have been disappointed. The first step is to identify malice, deceit, hypocrisy, envy, and slander when they emerge within our sphere and then put them aside and learn to abide in *Agape.* This *Agape* response was implanted in us in Seed form, but the Seed requires a favorable climate, needed nourishment, and proper moisture in which to grow.

Thoughts and Questions

🌱 In what ways have you encountered these five Christian sins?

🌱 Why do you think these five sins are part of the idiosyncratic nature of the fallen king?

🌱 What is the result of putting these five Christian sins aside?

ENDNOTE

1. Soanes, C., and Stevenson, A. *Concise Oxford English dictionary* (11th ed.). Oxford: Oxford University Press, 2004.

The Problem with Knowing it All

Knowledge makes arrogant, but love edifies (1 Corinthians 8:1).

WHEN we are convinced that we know something and then aggressively attempt to control people and events toward a certain end or desired behavior with that knowledge, we are taking on a superiority that is dangerous. Paul explained this danger to fallen kings when he said:

> ...*we know that we all have knowledge. Knowledge makes arrogant, (puffs up) but love (Agape) edifies. If anyone supposes that he knows anything, he has not yet known as he ought to know; but if anyone loves God, he is known by Him* (1 Corinthians 8:1-3).

Knowledge has a great tendency to create a vacuum of pride. In this Scripture, it is stated as arrogance. This is especially a problem in the academic and theological world. Have you ever met someone who lost 10 pounds and suddenly became the expert on weight loss and healthy eating? Or someone who just came back from the mission field and is now the self-appointed family and community evangelist? When people are rich, they think they really know everything. The problem is that we have the wrong understanding of wealth, which causes us to be drawn up into the vacuum of pride. The Psalmist said, *"If riches increase, do not set your heart upon them"* (Ps. 62:10). The word *riches* include several different meanings: army, strength, power, substance, and ability. Surrendering the control that comes with riches is not easy. False expectations in the realm of knowledge or ability may create the vacuum of rage because when people or circumstances do not do what we are fully expecting, we have the propensity to enter that sphere of rage, perhaps continuing until we are scandalized.

Agape has the ability to edify and impart life to another, but pride puffs us up, and it can happen individually and corporately. A vigilante mob is a corporate expression of both pride (we know he is guilty) and rage (it is our responsibility to do something about it). Whole cultures, including religious ones, have given themselves to pride and rage in the defense of their doctrinal or ethical convictions. The Jewish people felt intense pride and rage in response to the teachings of Jesus and Paul. Today we can see pride and rage in the radical Muslim who is more than willing to become a martyr for something he believes is absolutely true.

Pride causes failure to think clearly. When someone refuses to respond to what we consider truth, we respond in rage, which also causes failure to think clearly. When we think we know it all, we are much more susceptible to pride and rage. This is why religious radicals can do strange and unpredictable things, which Jesus identified when He said, *"They will put you out of (expel you from) the synagogues; but an hour is coming when whoever kills you will think and claim that he has offered service to God"* (John 16:2). If that is not pride and rage, I would not know how to explain it.

Thoughts and Questions

- ❦ What kinds of experiences have you had with a know-it-all?
- ❦ Explain why knowledge has a tendency to create the vacuum of pride.
- ❦ Why does knowledge create false expectations of others?

The Real Me

He must not be a new convert, or he may [develop a beclouded and stupid state of mind] as the result of pride [be blinded by conceit, and] fall into the condemnation that the devil [once] did (1 Timothy 3:6 AMP).

WE are not being real when we begin to believe our own advertising. It starts with a seemingly innocuous move out of our humanity into title, position, social standing, or wealth. It is pride in its purest form. We are, in a most self-deceiving manner, approaching the title, social standing, or possession of wealth as the "real me" when, in fact, we are most human and error-prone. We are and shall ever be mere humans before God. We are *assigned* spheres, roles, titles, and places of authority with the assumption that we are competent people. The danger lies in the temptation to cease seeing ourselves as really human and entering the sphere that carries us into believing our own advertising. The deception begins with the suggestion that we are really something other than and much different from all of those earth creatures—we are unique and need to be recognized. If you think this is overstated, give this Kingdom principle time! As we have observed, the most dramatic example of this is Herod in Acts 12:21-23, who was smitten with worms.

In The Brother's Karamazov, Dostoyevsky told the story of The Grand Inquisitor in which the Cardinal was accusing Christ of not playing fair. He understood the nature of *Eros* in that "There are three powers, three powers alone, able to conquer and to hold captive forever the conscience of these impotent rebels for their own happiness—those forces are miracle, mystery and authority. Thou hast rejected all three and have set the example for doing so."[1] Christ was fully human yet accomplished miracles with reluctance and used His authority not for Himself but to set others free. Christ did not play the religious game according to Pharisaical rules because His Kingdom was not a part of this world system.

Creation of the personality or persona comes from characters wearing masks in Greek plays. We take on a role and act, react, possess, acquire, and control because of who we *think* we are (i.e., I am the owner, the president, the mayor, the pastor, prophet, apostle, or elder). We have then essentially left our identity as a human being and assumed the identity of the personality of the office. When we act as though the personality is real, we are deceived. It reveals that the authority and driving force of our life is the power of the *arche* (the force of the created being) and not the King of the Kingdom. When we understand Kingdom reality, we know with certainty that we will be measured by a Man (see Acts 17:31). We will always be a human being in the presence of God; it is the human with whom God deals. He is impartial and does not respect any of our masks.

First Timothy 3 describes the qualities of a person who is *real* and *human*. This person is described as:

> *Above reproach, the husband of one wife, temperate, prudent, respectable, hospitable, able to teach, not addicted to wine or pugnacious, but gentle, peaceable, free from the love of money. He must be one who manages his own household well, keeping his children under control with all dignity* (1 Timothy 3:2–4).

Thoughts and Questions

- What are some signs that we are not being real?
- What is the difference between a created persona and the real person?
- What are some signs that we are being real?

ENDNOTE

1. Dostyevsky, F. The Brother's Karazmov. "The Grand Inquisitor". (ch. 36, 1879.) retrieved from http://www.online-literature.com/dostoyevsky/ brothers_karamazov/36/.

The Problem with Ordination

Do not be in a hurry in the laying on of hands [giving the sanction of the church too hastily in reinstating expelled offenders or in ordination in questionable cases],...keep yourself pure (1 Timothy 5:22 AMP).

SOMETHING eccentric, strange, and difficult to explain often happens to normal, healthy people when they are chosen for an office or position in ministry in a church body. Almost immediately after the "laying on of hands," they seem to leave the sphere of being *fully human* and take on the aura of the office. It seems to begin in the ungoverned thought process that goes something like this: *I am now an officer or leader. Because leaders are super-human, I, too, shall be the spiritual giant that everyone expects.* They begin to take their security, identity, and belonging from the office and the title rather than from their relationship to the Lord.

Essentially, they leave the realm of being human and exhibit a growing tendency to enter God's sphere by assuming a spiritual role based on unreality. This is a deceptive ploy of the enemy because they soon find themselves in spiritual unreality. If they continue in this deception, they eventually become inflexible, officious, obstructionist, and unreasonable. We have seen these symptoms in Scripture of those who were guilty of entering God's space. Re-read the book of Jude for a refresher course in leadership that missed its purpose. Rather than preserving their own humanity and taking on the assumed role of sheriff, judge, jury, and executioner, it is urgent that leadership in the larger body of Christ become increasingly caring and compassionate. Paul instructed Timothy regarding eccentric and unpredictable behavior in leadership when he said, *"He must not be a new convert, or he may [develop a beclouded and stupid state of mind] as the result of pride [be blinded by conceit, and] fall into the condemnation that the devil [once] did"* (1 Tim. 3:6 AMP).

In Bible school, Judith and I were assigned our summer ministry to a Native American Indian reservation in upper New York. We developed a friendship with the chief's son, who was a strong leader in the tribe. I decided that he should be ordained, so with little preparation, he was set in the congregation as an officer. The attention and authority soon caused him to be puffed up with pride with repeated bouts of rage. He began to crash and burn and was nearly totally injured by the condemnation. The congregation was confused between his church and cultural authority. How I wished I could have had an official "laying off of hands" for this young man.

As Hosea says, *"Their deeds will not allow them to return to their God"* (Hosea 5:4). Rebellion and deception take us into God's sphere, making it difficult to renounce, restrain, or retract ourselves. The moment we take our authority and usefulness from the title, office, or social position, whether religious or secular, we have entered the realm of self-deception. We are into the sphere of the satanic vacuum with the power to sweep us *up*. Should we effectively resist the upward sweep, the satanic vacuum will seek to cast us *down* into despair and rage. Whenever we begin to act in a capacity that is more than or other than human, we have, however unconsciously, begun to enter into God's own space. We then use the gifts of *miracle, mystery, and authority* as weapons in order to possess, acquire, and control.

Thoughts and Questions

- What phenomenon happens when someone is placed in an office in the church?

- In what ways is this phenomenon rebellion and deception? What does it keep us from doing?

- When we act in a capacity that is more than human, what is the result?

The Law of Sin and the Law of Christ

Bear (endure, carry) one another's burdens and troublesome moral faults,
and in this way fulfill and observe perfectly the law of Christ and complete
what is lacking [in your obedience to it] (Galatians 6:2 AMP).

THE law of sin involves inevitable movement up into God's sphere, resulting in pride, or movement down, resulting in rage. The law of sin leads us from being human to being inhuman because the result of sin (*Eros*) is becoming a predator or parasite. Sin isolates and destroys all relational potential, leaving us isolated and alone.

The law of Christ gives us the choice to repeatedly humble and empty ourselves and remove ourselves out of God's sphere because we know the potential of both pride and rage. We have the freedom to be fully human and still reveal God's DNA; this is God's victory in the human context. It is the essence of biblical Christology. *Agape* is unrewarded giving and unlimited forgiveness. It is *Agape* that gives us the ability to retract, restrain, and renounce so we can be free and allow God to function in His own freedom in our lives.

God comes at His own initiative and when it is safe. In other words, He knows when He can reveal Himself through you without injury to you. When we understand the Kingdom dimension and are securely in our sphere, the Father can properly relate to us. God as Father is cautious that He does not injure us. He knows that those who really love Him will keep His commandments. One of Jesus' disciples asked Him,

"Master, why is it that you are about to make yourself plain to us but not to the world?" "Because a loveless world," said Jesus, "is a sightless world. If anyone loves me, he will carefully keep my word and my Father will love him—we'll move right into the neighborhood!" (John 14:21-23 TM).

When we have been instructed in the laws of Christ, we practice the skill of abiding and know how to embrace by faith the rather drastic events that may be required to get us out of His space. The law of Christ requires humility and humiliation. The desert fathers knew there was no humility without the presence of effective humiliation. It is the cross that enables Christ's power to be revealed in our weakness.

We must be full of care (care-full) to see that we are relationally secure with others who are rooted in the Kingdom because those are the ones who know us and have the perception to guard and protect us from the vacuum that seeks to move us up or down. It is in relationships that we bear (endure, carry) one another's burdens and troublesome moral faults. Our spouses, family, and friends are the ones who know the moment we begin to move up or down and cease abiding as a real person. When we are motivated by *Agape* and function corporately in the law of Christ, His DNA is revealed through us.

Thoughts and Questions

- What is the law of sin?
- Why does God come to us when it is safe?
- Explain how the law of Christ is functioning in your life.

Reading 101

What Is the Skill of Abiding?

If you live in Me [abide vitally united to Me] and My words remain in you and continue to live in your hearts, ask whatever you will, and it shall be done for you. When you bear (produce) much fruit, My Father is honored and glorified, and you show and prove yourselves to be true followers of Mine (John 15:7-8 AMP).

ABIDING is a most critical principle; nothing is more valuable or more needed. This is why I risk irritation with the repeated use of the term. The biblical evidence about abiding is overwhelming. The Greek word for abide is used more than 120 times and in English it is used 67 times. It is translated: dwell, remain, continue, be kept, endure, be held, stand, and wait for. John, who reaches for maturity in *Agape*, uses it the most—25 times in his epistle.

We stated earlier that abiding is the *cessation of movement*. All temptation and every unexpected crisis are designed to move us from our position of abiding. Abiding is the ultimate faith posture because confidence in His person allows us to cease up or down movement. Movement ceases because God's grace is sufficient for us and His power is perfected in weakness (see 2 Cor. 12:9). It is a place of rest God intended in paradise and is a gift in the form of a Kingdom skill.

Enduring means to be left holding on to one's confidence after others have collapsed (see Heb. 10:35-39). We can only endure when we abide in Christ. Cessation of movement comes when we are wise as serpents in understanding the power and rewards of the Seven Giants. Since we are governed by *Agape*, we are denied employment of the giants for personal goals or for personal revenge; *our behavior must be harmless as a dove.* Rather than being victimized by movement that is up and down, *Agape* allows us to release and forgive so we *can* abide. Abiding is the single defense against the satanic upward and downward vacuums of pride or rage. When we are unmovable and unshakable, Kingdom fruit appears and Father's glory is revealed!

Wherever we find Jesus, we will find Him in action because *Agape* is risky, spontaneous, and unpredictable. Because abiding or paradise will is His home, Jesus can stand outside of the camp of Judaism and invite us to do the same (see Heb. 13:13). His life and ministry were characterized by servant-hood, and He chose to be a servant through an abiding relationship with His Father:

> *Look well at my hand-picked servant; I love him so much, take such delight in him. I've placed my Spirit on him; he'll decree justice to the nations. But he won't yell, won't raise his voice; there'll be no commotion in the streets. He won't walk over anyone's feelings, won't push you into a corner. Before you know it, his justice will triumph; the mere sound of his name will signal hope, even among far-off unbelievers* (Matthew 12:18-21 TM).

Thoughts and Questions

- From these definitions, summarize the concept of abiding in your own words.
- In what way is abiding cessation of movement?
- Explain why abiding is the single defense against pride or rage.

Abiding Doesn't Come Natural

The Son is able to do nothing of Himself (of His own accord); but He is able to do only what He sees the Father doing, for whatever the Father does is what the Son does in the same way [in His turn] (John 5:19 AMP).

ABIDING means that we only do what we see the Father doing. Kingdom believers are not permitted to *change the world with our wonderful plans and utopian visions.* The Kingdom must come in us prior to it coming through us. Abiding happens in the unshakable Kingdom. It is that which allows us to be unmoved though the mountains fall into the sea. It is based on our cultivated trust in the person of Jesus, who has all things in subjection under His feet and will accomplish all that He promised (see Eph. 1:21-23). Abiding is rest in declining prosperity, economic uncertainty, and outright danger, knowing that God provided something better for us—intimacy with God (see 2 Cor. 6:16; Heb. 11:40). When we abide with Christ, we do not have to *reach* for anything or anyone in an illegal manner (see Matt. 11:6; 1 Peter 3:21-22). Abiding has chosen to build its life and future on the three aspects of God's own nature because they are uncreated and eternal. They are: God is *Agape*; God is Light; and God is Spirit. Anything that does not include these three aspects of God's nature is suspect.

Abiding is a skill that has to be learned by faith alone; because we are human, it does not come naturally. We cannot abide if we are attempting to keep Moses' Law because we not capable of striving and abiding at the same time. Abiding is the rest Christ offered when He asked us to come to Him. It is *passive* righteousness alone that allows us to boldly enter into an abiding posture in the midst of a crisis, failure, or disruption. Because we are in

Christ, we can abide without condemnation even in the presence of guilt and failure. Abiding is the only effective antidote to the vacuum of pride or rage, including self-pity.

Abiding is Christ's gift to us so we may know the rest of God's paradise will in His New Creation. It is when we abide in the shadow of the Rock (see Ex. 33:22) that we can see His glory because *abiding is Father's chosen place where we are safe from the vicissitudes of life in a fallen world.* It is in abiding that God has chosen to reveal Himself as He wants to be known. The abiding life suspends itself in our time/space world because it is eternal. The transformation in us takes place as we behold Him *because* we are not continually moving up and down. Security, identity, and belonging are hidden in these words: abide in Me.

Thoughts and Questions

- Why does abiding involve doing only what we see the Father doing?

- In what ways have you been able to abide or rest in times of crisis, failure, or disruption?

- How is it possible to abide without condemnation?

READING 103

Abiding as Confidence

*Let us then fearlessly and confidently and boldly draw near to the throne
of grace (the throne of God's unmerited favor to us sinners), that we may
receive mercy [for our failures] and find grace to help in good time for every
need [appropriate help and well-timed help, coming just when we need it]*
(Hebrews 4:16 AMP).

ABIDING is being unmoved and resting in the completed work of Christ.
It means we are learning to recognize the craftiness of the enemy and
the early warning signs of both entering God's own space and seeking to
possess, acquire, or control. Our growing confidence also means that we are
less concerned that the Lord will have to humiliate us by using circumstances
and events to push us out of His space. The Look Good Giant demands to
be respected and honored. However, social titles, offices, and reputations are
forms of self-deception causing us to think more highly of ourselves than we
should. The only possible route that allows us to recover our *humanness* from
the snares of religious unreality is humility. If you are being humiliated, know
that no test or temptation that comes your way is beyond the course of what
others have had to face. *All you need to remember* is that God will never let you
down. He will never let you be pushed past your limit. He will always be there
to help you come through it, and at God's table there is no respect for social
distinctions (see 1 Cor. 10:13; Col. 3:25). John Newton, author of the song
"Amazing Grace," wrote an unusual explanation of what it means to abide:

> Another branch of blessedness is a power of reposing ourselves
> and our concerns upon the Lord's faithfulness and care, and
> may be considered in two aspects: a reliance upon Him that

He will surely provide for us, guide us, protect us, be our help in trouble, our shield in danger, so that, however poor, weak, and defense-less in ourselves, we may rejoice in His all-sufficiency as our own; and further, in consequence of this, a peaceful, humble submission to His will under all events which, upon their first impression, are *contrary to our own views and desires*. Surely, in a world like this, where everything is uncertain, where we are exposed to trials on every hand, and know not but a single hour may bring forth something painful, yea dreadful, to our natural sensations, there can be no blessedness but so far as we are thus enabled to entrust and resign all to the direction and faithfulness of the Lord our Shepherd. For want of more of this spirit multitudes of professing Christians perplex and wound themselves and dishonor their high calling by continual *anxieties, alarms, and complaints*. They think nothing is safe under the Lord's keeping unless their own eye is likewise upon it, and are seldom satisfied with any of His dispensations: for though He gratify their desires in nine instances, a refusal of the tenth spoils the relish of all, and they show the truths of the Gospel can afford them little comfort, if self is crossed. But blessed in the man who trusts in the Lord, and whose hope the Lord is. He shall not be afraid of evil tidings: he shall be kept in perfect peace, though the earth be moved, and the mountains cast into the midst of the sea.[1]

Thoughts and Questions

❦ What are some of the early warning signs of entering God's space?

❦ Why does God use humiliation?

❧ Summarize what John Newton was expressing.

ENDNOTE

1. John Newton, Letters and Sermons, "Vol II. Twenty Six Letters to a Nobleman," (Murray and Cochrane, Edinburgh. 1788.) p. 94-95.

Come Unto Me—
the Staying Power of *Agape*

Are you tired? Worn out? Burned out on religion? Come to me. Get away
with me and you'll recover your life. I'll show you how to take a real rest.
Walk with me and work with me—watch how I do it. Learn the unforced
rhythms of grace. I won't lay anything heavy or ill-fitting on you. Keep
company with me and you'll learn to live freely and lightly
(Matthew 11:28-30 TM).

THE word *come* has to do with movement toward, progress, development, and reaching a specified point. "Come to Me" is personal, voluntary, and never forced or coerced, but the rewards are immense! When we come, we embrace God's yoke, which is *Agape*—loving God with all our heart, soul, mind, and strength—in its most mature form. The yoke is a stabilizing factor that keeps us from continually responding to the satanic vacuum of moving us up in pride and down in rage. Jesus assured us that He would not lay anything heavy or ill-fitting on us. Our yoke of *Agape*, given us by Christ, is custom fitted and made especially for each of us. It is a call to Kingdom life as He intended it.

Jesus, as a human being (Son of Man) in the form of God (Son of God), does not reach up into God's sphere. Rather, He takes the journey down—seven steps down, which leads to seven steps up (see Phil. 2:1-10)—and says, "come unto Me." Jesus knew the Father loved Him because He freely laid down His life and was free to take it up again. He received this authority personally from His Father (see John 10:17-18). Because He was human,

He gives this authority to you and me. In both movements, He is in control rather than responding to the vacuum. We need to learn what it means to have our own personal authority restored in God's purpose.

When compassion speaks, DNA is released. Those who are physically and mentally sick, those who are harassed and cast down, as well as those who have been broken by life and the system can find healing. This is the meaning of Christ's appeal for us to come. It is His intention for us to minister His love to those who are hurting.

Oswald Chambers explained that "Come unto Me and I will give you rest" does not mean "do this" or "don't do that." It means that God will *stay* us. "Not—I will put you to bed and hold your hand and sing you to sleep; but—I will get you out of bed, out of the languor and exhaustion, out of the state of being half dead while you are alive; I will imbue you with the spirit of life, and you will be stayed by the perfection of vital activity."[1]

Thoughts and Questions

- Explain how the yoke of *Agape* can be a stabilizing factor in your life.
- Describe what "Come unto Me and I will give you rest" means to you.
- In what ways is abiding a staying force for you?

ENDNOTE

1. Oswald Chambers, *My Utmost for His Highest* (Dodd Mead & Co. 1935, renewed 1963 by the Oswald Chambers Publications Assn., Ltd., and is used by permission of Discovery House Publishers, Grand Rapids MI) June 11.

When Come Is Changed to Go

Go out and train everyone you meet, far and near, in this way of life
(Matthew 28:19 TM).

FATHER'S appeal to *come* is eventually changed to *go*. This is a very important transition because when the word to go comes from the Lord, it is always in perfect timing: not too soon and not too late. We are sent out when we have been properly prepared and instructed in the presence and principles of His government in the earth.

At the very beginning of my encounter with the Lord, the passion for missions began to pump in my veins. The one voice who sees this most clearly has been Oswald Chambers, who himself died on the mission field at a young age. He has been of the more authentic voices in the sphere of what it means for *come* to be changed to *go*. Oswald explains it better than anyone:

> The basis of missionary appeals is the authority of Jesus Christ, not the needs of the heathen. We are apt to look upon Our Lord as One Who assists us in our enterprises for God. Our Lord puts himself as the absolute sovereign supreme Lord over His disciples. He does *not* say the heathen will be lost if we do not go; He simply says—*"Go ye therefore, and teach all nations."* Go on the revelation of My sovereignty; teach and preach out of a living experience of Me.

> Then the eleven disciples went ... *"into a mountain where Jesus had appointed them"* (v. 16). If I want to know the universal sovereignty of Christ, I must know Him for myself, and how

to get alone with Him; I must take time to worship the Being Whose Name I bear. "Come unto Me"—that is the place to meet Jesus. Are you weary and heavy laden? How many missionaries are! We banish those marvelous words of the universal Sovereign of the world to the threshold of an after-meeting; they are the words of Jesus to His disciples.

"Go ye therefore. . . ." "Go" simply means live. Acts 1:8 is the description of *how* to go. Jesus did not say—Go into Jerusalem and Judea and Samaria, but, *"Ye shall be witnesses unto Me"* in all these places. He undertakes to establish the goings.

"If ye abide in Me, and My words abide in you . . ."—that is the way to keep going in our personal lives. Where we are placed is a matter of indifference; God engineers the goings. *"None of these things move me. . . ."* That is how to keep going till you're gone![1]

Thoughts and Questions

- 🦌 In what ways has Father's appeal to "come" been changed to "go" in your life?
- 🦌 What experiences in your life have prepared you for this call?
- 🦌 From Oswald's teaching, what does "go" really mean?

ENDNOTE

1. Chambers, *My Utmost for His Highest* (Dodd Mead & Co. 1935, renewed 1963 by the Oswald Chambers Publications Assn., Ltd., and is used by permission of Discovery House Publishers, Grand Rapids MI) Oct 14.

PART IX

Changing Directions

READING 106

Christlichkeit—Centered on Christ

For in Him all the fullness of Deity dwells in bodily form, and in Him you have been made complete (Colossians 2:9-10).

DISSIPATION and indulgence are most common in our day, with a multitude of voices and appeals coming from everyone and everywhere. Three German theological words will aid us in centering on the Kingdom: *Kirchlichkeit, Sachlichkeit,* and *Christlichkeit.*

Kirchlichkeit means centered on the Church. Please do not hear in this anything anti-Church; I love the Church because God does not build anything but Church, and she is the Body of Christ. However, it is more than possible to be so Church centered that we fail to be Christ or Kingdom centered. The Church can be shaken, but Christ's Kingdom cannot. Those who have been part of a serious church split know how shaken things can become. When we are Christ centered rather than Church centered, the Church can be extremely successful or a dismal failure without our being overwhelmed or in despair. We remain unshakeable. This will be increasingly important as we enter the post-modern phase of the Church.

Sachlichkeit means matter of factness or centered on what is real. We can be centered on good things like missions trips or helping the widows, orphans, and the poor but fail to be biblically centered on the Kingdom. A false center causes everything else in our sphere to be distorted and out of balance.

Christlichkeit means a life centered on the person of Christ. The Christ-centered life has more than one vital factor—the forgiveness of sin. The father forgave the prodigal before he even asked. Somehow, Christ-centered

268

has been substituted for forgiveness-centered. For several reasons, we have become so sin-conscious that we are incapable of being God-conscious. The larger body of Christ strongly needs less repentance and more faith. It is by *believing* that we stand in freedom. To be Christ centered means that we have discovered God has come to us in the form of *Agape* incarnate. *All things* are in His hand, which includes much more than forgiveness. When we have centered in Christ, human failure and the evening news cease to shake us. When we are centered on Christ and His Kingdom, all ministry and acts of service find their proper place in our lives.

God made a new covenant with us and put His laws within us and on our hearts so He could be our God and we could be His people (see Jer. 31:31-33). Behavior now comes from the DNA Seed of the new birth emerging from within rather than being imposed upon us from without. The result is the reception of a righteousness that is not out from ourselves. Jesus is unique in providing us this righteousness because He contains the fullness of the deity and the revelation of God the Father. He came for the purpose of much more than forgiveness. His job description is to make known the glory of God through Father's own family.

Thoughts and Questions

- Explain the three different ways we can become centered.
- What is one of the key factors in a Christ-centered life?
- In what ways do we need less repentance and move believing?

The Wedding Garment

For not knowing about God's righteousness and seeking to establish their own, they did not subject themselves to the righteousness of God (Romans 10:3).

JESUS told a parable about a man who came to the king's wedding feast without wearing the proper wedding clothes and was thrown out and cast into outer darkness. Because you and I do not have the proper garment and would be cast out ourselves, Christ was thrown out of the wedding feast on our behalf. He was bound, cast into outer darkness, and forsaken of God so we would never have to be (see Matt. 27:46). Christ's gift of the wedding garment is far better than anything we seek to gain on our own. It is righteousness enough; religion, Bible study, and praying will never make us more righteous. When we completely accept His gift of the wedding garment, He becomes responsible for dealing with the habits of sin in our lives. Like Paul, we need to embrace the wedding garment:

> *And that I may [actually] be found and known as in Him, not having any [self-achieved] righteousness that can be called my own, based on my obedience to the Law's demands (ritualistic uprightness and supposed right standing with God thus acquired), but possessing that [genuine righteousness] which comes through faith in Christ (the Anointed One), the [truly] right standing with God, which comes from God by [saving] faith* (Philippians 3:9 AMP).

The marriage feast is a metaphor of salvation. Like almost every other image in the Bible, the wedding is turned to profound spiritual use, becoming a metaphor for the relationship between God and His people. In this motif, God is the One who chooses believers to be the wife of His Son. Jesus is repeatedly called a Bridegroom. His earthly ministry is likened to a wedding feast. The parable of the king's wedding feast for his son depicts Jesus as the son/groom and a rejection of the invitation as a rejection of Jesus Himself.

Faith alone releases us from all of our *essential* self-centeredness so we are capable of giving ourselves to this Bridegroom. Our problem is that when we are in trouble, we have been taught to repeatedly look within ourselves for righteousness, which comes out of our own obedience. Failure, sin, selfishness, and other problems are all evidence of the reality of this. Instead of believing, we rely on ourselves to figure out what we can *do* to make the problem go away. When we cease looking inside ourselves for freedom and starting looking to the righteousness of Christ, the supernatural is released. Once our whole understanding of merit and reward disappear and we stand on faith alone, we will discover the need for less repentance and more believing. When you are in trouble, intentionally believe that He has declared you righteous and made you ceremonially clean. God made a covenant like none before it in which Jesus was provided as the source of man's freedom even in the darkest sin and failure.

If you struggle believing in the wedding garment, try saying out loud, *"Because of Christ's righteousness, I am clean before God. There is nothing I can do to be more righteousness, and there is nothing more righteous than Christ's righteousness."* Paul called this the *"power of God"* (Rom. 1:16).

Thoughts and Questions

- Describe your understanding of what Christ's wedding garment does for you.
- How does Paul describe his wedding garment?
- How can you see Christ's righteousness as the power of God?

Christ Was Judged For Us

For Christ (the Messiah) has not entered into a sanctuary made with
[human] hands, only a copy and pattern and type of the true one, but [He
has entered] into heaven itself, now to appear in the [very] presence of God
on our behalf (Hebrews 9:24 AMP).

IN the same manner that we were "in Christ" when He was crucified and
resurrected and experienced the breaking of the power of sin and release
of God's forgiveness, so we were "in Christ" when He appeared before the
Father. It should bring great comfort to know that we have already arrived in
Heaven and appeared before the presence of God Himself.

Many Christians have developed a fear of future judgment. Because of
what has been preached, judgment hangs over our head like Damocles sword.
The good news is that Christ has already been to the judgment seat for us. He
came back in resurrection, bringing with Him the wedding garment, which
is God's righteousness. Christ earned it through His death, separation from
God, and resurrection. We have actually and literally already faced future
judgment, so the fear of it should lose its power. His wedding garment cannot be added to or subtracted from. We are complete and lacking nothing
in the Person of Christ. The severity of God's judgment was exhausted on
Christ, so there was nothing left to judge. As *Agape* is brought to maturity in
us, all *fear* is displaced by the presence of God's own *Agape*. Fear of judgment
is mitigated into assurance and confidence by having walked in *Agape*. *"In*
this [union and communion with Him] love is brought to completion and attains
perfection with us, that we may have confidence for the day of judgment [with

assurance and boldness to face Him], because as He is, so are we in this world" (1 John 4:17 AMP).

The fact that Jesus came to convict the world concerning sin because they do not believe in Him has been mistakenly applied to believers. Under Christ's righteousness, we are acceptable to God and made perfect in His sight. For the believer, we experience judgment every day in the manner in which we respond to the expectations and requirements of *Agape*. This is the Cross confronting all that is self-referential and unreal in us. We can only die with Him and wait for the resurrection. After all the deals, promises, and vows we try to make with God, we still must die to what is self-referential in our own person.

Paul states that Christ is not primarily concerned with sin in the flesh. There is no condemnation for those who are in Christ Jesus because He annulled sin's effect in God's presence (see Rom. 8:1-3). The power of it was taken away by Christ's righteousness, which became ours by faith alone. By our love for Christ demonstrated as preferential choice, we reach into His righteousness and embrace all God has done on our behalf. If we fail to access this righteousness, we fail in the transformation process.

Thoughts and Questions

- In what ways have you tried to add to your wedding garment?
- What is facing you at the judgment seat?
- Describe what embracing the Cross/*Agape* does for you.

Word of the Cross

For the word of the cross is foolishness to those who are perishing, but to us who are being saved it is the power of God. For it is written, "I will destroy the wisdom of the wise, and the cleverness of the clever I will set aside."...
But we preach Christ crucified, to Jews a stumbling block and to Gentiles foolishness, but to those who are the called, both Jews and Greeks, Christ the power of God and the wisdom of God. Because the foolishness of God is wiser than men, and the weakness of God is stronger than men
(1 Corinthians 1:18-25).

THE Jewish religious system has a strong merit system. External symbols and feast days hold sway over the hearts of God's people. The word of the cross destroys the wisdom of the wise and the merit system of Jewish religion. This is why the word of the cross was such an offense to the Pharisees. Paul's courage to embrace 39 stripes and then go back into the local synagogue to preach Christ was out of *Agape* for his own people. He was driven to declare that through the cross Christ had, once and for all, made all outward and external forms of spirituality lose their redemptive value. Apart from the internal working of the cross, we continue to *acquire, possess, and control* in either sensual or religious ways. Paul referred to this as being *"enemies of the Cross of Christ"* (Phil. 3:18).

The cross is an intricate part of the Christian life because it is the crucified Christ who we are following. His death was more than our free ticket to Heaven. Through the cross, we look in depth to the heart of God, as Father, who is seeking to restore us to Himself as the human created in His own image. In giving us His Love in crucified form, we are able to see the Kingdom and understand how God wants us to act and respond to the issues of real life. It is the cross alone that has the ability to shape our person and our world. Vocational suffering emerges as a natural result of the way in which we have chosen to walk. Our call is to recognize and embrace the irrational and painful manner in which life unfolds for those who have not known Christ. Identity with a hurting world is our vocation. That calling requires being equipped to absorb the pain and confusion of those to whom we are being sent.

Unfortunately, *Eros* has the capacity to use both Moses' Law and the cross of Christ to our own advantage. A lot of people wear crosses and get cross tattoos, seeking to use the cross as a magic charm to keep them from harm or poverty. The Christian message becomes one of triumphalism, prosperity, and condescension. We speak from above to those who are yet trapped in ungodly circumstances rather than being one with them in identity and compassion.

When we reach into God and say, "I know I failed in this thing, and I'm asking You, in Jesus' name, to let the righteousness of Christ prevail on my behalf," we are embracing a working form of repentance. We are learning to stand in the righteousness of Christ on faith alone. When we are grieving, angry, or in isolation, we must abide by faith alone and embrace the word of the cross as it comes to us in resurrection. The alternate is religious or sensual/condescending *Eros*. This Kingdom conduct takes the relationship with Christ out of the subjective into the objective. Through the Cross, Christ takes us out of ourselves into His purposes.

Thoughts and Questions

- Explain why the word of the Cross was an offense to the Jewish religious system.
- In what ways does the Cross keep us from acquiring, possessing, and controlling?
- What are some results of embracing the Cross?

Changing Directions

And cut through and make firm and plain and smooth, straight paths for your feet [yes, make them safe and upright and happy paths that go in the right direction], so that the lame and halting [limbs] may not be put out of joint, but rather may be cured (Hebrews 12:13 AMP).

WHEN God created man, His ultimate intention was for creation to have an outward center—God Himself. The entrance of sin and death *changed the direction of the entire human race.* Mankind's change of direction was an offense to God. It was so total and complete that God's nature had to be revealed through the Incarnation. Christ Jesus is the one Man who absorbed God's offense. Not only does our universe turn in on itself, but it also contracts to the point of death.

In years of helping others, I have watched people, including myself, enter obsessive-compulsive prisons simply because we have changed directions. When I was 12 years old, I changed directions on the Lord, intentionally rejecting His presence in my life. Since my encounter with the living Christ in 1954, I have never changed directions on Him again. When the pressure or personal cost of following Jesus becomes too much, our tendency is to move centrifugally away from an *Agape* center. The entire human race is so moving away from center and turning in upon itself that consistency is, of itself, evidence that the Kingdom has come.

Every one of us stands on a razor's edge of personal preference. We can either turn in on ourselves and save our own skin for personal advantage or remain faithful to an *Agape* center and find a new measure of freedom. The power of darkness always stands ready to force a compromise or attempt to extinguish the Seed of the Kingdom. *The successful act of reversal of direction and leaving our love for darkness and turning toward Light is supernatural.*

The sinless Son of God never changed directions at any time, for any reason, or due to any pressure. Jesus never changed directions on His Father, not even when it was time to go to Jerusalem and face betrayal, Gethsemane, and Calvary. He always moved outward to a hurting world and always fulfilled His Father's mission. He came to do the will of His Father irrespective of the cost. By following Him, we move outward from an *Agape* center. One of the signs that we have been born of God and are moving outward is our love for others.

Nicodemus saw Jesus do miracles and wanted to know the Kingdom. Jesus told him that he couldn't understand the Kingdom unless he had been born from above, encountering a source of life of which he was totally ignorant. Nicodemus could not follow Jesus because, as a teacher of the Jews, he was moving in the wrong direction. Jesus was heading toward a well in Jerusalem to reveal Father's love to a Samaritan—an inconceivable act to a Jew. Without the new birth, loving the unlovable is unthinkable. When we are born of the Spirit, it changes our direction. As the incarnate Eternal Seed of *Agape* is implanted and nourished within us, we discover the capacity to remain faithful in circumstances that would pressure us toward betrayal of the person of Christ.

Thoughts and Questions

- Explain why changing directions is so offensive to God.
- What is the end result of turning in our ourselves?
- Why was Nicodemus unable to follow Jesus?

Kingdom Is a Person—Follow Me

Now we look inside, and what we see is that anyone united with the
Messiah gets a fresh start, is created new. The old life is gone; a new life
burgeons! Look at it! ...Most people around here are looking out for
themselves, with little concern for the things of Jesus!
(2 Corinthians 5:17; Philippians 2:21 TM)

THE new birth is new in the sense that it is unique. It is the Eternal Seed being implanted in us. In order to change directions, the Eternal Seed must be cultivated, guarded, and nourished. The Kingdom is not a place, location, or destination; the Kingdom is a person. If we are following Him, we are moving outward from an *Agape* center. If we are not following Him, we are turning in on ourselves.

If we follow Jesus, where is He going to take us? Follow Me is directional, and as ones who "follow after," we have to buckle our seatbelts for the journey because He's taking us against the moral and social current of darkness. The whole world is *turning in* on itself, while God is seeking to *take us out* of ourselves. When someone asks if I am a Christian, I usually tell them that I am a follower of Christ, adding that some days I am able to follow Him more completely than other days! Followers can be identified by watching their feet, not their words.

Paul was alarmed that the Galatians were preparing to change directions; they began to use their freedom erroneously, missing their Kingdom inheritance. He wrote, *"Are you going to continue this craziness? For only crazy people would think they could complete by their own efforts what was begun by God. If you weren't smart enough or strong enough to begin it, how do you suppose you could perfect it? ...Christ has set us free to live a free life. So take your stand! Never again let anyone put a harness of slavery on you"* (Gal. 3:3; 5:1 TM). Look at the direction in the following Scripture:

> *It is obvious what kind of life develops out of trying to get your own way all the time: repetitive, loveless, cheap sex; a stinking accumulation of mental and emotional garbage; frenzied and joyless grabs for happiness; trinket gods; magic-show religion; paranoid loneliness; cutthroat competition; all-consuming-yet-never-satisfied wants; a brutal temper; an impotence to love or be loved; divided homes and divided lives; small-minded and lop-sided pursuits; the vicious habit of depersonalizing everyone into a rival; uncontrolled and uncontrollable addictions; ugly parodies of community. I could go on. This isn't the first time I have warned you, you know. If you use your freedom this way, you will not inherit God's kingdom* (Galatians 5:19-21 TM).

This is a description of most of the Western culture. As a nation, as well as the modern Church, we are in danger of missing the Kingdom because we are not following the Kingdom as a person. Following Jesus requires turning from an inward center and moving outward to share the Eternal Seed with a hurting world. Thus, we grasp the intent of *Agape*: God loved and God gave.

Thoughts and Questions

🌱 Describe the Kingdom.

🌱 What must we do to change directions?

🌱 Describe the problem with the Galatian church.

The Fruit of Changing Directions

When you attempt to live by your own religious plans and projects, you are cut off from Christ, you fall out of grace (Galatians 5:4 TM).

FOLLOWING Christ means we are entering the Kingdom. It is not static; it is a relational journey because the Kingdom is a person. Being in Christ is both a position and an experience. Moving with and following Him who is going in a *totally opposite direction* creates complexity, persecution, and difficulty. As long as we are moving in a direction that preserves our comfort level—save me, heal me, help me, bless me—we have very few problems. The Kingdom issues start when we decide to literally and intentionally follow Christ, knowing that the *Agape* Seed will take us places we would not necessarily choose for ourselves, but due to the compassion of God the Father, we find ourselves compelled to go.

The quintessence of all spiritual warfare, temptation, and ungoverned desire is to cause us to change directions. At the *existential moment* when we choose to change direction, our minds, emotions, and willpower are flooded with multiple reasons why we have made the right choice, but the result is darkness, which eagerly waits to fill the vacuum. It is movement inward and downward that results in falling out of God's grace. Once we change directions, we are capable of *anything*: denial, betrayal, and murder—we crucify Christ all over again. The fruit of changing directions is always death by degrees.

Never change directions at any time, for any reason, or due to any pressure. Judas changed directions on Jesus, thinking no one knew it. Although marital relationships sometimes need adjustments, changing directions in a marriage is another matter. Going to marriage counseling is making adjustments; having a girlfriend across town is changing directions.

After some hard words from Jesus, many people decided to go a different direction. Jesus asked the disciples if they wanted to go too. Peter answered Him, *"Lord, to whom shall we go? You have words of eternal life"* (John 6:68). Fortunately, God made room for us changing directions: *"If we confess our sins, He is faithful and righteous to forgive us our sins and to cleanse us from all unrighteousness"* (1 John 1:9). The world waits for cohesion, but changing directions creates the opposite effect. What makes the church a safe place is an increasing and unshakable degree of cohesion. Even in a crunch, a follower of Jesus will not change directions on you!

Thoughts and Questions

- What is the end result and some of the signs that we are following Christ?
- What are some of the fruits of changing directions?
- Why did some of Christ's followers want to leave?

READING 113

Piously Changing Directions

I tell you that crooks and whores are going to precede you into God's kingdom
(Matthew 21:31 TM).

THE reason it is easier for crooks and whores to repent, change directions, and follow Christ is because they *know* they are sinners. It is
irrelevant whether our journey is religious or secular; the issue is the act of
changing directions. J. Jeremias said, "Repentance was hardest for the pious
man because he was separated from God not by crude sins but by his piety.
Nothing separates a man from God so radically as self-assured holiness."[1]

Because of his own devoutness, Nicodemus was almost unable to change
directions to follow Christ. This is what Matthew was talking about when he
said, *"You're hopeless, you religious scholars and Pharisees! Frauds! You go halfway
around the world to make a convert, but once you get him you make him into a rep-
lica of yourselves, double-damned"* (Matt. 23:15 TM). They were already mor-
ally blind—add religion and they were doubly blind. If you have ever talked
to someone fully enclosed in a religious system, you will see why there is cause
for alarm. It is especially painful to see evangelism take on the *Eros* dimension
of possess, acquire, and control. Not all evangelism is *of God*; as fearful as it
sounds, much that looks like evangelism is motivated by the innate and compulsive desire to conquer others for our own agenda. Many people in Israel,
the church, and various religious groups want to claim Him but refuse to
acknowledge His demands in order to follow Him. Jesus went first to the lost
sheep of Israel because religion nearly destroyed them and is still doing so.
When Jesus spoke of the Kingdom agenda toward the blind, oppressed, and

brokenhearted, He was speaking in a synagogue where these people attended. The promise of the Kingdom was that this would be changed!

Post-modern pressure forces us into a Kingdom posture. Jesus said this in the synagogue: *"The spirit of the Lord is upon Me, because He anointed Me to preach the gospel to the poor. He has sent Me to proclaim release to the captives, and recovery of sight to the blind, to set free those who are oppressed"* (Luke 4:18). Ask God to turn you from exclusive to inclusive, from pious religion to post-denominational and post-doctrinal. Rather than expanding, we must learn to contract. Love people without condition until they give concrete evidence that they do not want or intend to follow Jesus. It matters little how strange, weird, or off the wall they are. The issue is: Do they want to follow Him? Watch their feet, not their words.

If we expand rather than contract, it can become expensive. The issue is: which way are we going? We should be expanding, going to the ends of the earth, not contemplating our spiritual health or well-being.

Thoughts and Questions

- Why do you think it is easier for sinners to get into God's Kingdom?
- What are some of the results of pious religion?
- What do we learn by watching someone's feet, not their words?

ENDNOTE

1. Paul Servier Minear, *Christians and the New Creation*. (Westminster John Knox Press. Louisville, KY. 1994) pg. 142

READING 114

Movement, Direction, and Velocity

*Because this people draw near (movement) with their words and honor Me
with their lip service, but they remove their hearts far from Me, and their
reverence for Me consists of tradition learned by rote* (Isaiah 29:13).

I'VE learned that you can get a rocking chair up to 20 miles per hour if you
really try. It seemed I had mine up to about 60 miles an hour and I put
about 5,000 miles on it while I was asking God to show me the Kingdom. At
about the 4,000-mile mark, I had a mental picture of *Eros* as *movement, direction,* and *velocity.* I saw that these three were really important components in
understanding the Kingdom because if we are moving toward *Eros,* we are
moving away from God into ourselves. Many people move toward God with
their words but moving away from Him in their affections. This is movement,
direction, and velocity in the wrong direction.

A friend of mine experienced movement, direction, and velocity when he
went through the pain and pressure of an ugly divorce. He told me that he
wasn't just backslidden; he was doing back flips, and everything in him was
trying to escape. The velocity of our running from God can increase. Jonah
certainly experienced this. It is hypocritical to move toward God with our
words and keep saying the right things while we move away from Him in our
hearts, but each one of us has managed to accomplish this. *This is the Eros shift*
(See Appendix A *Eros* Shift Chart).

Even though Peter could see the glory of God in the face of Christ, he still
needed an *Agape* conversion—really changing directions so he could strengthen
his brothers. Shortly afterward, Peter went through a personal crisis, totally failed

Jesus, but found his way through to repentance and was able to change directions (see Luke 22:32; John 21:15). The only time he ever compromised after that was when he was eating with the Gentiles and the elders were coming down from Jerusalem. Because he had something to lose, his movement and direction changed, and he denied his association with the Gentiles. Paul confronted him because his change of directions brought confusion to the church. Changing directions is a very critical and important concept. Just because you are a Christian doesn't mean you're not experiencing movement, direction, and velocity in an *Eros* shift; there are selfish believers moving in the wrong direction everywhere.

When God comes to us in an *Agape* reformation, our direction changes, and we start to move toward God. The Greek word for changing directions is *metanoia,* meaning to repent. It involves a change in thinking, not the removal of your mind. Paul stated this well when he said, *"Don't become so well-adjusted to your culture that you fit into it without even thinking. Instead, fix your attention on God. You'll be changed from the inside out. Readily recognize what he wants from you, and quickly respond to it. Unlike the culture around you, always dragging you down to its level of immaturity, God brings the best out of you, develops well-formed maturity in you"* (Rom. 12:2 TM).

Thoughts and Questions

- ❦ Describe a situation in your life where you experienced movement, direction, and velocity.
- ❦ Why do you think Peter changed directions when the elders paid a visit?
- ❦ What causes a change in our direction?

Kingdom Philosophy of Life

Since you have in obedience to the truth purified your souls for a sincere love (phileo) of the brethren, fervently love (Agape) one another from the heart, for you have been born again not of seed which is perishable but imperishable, that is, through the living and enduring word of God (1 Peter 1:22-23).

BECAUSE we were all born in sin, every child thinks he or she is the center of the universe. Original sin turns us in upon ourselves; that is the *direction* in which we are headed at birth. However, when we are born again, we receive an impartation of the incorruptible Seed. Because we have been born again of Seed that is imperishable, we learn to *Agape* one another from the heart. The new birth is the source, cause, or reason for our initial change of direction. When we meet Jesus, He starts to unwind the whole direction of our life; thus, the prisoner is being set free as He promised. The center of our world becomes the Kingdom, and He focuses us on the poor and hurting people. Our whole world changes directions, and we begin to understand Father's initiative and His indefectible mercy.

A Kingdom philosophy of life is a vision of the Kingdom. It gives us a compelling reason and desire to change directions. Nicodemus couldn't even see the Kingdom because his whole life was going in the wrong direction. This is *Eros* blindness. I'm sure you can remember times when you were blind as a bat—absolutely so self-centered you couldn't see anything. Denominationalism is like a fish bowl, while the Kingdom is the sea. When we have a vision of the Kingdom, compassion begins to develop for those who consider themselves free but are, in fact, possessed, acquired, and controlled by the limitations of imposed doctrinal restraints. I know this is inflammatory. My heart yearns for the day when this statement will seem normal rather than reformational.

Only a Kingdom philosophy can give us the desire to deny ourselves. An 18-year-once said to me, *"Mr. Mumford, I no longer see why I should help anybody but myself."* Her philosophy was to party, drink, and live it up, for tomorrow you die. I believe that if the youth of America could see a Kingdom vision, they would respond to it. There is something in us that *wants* to respond to challenge and sacrifice if it's for the right thing. True wealth can be measured by having something for which we are willing to die. Apart from the revelation and the illumination of the Gospel of God and the influence of His Kingdom, there is nothing that stands in the way of us becoming a predator or a parasite. Because our core nature is to turn in on itself, an *Agape* culture is the only thing that can possibly serve as an antidote to the poison of *Eros.* Malcom Muggeridge stated that fourteen civilizations have disappeared from the earth because they turned in upon themselves and disappeared. This is certainly true in the history of Rome.

Entering the Kingdom is a matter of direction. We must head toward an *Agape* conversion.

Thoughts and Questions

- ₮ What allows our initial change of direction?
- ₮ What is a Kingdom philosophy of life?
- ₮ In what ways has a Kingdom philosophy allowed you to deny yourself?

Movement and Direction in the Life of Christ

But [Satan is coming and] I do as the Father has commanded Me, so that the world may know (be convinced) that I love the Father and that I do only what the Father has instructed Me to do. [I act in full agreement with His orders.] Rise, let us go away from here (John 14:31 AMP).

AT Christ's birth He was God made flesh—incarnate. Then He identified with us in the waters of baptism. Immediately after He was baptized, He encountered and conquered the three temptations in the wilderness. These encounters with the satanic were designed to tempt Him to change directions. Through the temptations, Jesus learned obedience and was perfected by the things He suffered, resulting in boldness and courage. After these temptations, He had several major encounters with the whole religious system (see John 5). Standing in front of the temple, He said that in three days the temple would be destroyed and rebuilt, and they went crazy! If He had stood anywhere else and said that, He would not have been nearly as misunderstood. Jesus intentionally watched for sick people so He could heal them on the Sabbath. The people wanted to make him King, which involved all the Abrahamic, Davidic, and messianic fulfillments. It was not a light temptation, but Jesus would not change directions.

When I was in Bible college, I was somewhat older than the other students, so many of the instructors would ask me to substitute teach in their classes when they were away. A pastor from south Philadelphia came to the college to see me and asked that I visit his church as soon as I graduated.

When I walked into the huge building, I was overwhelmed at the posh, elevated seats and the thick rug. I was salivating internally and thought, *If I could have built a church, it would have looked just like this!* The pastor was watching me and said, "This church is in my name, and I hold the title. If you will come be the pastor, I'll give you the entire church, building, title, and all." When the Lord allows a temptation, it is not usually a dead fish but a live one. We all know that the fish can only see the bait and not the hook! I looked at that church building in pain, agony, and despair because I knew that this was an attempt to make me "king" and divert me from the real purposes God had for me. God gave me the grace to decline the pastor's offer.

Jesus, in His humanity, was very close to changing directions in Gethsemane. He prayed, as many of us have, "Father, is there any other way to do this?" Instead of changing directions, He faced all the pain, agony, and shame and stayed on course. Christ's refusal to change directions is part of what made Him the sinless Son. Jesus created an example for us to follow. He never changed directions but intentionally moved from an *Agape* center.

Thoughts and Questions

- What was the purpose of the three wilderness temptations?
- Describe some other situations in which Jesus refused to change directions.
- Why would Jesus be considered sinless for refusing to change directions?

God's Worldview

Yes, Father, for this way was well-pleasing in Your sight. All things have been handed over to Me by My Father; and no one knows the Son except the Father; nor does anyone know the Father except the Son, and anyone to whom the Son wills to reveal Him (Matthew 11:26–27).

THE Kingdom involves a true and full embrace of God's worldview; as such, the Kingdom produces an *inner victory over self-concern*. When I was born of the spirit at 12 years old, the first thing I experienced was the rather violent circumstances attempting to steal the seed of the Kingdom. The construction workers who worked for my father were unmerciful; they mocked and persecuted me for my newfound faith until I actually changed directions. In Jesus' parable about the birds eating up the seed, we usually think of an obnoxious black crow (like the construction crew), but the thief *could* be a beautiful canary in a fancy yellow dress and wearing expensive perfume. In either case, if the seed is stolen, we lose our desire, motivation, and vision for the Kingdom. Loss of our Kingdom inheritance could be defined as the loss of that participation of Father's activity and unfolding purpose in the earth. To lose that is more expensive than one could imagine.

Sometimes the *cares of the world* are more powerful at stealing the seed than persecution. This is not sin in the classic sense. The pressure to manage our accounts, make more money, and get things done is more insidious than having abuse of alcohol or compulsive use of drugs stealing the seed. There are people whose whole lives consist of horses, golf, or fishing. None of that is illegal unless it captures us. When we experience the spiritual and physical needs of the poor, it causes us to look at a new set of golf clubs in a whole new light.

Anything that causes the Eternal Seed of the Kingdom to be stolen moves us away from our chosen direction. If the Seed is stolen right from the start, it essentially could be understood as a still birth. Christian historians state that there are somewhere between 20 and 40 million born-again Christians in America! Most of these have had their Kingdom Seed stolen. Please hear me when I say another 20 million just like them will not make any difference to the Kingdom agenda. Our commission is to see that the will of God is done on the earth as it is in Heaven. There are very few churches that understand and preach the Kingdom. They preach church growth, bribe us with heaven, and blackmail us with hell.

We can change direction or turn back and still be saved. Repentance is what causes us to find our direction again. Have you ever been running from God when the Lord starts saying something to you that you don't want to hear? This is the beginning of God extending His *grace* of repentance. The Kingdom as *Agape* brought to its full intention involves a full embrace of God's worldview. Because of Father's DNA nature, He does not injure or confuse us by circumstances; He is always intentionally leading us to a place of freedom, giving us His perspective and worldview, and allowing us to eagerly and effectively seek the Kingdom first.

Thoughts and Questions

🐦 What are some of the signs of having God's worldview?

🐦 In what ways can persecution steal your Kingdom Seed?

🐦 Why would more believers without God's worldview not make much difference?

PART X

Offense

Being Scandalized

Blessed is he who does not take offense at Me (Matthew 11:6).

BEFORE you have finished this book, you will have been carefully and methodically instructed in three words: *Agape*, abiding, and offense. My intention is not only that Father would make each of our lives count but that in our response to His call, we would not become offended and consequently, become victims.

Years ago, people would build a trap in order to capture birds. A box would be balanced on a stick tied to a rope and birdseed or other food was placed under the box. When the birds came to eat the seed, the stick would be pulled out and the box would fall on the unsuspecting birds. In Greek, the stick that held up the box was called the *skandalizo*, which is most commonly translated "to offend." The root of the word is a term used to describe the bait in a trap that was used to snare animals. A "scandal," then, is a situation that causes one to be trapped or ensnared.

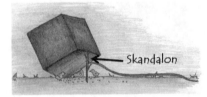

This happened to me. It never occurred to me that Father would give anyone the privilege of saying no to God. However, when I was 12 years old, I did. My father had several very rough and rather uneducated men who worked for him in the construction business. When I came to Christ at the age of 12, they began to mock, harass, persecute, and undermine the joy I was experiencing. As the mocking and mimicking continued day after day, I became frustrated, angry, and full of resentment, so I stood in the middle of the street and very boldly told God, "I do not *want* to be a Christian! I do not *want* to live like this! Take Your presence *away* from me so I can live my own life!" I was what Scripture calls *offended.* I chose to deny, refuse, and then distance myself from what was causing the pain. When I returned to the Father after 12 longs years of estrangement, I came back like a heat-seeking missile; something in my heart had changed. No was taken out of my vocabulary. In Strong's definition of *offense* (Strong's #4624), we can see how offense can be both given and received:

> To put a stumbling block or impediment in the way, upon which another may trip and fall. To *entice* to sin, apostasy or displeasure. To cause a person to begin to distrust and desert one whom he ought to trust and obey. To cause to fall away. To be offended in one, i.e. to see in another what I disapprove of and what hinders me from acknowledging his authority. To cause one to judge unfavorably or unjustly of another. One who stumbles or whose foot gets entangled feels annoyed. To cause one displeasure at a thing. To be displeased, indignant.

A stumbling block brings to mind the mental image of some small obstruction that catches our toe when we are walking and puts us flat on our face in the dirt. It is more than a simple hindrance or confusion about the way to go; it totally stops us in our walk with others, in our pursuit of a particular truth, or in our personal relationship with God. A stumbling block may only be an inch high, but it can be just as effective as a range of mountains.

Thoughts and Questions

In your own words, describe what it means to be offended.

- What did Jesus mean when He said, "blessed is he who does not take offense at Me"?

- In ways have you been offended? How did that work for you?

Offended at God

These things I have spoken to you that you may be kept from stumbling
(John 16:1).

IF you have ever been scandalized, you know it is a serious issue, especially if the anger is directed at God. When we refuse or are unable to hold our position of abiding, the force fields of pride or rage come into play. I remember driving into a gas station one time and saying to the mechanic, "Oh, what I beautiful day God created!" His response was, "Don't talk to me about God!" and out came all the anger and bitterness about how his son had been killed in the military. He prayed that God would keep his son safe, and he felt that God had let him die. Then he said, "Where was God when my son was killed?" I said, "The same place He was when His Son was killed." When *skandalizo* becomes your portion, and it will, and you find yourself in a spiritually or emotionally dark box from which it is difficult to recover because when the enemy gets involved, it is like fighting a tar baby. Every move is the wrong one. Every prayer sounds like a poorly verbalized whimper. All counsel and advice seem petty or counterproductive.

Being scandalized or offended is one of the deepest and most binding traps into which a believer can fall. In many ways, it goes far beyond simply being hurt, deceived, or ensnared by carnal sin; it has the capacity to *totally undermine and destroy our walk with the Lord.* Some of the strongest teachings of the New Testament, including the direst warnings of our Lord Jesus, have to do with avoiding the snare of being scandalized or offended. Once we have been scandalized, we really do not care what anyone thinks. We feel the force field of the early signs of deeply brooding anger, and if we are not careful, we are rapidly sucked down into the vacuum of rage and depression. We have the sensation or feeling that this event or circumstance is pulling us down into its control.

Just before a young bride walked down the aisle, one of God's little helpers with a questionable reputation for receiving words from the Lord, whispered in her ear, "Dear, the Lord has shown me that this marriage will not last." What she had been so sure was the will of God only seconds before now brought total doubt. She went through the ceremony panic-stricken, unsure whether she was fulfilling the will of God or stepping out from under His favor. Each time this couple encountered the normal pressures in a young marriage, this false word of snare and scandal would sweep over her. The more she believed it, the more she expected problems until she had convinced herself that the word had been true. The couple finally separated, and the young wife *stumbled*, both in her relationship with her husband and with the Lord. How could she trust a God who would deceptively lead her into a wrong relationship and then abandon her? She had mistakenly received a word from the adversary as if it had come from the Lord, and the resulting *offense* against the Lord cost her dearly.

Jesus gave us several warnings about not being offended. God can do things we would never expect or anticipate. Maturity includes a biblical guard against stumbling, falling into sin, or giving up our faith because our expectations were unmet.

Thoughts and Questions

- 🦌 In what ways have you been offended at God?
- 🦌 What are some of the signs of being offended?
- 🦌 Why did Jesus warn us about not being offended at God?

Reading 120

Expectations and Offense

And blessed (happy, fortunate, and to be envied) is he who takes no offense at Me and finds no cause for stumbling in or through Me and is not hindered from seeing the Truth (Matthew 11:6 AMP).

THERE are several basic factors involved when a believer is scandalized. In almost every situation, the process of being offended begins with unrealistic expectations. An *Eros* imagination knows just how this is going to happen, what the results will be, and how the Lord will handle this circumstance. When it does not happen—the parent dies, the child is lost, or the prophetic word does not come to pass—we are left not knowing what to believe and thinking the whole Christian walk is a deception.

One of the more graphic examples of false expectation is in the Old Testament when Naaman, the captain of the army of Syria, came to Elisha to be healed of his leprosy. When Naaman and his entourage arrived at Elisha's door, the prophet did not even go out to greet the mighty officer; he simply sent out a servant and told him to go wash himself seven times in the Jordan River. Needless to say, Naaman was *scandalized!* He stormed away from the prophet's house in a rage. In his false expectations, Naaman *thought* that Elisha would come out and call on the name of the Lord his God, wave his hand over the place, and cure the leper (see 2 Kings 5:11). Naaman's expectations left him open to being scandalized when they did not happen *like he thought they should*. Had it not been for a faithful servant girl who could reason with Naaman, he would have lost not only his healing but possibly his life as a result of this offense.

In the New Testament, we find that John the Baptist, for all his spiritual stature and insight, was nearly *scandalized* by Jesus Himself. John's expectations of the Kingdom of God, Jesus' ministry, and his own circumstances had set him up to be offended. John had seen the Kingdom as fire and judgment—the axe coming to the root of the unfruitful tree. However, Jesus did not fulfill his expectations of being a national liberator, nor had He thundered forth the expected judgment against Israel's unrighteousness. Instead, Christ spoke of love and the fatherhood of God, and this was *not* what John had in mind. The reports he was receiving in prison about Jesus accepting invitations to feasts and actually eating and drinking with publicans and sinners were more than the prophet could endure. So, John, in desperation, sent word to Jesus: *"Are You the One Who was to come, or should we keep on expecting a different one?"* (Matt. 11:3 AMP). Christ's answer to John was a simple appeal to scriptural evidence that confirmed His identity. Jesus had to adjust John's expectations of the nature of the coming Kingdom, for John's difficulty was based not on what Christ did but on *what he expected* Christ to do. Jesus knew that if John became totally offended by Jesus' ministry, the prophet could be deeply wounded and perhaps even lost to the purposes of God.

We must remember that John's difficulty was not some great character weakness or lack of spiritual strength. Rather, he had wrong expectations about what Jesus was going to do when He set up His Kingdom. If we were scandalized every time the Lord surprised us, it would be next to impossible to walk in this life without continually stumbling and falling on our faces. May the Lord Jesus help us adjust our expectations so that we do not miss the Kingdom.

Thoughts and Questions

- ❦ What was the basis of Naaman's offense?
- ❦ After seeing all of Jesus' signs, why was John asking if He was the coming one?
- ❦ Why is it easy to be scandalized when Jesus does something surprising?

Three Roots to Being Scandalized

The Pharisees were offended... (Matthew 15:12).

CERTAIN "roots" in us make us vulnerable to being scandalized when our expectations are not met: personal opinion, personal advantage, and personal convenience.

Personal Opinion. The root of strident personal opinion is an *unhealthy desire to be right.* This aspect of the Be Right Giant privately interprets God's actions and written Word in a way that is narrowly individualistic and biased. Most often the more strongly opinionated a person is, the more easily he is offended when things do not go his way. God may answer a prayer for someone we feel does not deserve it or *not* answer a prayer for someone we feel *does* deserve it.

Personal Advantage. "What's in it for me?" is often the bait used to trap us. Although we would like to think our motives for following the Lord are pure, very often we are guilty of following Him as a means to personal prosperity, glory, or even for the fame and excitement. Many of us are "Bread Christians"—we follow Him for what He gives and what we may receive. The disciples asked: What do we get for following? Personal Advantage was a stumbling block for Peter. Soon after the Lord began to tell of His impending arrest and crucifixion by the authorities, Peter interrupted, telling Him that this *must not happen to Him.* On the surface, it would seem that Peter was concerned about the personal safety of the Lord, but we must remember that this is the same Peter who argued with the other disciples about who was the greatest and who now saw himself as the cornerstone of the coming Kingdom. His *expectation* was that Jesus would vanquish the Roman conquerors, remove the offensive existing religious order, and set up a powerful earthly kingdom. Jesus' talk of crucifixion suddenly brought an end to all of his personal plans and set him up for being scandalized. Because of Peter's desire for personal advantage, he became an offense to the Lord Jesus Himself.

Personal Convenience. Most of us would prefer not to have our comfortable and self-centered lifestyles interrupted by the inconvenient and uncomfortable demands of the Gospel. This is why the rich young ruler turned away from Jesus. If we were to take seriously Jesus' commands about the poor, the orphan, and the widow, we might find our own lifestyles inconveniently interrupted. Very little about the Gospel of the Kingdom is convenient. Nothing is comfortable about bearing a cross. We would much rather hear about God's blessing, prosperity, and care. Jesus spoke directly to this problem when He taught that it was better to lose a hand, a foot, or an eye than to be scandalized. This teaching may be offensive to the modern mind, but it presents a crucial truth. Those who are not prepared to restrict without reservation what they *do* (the hand), where they *go* (the foot), and what they *watch and desire* (the eye) are setting themselves up to be offended. Pastors who teach, "You *can* have it all!" are setting their people up to be scandalized.

Our natural desires for personal opinion, personal advantage, and personal convenience are the bait the enemy uses to spring the trap. The cost is the possibility of losing our inheritance in the Kingdom.

Thoughts and Questions

- ❦ Which of these three personal problems has been the greatest issue for you?
- ❦ In what ways can you see how "What's in it for me?" can be the bait in a trap?
- ❦ Why are the hand, foot, and eye keys to keep from getting offended?

Symptoms of Being Scandalized

... many of His disciples withdrew and were not walking with Him anymore (John 6:66).

TWO symptoms can help us diagnose whether we have been scandalized in a given situation. They are disillusionment and disengagement.

Disillusionment. Before we can be disillusioned, we must first have certain illusions. These may include an unrealistic image or idea about who God is and what we should expect from Him or an unrealistic standard of how others should act, particularly professional, political, business, or religious leaders. Disillusionment often comes when our personal opinions, advantage, or convenience are confronted by reality. When the Lord does not seem to cooperate by fulfilling our expectations, we find ourselves *scandalized* and doubting the character of God. These expectations can be strong. God said to Job, *"Will you condemn Me, so that you can be justified?"* (Job 40:8).

At first, the early followers of Jesus were delighted by His gracious words and miracles and the love of the Father that flowed from Him. However, the longer they followed Him, the more they found the things He was saying and doing increasingly less enchanting. After several hard sayings, Jesus asked them, *"Does this cause you to **stumble?**"* (John 6:61). Evidently, many of the disciples were literally offended at His words because they withdrew and did not want to walk with Him anymore. They were disenchanted or in our words, disillusioned, with Jesus because His ministry was not all broken bread and multiplied fish. One of the most difficult problems to deal with in Christians is what could be identified as "Christian idolatry." The second commandment is, *"You shall not make for yourselves idols"* (Lev. 26:1), which includes both *physical* and *mental* images. It is often easier to break up little copper baals than to break down some of the mental images Christians have of the Lord and what He should or should not do. Quite often, the false images we set up in our minds become a source of disillusionment once God does not fit the image we have created for Him.

Disengagement. Disengagement is the natural response of distancing ourselves from an offending person or party. Before we can be scandalized by someone, we must first be attracted to him or her. The Pharisees were attracted to Jesus because of His miracles and the wisdom with which He taught. The disciples were attracted to Jesus because He was a source of life and grace. These were all legitimate reasons for following Jesus, but once the *offense* came, the attraction was lost, and they began to disengage themselves from the Lord. Naaman's first response to Elisha's command to "go and wash" was to *reject* the offending prophet. In the same way, the followers of Jesus were offended when He told them that they must eat His flesh and drink His blood.

Many who walk with the Lord become scandalized. They start their journey with Christ but because a particular group of Christians does not measure up to the *standards they have set*, they must distance themselves from God, His people, or both. Such isolation ultimately results in a departure from active fellowship with the Lord Himself. Offenses are unavoidable. Our response to offense is the critical issue.

Thoughts and Questions

- What illusions of God's character and actions have you set up for yourself?
- Describe a situation in which you became disillusioned.
- In what ways have you disengaged from the Lord because of being offended?

Reading 123

Giving and Taking Offense

And blessed (happy, fortunate, and to be envied) is he who takes no offense at Me and finds no cause for stumbling in or through Me and is not hindered from seeing the Truth (Matthew 11:6 AMP).

WITH over 12,000 biblical references to offense, we do not need a rocket scientist to tell us that this is a significant biblical principle. In a room full of religious people, Jesus spoke to the disciples who were following John and encouraged them not to take offense at Him. John had his own ideas of what Jesus would or would not do. When Jesus appeared on the scene with an agenda that did not fit into John's preconceived ideas, John came close to being offended. Jesus was saying something very direct to them: *You are blessed if what I do and the manner in which I do it do not cause you to become offended.* For safety reasons, it is our responsibility not to allow offense to occur. Like nitroglycerin, it needs to be handled with care.

Offense has been around a long time. Romans 5:14 says, *"Nevertheless **death reigned** from Adam until Moses, even over those who had not sinned **in the likeness of the offense of Adam**, who is a type of Him who was to come"* (Romans 5:14). This verse leads us to believe that God the Father was actually *offended* at the conduct of Adam and Eve and dismissed them from the Garden.

When Jesus was traveling toward Jerusalem and the Samaritans did not receive Him, the disciples, because they were nursing past offenses, asked if they should call down fire from heaven on them. Jesus Himself was *offended;* turning, He rebuked them, saying, *"You do not know what kind of spirit you are of"* (Luke 9:55). It is kind of shocking, but Christ was also *offended* at

Peter when he said, *"Get behind Me, Satan! You are a stumbling block to Me; for you are not setting your mind on God's interests, but man's"* (Matt. 16:23). Peter especially was manifesting unrighteousness, and that was offensive to Jesus in a positive way. Jesus was not scandalized; He did not embrace the offense, but with His rebuke, He recognized that the offense existed and immediately dealt with it. He handled the offense on the spot so that neither of them carried it any further; they both walked away free. This puts the idea of giving and taking offense in a whole new arena.

"For we all stumble in many ways. If anyone does not stumble in what he says, he is a perfect man, able to bridle the whole body as well" (James 3:2). If we can speak and listen without offending anyone or without becoming offended, it is evidence that we are maturing in Christ.

Thoughts and Questions

- Why is it our responsibility not to allow offense to occur?
- In what ways was Jesus' offense positive?
- How can you tell you are maturing in Christ?

Occasions for Offense

It is inevitable that stumbling blocks come (Matthew 18:7).

THERE are numerous occasions for stumbling that lie in our path. One of the most common stumbling blocks is the misconduct of a believer we hold in high esteem. This behavior might be actually immoral or unscriptural conduct, or it might be the abuse of Christian liberty by indulgence in things that, though proper for them, may cause our own conscience to be violated before the Lord.

Many times a presumptuous prophecy or some other false "guidance" may set us up for false expectations that never come to pass. A voice may tell us, "I will use you to evangelize your whole city." Then, when our city is still unevangelized ten years later, we question the faithfulness and character of God. If we misinterpret, misunderstand, or misapply a prophetic word, we can easily become scandalized.

Like Job's wife, we may ultimately assign to God that which is satanic activity, stumble in our walk with Him, and end up disengaging ourselves from everything God is doing in our life. We must be continually alert to the fact that malevolent forces are at work in the universe, and we are *required* to discern leadings, circumstances, and events that result from false direction and impure initiative.

One of the primary areas of offense is in the area of promised or claimed healings that never seem to come to fruition. Because the issue of healing is usually urgent by virtue of the pain and discomfort, problems of personal convenience and advantage frequently surface. How much more convenient it is to have God heal us (or a loved one) than to go through days and weeks of pain or watching someone we love suffer. This is not to say that it is God's *desire* to see His children suffering but that we need to discern the difference between a settled, peaceful conviction of what God will do based on the covenant blood of Jesus and some super-heated extraction of a promise from God that will make our pain go away. There is a direct relationship between seeing a desperate need and hearing a voice giving relief to that need. We can speak to ourselves in Jesus' name and take ourselves beyond the intended will of God for a given situation.

Our first son was born with an umbilical hernia, and my wife and I would keep tape over it so his intestines would not pop out. At the time, our family lived on my teaching salary of $150 a month, and we were quite heavy into healing and miracles. Judith fasted and prayed and asked God to heal him. A few days later, she came to me and said, "God spoke to me this morning that Bernard is healed," and we rejoiced. When she pulled the tape off the hernia, the intestines popped right out, and I saw something in her face that scared me. She whispered, "But God said…." The *skandalizo* stick was pulled, and the box nearly came down over both of us. We could feel the darkness. It was abiding that managed to hold us steady. Later that day, we made an appointment for surgery. It took several months to work ourselves clear from offense until we were able to say, "God, we don't understand, but we trust You!" There emerges a confidence where we can rest in the circumstances as He brings into our life "all things" designed to conform us to His image.

Thoughts and Questions

- 🕯 Describe a time when you were offended by the conduct of another Christian.

- 🕯 In what ways have you been scandalized by the misinterpretation of a prophetic word?

- 🕯 Why do you think God does not always grant our requests?

Other Occasions for Offense

Yet it has no real root in him, but is temporary (inconstant, lasts but a little while); and when affliction or trouble or persecution comes on account of the Word, at once he is caused to stumble [he is repelled and begins to distrust and desert Him Whom he ought to trust and obey] and he falls away
(Matthew 13:21 AMP).

THERE are multiple occasions for offense. It took some effort for me to embrace His statement that offenses must come. One of the more difficult situations is when we intentionally *take up an offense* against another. It is often an offense on behalf of someone we love. God may give grace to the person offended to overcome the offense, but because the offense was not ours, we may *not have the grace* to forgive and walk out of the situation ourselves. Whole denominations or groups of people can become offended at a man or another group of people simply because a leader burdens his followers with his personal offense.

A wife can take offense when something happens to her husband or children. It can be very difficult to get free, because this kind of offense seems to cling in some inexplicable way. Corporate offense is deeper and more common than we know. I remember a rather influential church in our city became offended over the emphasis of the church in the home and made that offense well known. A few months later, a fire burned many of the classrooms in that church. We took up a healthy offering for the repairs, which gave us access to their leaders, and the offense was cleansed and freedom restored.

Jesus said that persecution would be a source of offense. Those who have suffered persecution for their testimony of the Lord Jesus often experience periods of disillusionment with the Lord because they had falsely expected reward, gratitude, and blessing rather than complexity and difficulty. Offenses often happen when our expectations need adjustment. Like John the Baptist, we may question the justice of God if some believers are allowed to suffer while others seem to be inordinately prospered by the Lord. We are especially vulnerable to this attitude when we go through financial difficulty while being faithful to the Lord yet observe someone else who does not seem nearly as spiritual experiencing an apparent abundance of financial blessing.

Countless doctrines, when taken out of their proper perspective or overemphasized, can also become the source of offense to us and others because they do not produce the expected results. Simplistic teachings on healing, deliverance, secrets for receiving the blessing of the Lord, discipleship, overcoming, seven steps to unlimited prosperity, and other current teachings can become a source of our own personal stumbling if we look to the doctrine or teaching as the source of personal fulfillment or an answer to all our problems instead of the Father Himself. To avoid occasions for offense, we must build on the foundation of Father's nature: God *is Agape*, God *is* Light, God *is* Spirit. We must continually return here because only this foundation is unshakable.

Thoughts and Questions

- Describe a situation where you took up an offense for someone else. How did it work out?
- Why did Jesus warn us that persecution would be a source of offense?
- In what ways can simplistic teachings cause us to stumble?

Four Categories of Offense

A stone of stumbling and a rock of offense (1 Peter 2:8 KJV).

JESUS is identified as a stone of stumbling and a rock of offense. This gives clear biblical precedent for the four following statements that could lead to our being offended or being an offense to others if we don't understand them and make adjustments to our expectations:

1. God intends, inexorably, to *"make all things new"* (Rev. 21:5 KJV). Our possible offense lies in giving real, existential answers to the following questions. What aspects of my life does He intend to make new? How could the process offend me? How much turbulence am I willing to endure in the process?

2. God requires us to surrender all of our past, present, and recurring offenses in a manner similar to that which He expected of the disciples. A recurring offense is being offended at something specific—like offense toward our parents—dealing with it, but six months later realizing the offense has re-appeared. Sometimes we have to deal with deep offense in layers. Are we willing to surrender past, present, and recurring offenses?

3. The Kingdom expects and anticipates an effective transformation of our total personality, our nuclear family, our church family, our nation, and ultimately, the entire universe (see Rom. 8:19-21). The Lord may do something in that process that we do not understand.

4. Mental and attitudinal sins are realms without rules that affect both Christians and pre-Christians. These can be gateways for

offense. Faith and abiding are forms of intellectual surrender. The Kingdom asks for a full transformation of our intentions, desires, thinking, and motivations. This includes transforming *tears that we shed for ourselves into tears of intercession for others.* There is an urgent need to bow our knee before the Lord of glory and trust Him to take us where He wants.

In light of this necessary internal transformation, these four points must be embraced as necessary preventative measures to avoid our taking or giving offense. God the Father uses misunderstanding as an instrument to perfect us. In these circumstances, we can either choose to be offended or choose to release the offense. We must learn to have the proper response if we are to live above offense.

Mumford's translation of Matthew 11:6 can help us effectively diagnose and understand the process of mental and attitudinal sin: Blessed (to be envied) is the person who does not become offended at the manner and the procedures that I have chosen to transform and make all things new. Be assured, causes of offense will come. The fallen human cannot be happy in the transformation process. Therefore, we must take the fallen human will daily and repeatedly to the cross of Christ. Compare the offenses of Cain, Esau, and Judas Iscariot with the sheer joy of the treasure and the pearl and of selling all to buy the Kingdom! The freedom of the entire created universe is in some mysterious way waiting for us to find our own freedom and release.

Thoughts and Questions

- ❦ Are you willing to surrender past, present, and recurring offenses?
- ❦ In what ways can you see the Lord doing something that you do not understand or of which you would disapprove?
- ❦ How can you see offense entering through your mental and attitudinal gateway?

Offense: Mental and Attitudinal Sin

Let this same attitude and purpose and [humble] mind be in you which was in Christ Jesus (Philippians 2:5 AMP).

I have not consciously said no to God since I was a young teenager and stood in the middle of the street and dismissed Him. I have failed, missed it, confused the issues, and attempted things in God's name that He would not claim as His own, but it has seldom occurred to me to say no. However, when a series of relational pressures began to surround me and an unrestrained flood of mental and attitudinal sins began to manifest, I came very close to saying no to God. Whatever was going on in me was very real, extremely ugly, and seemed unmanageable. Over the years, I have learned the importance of abiding, so abide I did. With great tenacity, urgency, and spiritual determination, my intention was to allow the internal and external circumstances to press me into the person of our Lord Jesus. This internal conflict went on for months, seemingly without resolve or lessening of intensity. By God's grace, I did not "kill any Egyptians" or do anything stupid that would increase my stay in the wilderness.

One day, an illumination came like a lightning bolt from heaven. I could see I was on the brink of being offended and was about to go around the bend. I was generally angry and irritated for no specific reason, disappointed in myself, fuming at the series of events, and anxious because I could not seem to control my mental and attitudinal processes. I discovered the deeper meaning and significance of what it means to be scandalized. Many thoughts filled my mind. Lessons on vocational suffering became a kind of refuge for me. On a mental and attitudinal level, I began to understand more comprehensively the biblical concept of being offended. Addressing the idea of mental and attitudinal sin is critical because they are not outward transgressions, so they cannot be seen; *they are the realm without rules.*

Getting free from an offense is good, but *preventing* our embrace of the offense is better. The latter requires a transformation of our inner person, which is deeper than outward change or acceptable Christian behavior. *Change* is an external rearrangement of the present circumstances. *Transformation* involves the cross and necessary spiritual death because it is an internal metamorphosis in character. Transformation comes as a result of our *refusing to accept* the offense. Mental and attitudinal transformation signifies the cessation of our human attempts to possess, acquire, and control. Paul explains this transformation when he encourages us to have *the same attitude that Christ did.* When our human thought processes and attitudes have been transformed, it signifies that our very thinking is being redeemed. There is a maturity we have sought and have faithfully attempted to impart—internal spiritual integrity that can only be understood as *"Christ formed in you"* (Gal. 4:19). This is *Agape* actually functioning as the motivation of our most secret and internal person. The only thing that prevents us from embracing offense is the presence of Christ who dwells in us. Transforming our thoughts is the process of being governed by *Agape.* We can know that transformation of our mental and attitudinal sin is happening when we no longer cry for ourselves but begin experiencing intercessory tears for others.

Thoughts and Questions

- In what ways have you been offended in a mental or attitudinal manner?
- How can you prevent embracing offense?
- How does *Agape* practically transform you and keep you from being offended?

Consequences of Taking an Offense

*We put no obstruction in anybody's way [we give no offense in anything], so
that no fault may be found and [our] ministry blamed and discredited*
(2 Corinthians 6:3 AMP).

TO be forewarned is to be able to see and hear. When we wrongly respond
to or embrace offense, several clear events follow:

1. We experience a measurable increase in agitation, irritation,
    moodiness, and touchiness, and we become increasingly
    impossible to please. When not dealt with, this can erupt in rage,
    which is what happened to my missionary friend in Peru who
    became so offended with his 12-year-old servant girl that he beat
    her. His offense destroyed him.

2. We are then inclined to collect offenses. We seem to wait for or
    anticipate the next broken promise, lie, or disappointment, which
    proves and reinforces the nature of the offense. If our thought
    process progresses to, "See, I knew you would do that!" we are
    collecting offenses.

3. We question and re-examine each opinion and every statement
    and perceive people negatively, however simple and well meaning.
    This turns us in upon ourselves.

4. We unavoidably begin to experience a downward cycle of cynicism
    and self-defeat that is based on the strange paradox of paranoia,
    which says: "Just because you are paranoid does not mean that
    they are not after you." We begin to enter the world of suspicion.

5. Once the offense—from whatever source—has been deeply and completely received, the only thing that could possibly relieve our discomfort is to remove the perceived source of offense from the face of the earth! When we are offended because we failed to get what we wanted when we wanted it, there follows abuse, violence, and eventually actual thoughts of murder. This includes believers, whether that makes you uncomfortable or not.

Like the offended disciples who were ready to call down fire (see Luke 9:54), our only possible answer is to remove those who offend us from the face of the earth. The daily news gives us reports of religious, political, and economic upheaval of personal abuse, violence, and literal murder that are motivated by deep offense. The end result of receiving offense seems to function on the sowing and reaping principle that overtakes our intentions and desires. We have the freedom to choose being offended; *we do not have the freedom to choose the consequences of that offense.*

Thoughts and Questions

- ❧ What are some of the signs of being offended?
- ❧ In what ways have you collected offenses?
- ❧ After offense has spiraled down into an *Eros* prison, what is the end result?

Unintended Consequences of Offense

Where do you think all these appalling wars and quarrels come from?
(James 4:1 TM)

FOLLOWING are some personal observations of the unintended consequences of offense I have made over the years. These are not absolutes; they are experiential rather than doctrinal.

- ❦ Those offended at God discover a frightening, hidden capacity to crucify Him afresh.

- ❦ Those who are offended at society are likely to be loners, becoming increasingly isolated, resulting in varying degrees of sociopathic responses. One example is the "BTK killer," who was an elder in his church.

- ❦ Those offended at their parents discover themselves wrestling with personal anarchy, rebellion, and a tendency toward crime. This is the opposite of honoring your parents.

- ❦ The offended wife or husband will settle for nothing less than divorce, almost always accompanied by bitter animosity.

- ❦ Offended females lean toward masculinity and lesbianism; offended males lean toward effeminacy and homosexuality. It is often a departure from what has offended.

🦌 Like the offended postman who murdered several at his coworkers at the post office, those offended at the system, the company, or coworkers give meaning to the term "go postal."

🦌 Those offended by the Church often reject God as Father because of the Church's failure. Unable to discern the difference, we throw out the baby and the bath water.

Hollywood gives us examples of deep offense in many movies. *The Phantom of the Opera* was offended at society. The story lines from *Count of Monte Cristo* and many others are often based on the lead characters' offense. Remember that *offense is probably the major, most identifiable source of depression leading to violence, abuse, murder, and divorce.* For one who is deeply offended, reconciliation is out of the question; those who have offended me must be removed from the face of the earth. This is what happened to Christ. His whole trial was a farce. The Jews of that day were so *offended* at Christ that the only thing that would appease them was to crucify Him. James describes it well:

> *Where do you think all these appalling wars and quarrels come from? Do you think they just happen? Think again. They come about because you want your own way, and fight for it deep inside yourselves. You lust for what you don't have and are willing to kill to get it. You want what isn't yours and will risk violence to get your hands on it. You wouldn't think of just asking God for it, would you? And why not? Because you know you'd be asking for what you have no right to. You're spoiled children, each wanting your own way. You're cheating on God. If all you want is your own way, flirting with the world every chance you get, you end up enemies of God and his way* (James 4:1-4 TM).

Nearly every commentary wants to modify literal murder to something less offensive. However, the original language clearly tells us the serious nature of what it means to give or take offense. Unguarded and untreated, offense leads to depression, abuse, violence, and murder.

Thoughts and Questions

- What are some of the unintended consequences of offense that you recognize?
- Can you think of any stories that depict deep offense?
- Why does deep offense lead to murder?

Offense Hinders Our Following Christ

Where I go, you cannot follow Me now; but you will follow later
(John13:36).

WHEN Jesus said to the disciples, "you cannot follow Me now," I always thought He meant that He was going to die and go to heaven and that we could not (were unable) to follow Him where He was going. Although this is certainly one interpretation, there is another possible way to apply this verse. In following Christ, there lies the possibility of our being offended. Like the disciples, once I am offended, I do not want to walk with Him anymore (see John 6:66).

Nicodemus, a leader of the Jews, could not follow Jesus where He was going because Jesus was intending to go to people like the Samaritans. Every Jew of that day understood that accepting or receiving help from a Samaritan would delay the coming of the Kingdom! The *offense* between the Jews and the Samaritans was so deep and intense that many scholars say it is nearly impossible to exaggerate the degree of animosity. It would be similar in intensity to the conflict between Muslims and Jews today.

Many commentators, including Ulrich Luz, make a most interesting observation of Jesus' statement *"love your enemies"* in the Matthew 1-7 passage. The Jews of His day saw this command as absolute treason, disrespect, and disloyalty to the covenant. In their culture, "your enemies are my enemies." When Jesus came "making all things new" and dealing with past, present, and recurring offenses saying love your enemies, the implications *offended* them.[1]

Immediately after His encounter with Nicodemus, Jesus visited the Samaritan woman at the well. To this most unlikely candidate, the Master of the universe says to the first person ever, *"I am He." "The disciples were shocked. They couldn't believe He was talking with that kind of woman"* (John 4:26-27 TM). If we hang on to our offense, the Lord Jesus is not able to send us to whom He will because our offense is what *rules* us, not the person of the Lord Jesus. Our *offense* keeps us from following Him. Thus, *offense* is a loss to us and to the greater purposes of God in the earth.

Think about the absence of offense in the life of Mother Theresa. To her, the poorest of the poor deserved to receive the life and love of our Lord Jesus. Think of our offense toward Native Americans in the birth of our nation and our statements that "the only good Indian is a dead one." Think of the depth of the offense between the African American and the Caucasian that has caused so much deep hurt, rejection, and bitterness. Offense, given and received from both whites and blacks, has resulted in countless murders. Understanding offense helps us see into the age-long conflict between Roman Catholic and Protestants. Year after year people keep wounds of offense open and bleeding. We use slurs and verbal and literal assassinations, hoping to remove them from the face of the earth. As we learn to release offenses, we become true followers of Christ and become more and more conformed to His image.

Thoughts and Questions

- In what ways was Jesus saying that the disciples could not follow Him?
- Why would Jesus asking that we love our enemies be cause for offense?
- Explain why release from giving and receiving offense conforms us to Christ's image.

ENDNOTE

1. Ulrich Luz. Matthew 1 to 7: A Commentary. (Augsburg Fortress, Minneapolis, MN. 1989) p. 337-351.

READING 131

How to Prevent Being Scandalized

*If your hand causes you to stumble, cut it off; it is better for you to enter life
crippled, than, having your two hands, to go into hell,
into the unquenchable fire* (Mark 9:43).

S CRIPTURE not only warns us of the dangers of being scandalized; it
also gives us some clear guidelines to help us avoid stumbling blocks and
get back on our feet should we become offended.

Prepare yourself. We must be mentally and spiritually prepared for personal pruning in life and conduct. Jesus has given us our own responsibility
for removing certain sources of stumbling from our own lives. He said clearly
that if our eye causes us to stumble, we would be better off to pluck it out
than to allow ourselves to stumble in our walk with Him. He intends for us to
develop the sensitivity and maturity necessary to deal with stumbling blocks
that would hinder our spiritual growth and freedom regardless of what it
might cost us.

Forewarned and forearmed. We must prepare ourselves for people and situations that will cause offense and stumbling. Jesus said it was *inevitable* that
stumbling blocks come. Our challenge is to guard ourselves against stumbling and when possible, avoid the situations in the first place. Equally, we
seek to avoid any action or attitude that would give offense.

Allow God to be God. We must develop a healthy attitude that allows God
the absolute freedom to function in a way that is different from our expectations. After all, *"our God is in the heavens, He does whatever He pleases"* (Ps.
115:3). He is answerable to no one for what He does. The pot does not ask

the potter why it was made a certain way; neither do we have the right to call God into question for His sovereign actions. He is not limited by our preconceptions or our personal opinions. Certainly, He is not offended at those people with whom we are offended.

Caring relationships. A caring relationship with other believers will give them opportunity to speak clearly to us when we are being offended. Naaman's servant was faithful to adjust his master's perspective when he was offended by the conduct of Elisha. Ecclesiastes tells us that two are better than one because if one stumbles, the other can lift him up. If in our walk we trip over a stumbling block, what a blessing it is to have another believer upon whom we can confidently lean until we regain our spiritual equilibrium.

Overview. We must maintain an overview of life and circumstances in line with God's eternal perspective. Jesus' discourse to His disciples in John 14–16 was given primarily to help them place His coming crucifixion and death into an eternal perspective and keep them from stumbling. All too often, a personal crisis, such as the death of a loved one, a financial collapse, war, a painful divorce, or some deep personal tragedy, can cause people to be scandalized. The failure to put such tragic events into an eternal perspective can be fatal. Somehow, we must rise out of the present circumstances and realize that God was on His throne *before* the tragedy occurred, and He will continue to be on His throne *after* it has passed.

Thoughts and Questions

- Explain why preparing and being forewarned helps you prevent being scandalized.

- In what ways have you allowed God to be God in your life?

- What relationships do you have on which you can lean when you stumble?

Agape Keeps Us From Stumbling

*Those who love Thy law have great peace, and nothing
causes them to stumble* (Psalm 119:165).

FOLLOWING are additional guidelines to help us avoid stumbling
blocks and get back on our feet should we become offended. Like Moses
holding up the serpent on the pole, we may look and be healed.

Love for God's law. God said of lawless Israel, "*They have not listened to My
words, and as for My law, they have rejected it also...behold, I am laying stumbling
blocks before this people, and they will stumble against them*" (Jer. 6:19, 21). On
the other hand, *Agape* keeps us from stumbling. Loving the law of God is not
so much intellectual assent to a set of Scriptures as it is a deep personal desire
to be conformed to God's character and will. When we are driven by *Agape*,
we are able to see and understand stumbling blocks as they come into our
path and deal with them before we get scandalized.

Avoid the sin of presumption. We must avoid presuming upon the will of
God. Though it is easy to say that God will do a certain thing (particularly
when it involves our own personal advantage or gain), we must always leave
God the option of changing our plans, desires, or opinions. Proper response
to disappointment is clear evidence of spiritual maturity.

Love your brother. "*The one who loves his brother abides in the Light and
there is no cause for stumbling in him*" (1 John 2:10). As we set our *Agape* upon
someone, we find that we begin to focus on their person and what we can do
to help them. We become more concerned about maintaining the relationship than preservation of personal opinion, advantage, or convenience. An

offended person needs someone who understands and cares. Someone who is scandalized really is harder to be won than a strong city. He or she is hurting badly and needs someone to reach under, bring light into the darkness, help lift the box off them, and take them out of the snare of the enemy. That is one of the roles of being a priest. Whatever you do, do not quote Scripture to someone who has been scandalized. Give of yourself, but limit it to what is real.

If Jesus wants us to follow Him, are we willing to work through our offenses and actually follow Him wherever He sends us? What if He sends us to our in-laws or siblings we have not spoken to in decades? What if He asks you to extend His love to the neighbor two doors down who offended you five years ago? When Jude says, "keep yourself in the exact center of God's *Agape*," he is giving us his antidote to being offended. *Agape* is the transformation of our intention, desire, and mindset that allows us to live above the sources and causes of offense both given and taken. Paul describes this as being seated with Christ in heavenly places (see Eph. 2:6). Only the *Agape* of God has the sufficient spiritual strength to perform the laser surgery necessary for our spiritual eyes and ears to see and hear the significant issues of the Kingdom.

Thoughts and Questions

- Why does *Agape* keep us from stumbling?
- Why is it not good to quote Scripture to someone who is scandalized at God?
- Are you willing to work through any offense so you can follow God wherever He sends you?

The Fruit of *Agape*

"...bearing fruit in every good work and steadily growing and increasing in and by the knowledge of God" (Colossians 1:10 AMP).

YOU and I are sons and daughters of the living God because of the Seed that was inseminated into our person at our new birth in Christ. When we respond to the Eternal Seed of the Kingdom within us, we become one with Christ, and the desire to produce the fruit of *Agape* in our lives begins to emerge. When the Seed permeates our personality, something begins to happen because the Eternal Seed contains the mystery of the Kingdom. Through the water of God's Word we nourish the Seed in us, enabling us to hear and do the promptings of the Holy Spirit. Cultivating and nourishing the Seed allows it to grow, producing after its kind and crowding out every other seed that is not *Agape* in our lives.

Following Jesus means giving expression to the eternal and incorruptible Seed of *Agape*, and *Agape* involves spontaneity and risk. The results are pure joy. We have been raised up and seated with Him in the heavenly places (see Eph. 2:6). However, remaining in the chair of *Agape* is an intentional choice. It involves suffering because it requires us to act against ourselves and embrace the cross. It is only *Agape* that can transform us from takers into givers and keep us from stumbling or being offended.

Agape is behavioral; when Christ is fully formed in us, God's *character* (fruit of the Spirit) shows up in our behavior. It is never our possession; it is God's. His love comes to us and then *through* us to a hurting world. We love because He first loved us. We have a responsibility as Kingdom gardeners to water, nourish, guard, and speak edification and comfort to ourselves and others in whom the Seed has been inseminated so we can bring forth God's inheritance. Remember, the power is in the Seed, not in the person.

Bob Mumford

Appendix A : *Eros* Shift Chart

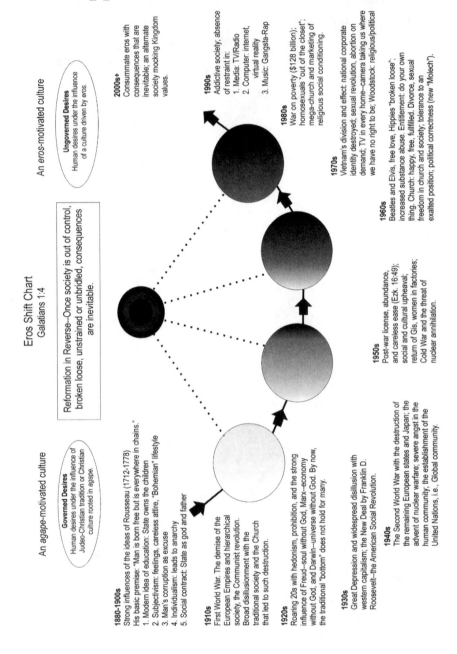

An *agape*-motivated culture

Eros Shift Chart
Galatians 1:4

An *eros*-motivated culture

Governed Desires
Human desires under the influence of Judeo-Christian tradition or Christian culture rooted in *agape*.

Reformation in Reverse—Once society is out of control, broken loose, unstrained or unbridled, consequences are inevitable.

Ungoverned Desires
Human desires under the influence of a culture driven by *eros*.

2000s+
Consummate eros with consequences that are inevitable; an alternate society mocking Kingdom values.

1990s
Addictive society; absence of restraint in:
1. Media: TV/Radio
2. Computer: internet, virtual reality
3. Music: Gangsta-Rap

1980s
War on poverty ($128 billion); homosexuals "out of the closet"; mega-church and marketing of religious social conditioning.

1970s
Vietnam's division and effect: national corporate identity destroyed; sexual revolution, abortion on demand; TV in every home—camera taking us where we have no right to be; Woodstock: religious/political

1960s
Beatles and Elvis, free love, Hippies "broken loose", increased substance abuse. Entitlement: do your own thing. Church: happy, free, fulfilled. Divorce, sexual freedom in church and society; tolerance to an exalted position; political correctness (new "Molech").

1880-1900s
Strong influences of the ideas of Rousseau (1712-1778)
His basic premise: "Man is born free but is everywhere in chains."
1. Modern idea of education: State owns the children
2. Subjectivism: feelings, careless attire, "Bohemian" lifestyle
3. Man's corruption as excuse
4. Individualism: leads to anarchy
5. Social contract: State as god and father

1910s
First World War. The demise of the European Empires and hierarchical society, the Communist revolution. Broad disillusionment with the traditional society and the Church that led to such destruction.

1920s
Roaring 20s with hedonism, prohibition, and the strong influence of Freud—soul without God, Marx—economy without God, and Darwin—universe without God. By now, the traditional "bottom" does not hold for many.

1930s
Great Depression and widespread disillusion with western capitalism; the New Deal by Franklin D. Roosevelt—the American Social Revolution.

1940s
The Second World War with the destruction of the remaining European states and Japan; the advent of nuclear warfare; severe angst in the human community, the establishment of the United Nations, i.e., Global community.

1950s
Post-war license, abundance, and careless ease (Ezk. 16:49); social and cultural upheaval; return of GIs, women in factories; Cold War and the threat of nuclear annihilation.

328

Appendix B—Book Recommendations

Enthusiasm by Ronald Knox

Outlines of Theology by Archibald Alexander Hodge

When Religion Is an Addiction by Robert Minor

Eros and Agape by Anders Nygren

Unchanging Person and the Unshakable Kingdom by E. Stanley Jones

The Eclipse of Christ in Eschatology by Adrio Konig (Eerdman, 1989)

About Bob Mumford

BOB Mumford is a dynamic Bible teacher with a unique and powerful gift for imparting the Word of God. His anointed messages are remembered for years afterwards, because he captivates his audiences with humor in the form of word pictures, which penetrate deep into hearts with incredible authority, clarity, and personal application. Since 1954, thousands of Christians worldwide have attributed their spiritual growth and determination to follow Jesus Christ to his prophetic teaching, helping them understand Father God and His Kingdom.

Bob has written for major Christian periodicals both in the United States and abroad and published several books, including *Agape Road, Take Another Look at Guidance, The King & You, Fifteen Steps Out, Living Happily Ever After,* and *The Purpose of Temptation.* He has also published numerous booklets called *Plumblines,* including *Renegade Male* and a series on *Inheritance*

Bob has a heart for backsliders, having come to the Lord at age 12 only to stray from God a few months later. During this time, when he was 13, his parents divorced, creating the need for him to quit school and work to help support his mother and five sisters. At 20 years old, he joined the US Navy as a medic. Bob would go with his Navy buddies to the bar and end up preaching to those in the bar the necessity to repent of their sins and come to Christ. Even then, Father God was pursuing him!

While on leave from the Navy, Bob attended a church service one evening where he was overcome by the conviction of the Holy Spirit and literally ran to the altar. After being away from God for 12 years, the Lord cleaned up his heart and gave him a new purpose and direction, calling him specifically to "Feed My people".

After completing his high school education in the Navy and then graduating with a Bachelor of Science degree from Valley Forge Christian College, Bob attended the University of Deleware and then received his Masters of Divinity degree from Reformed Episcopal Seminary in Philadelphia. Over the years, he has served as pastor, as a Dean and Professor of New Testament and Missions at Elim Bible Institute. In 1972 he founded Lifechangers, Inc. to distribute his teaching materials all over the world; his materials have been translated into more than 20 different languages.

Bob has traveled extensively to some 50 nations as an international conference speaker, and today he is considered to be a spiritual "Papa" to thousands of Christians. His ministry has been to prophetically proclaim and teach the sufficiency of Christ Jesus and His Kingdom in a manner which promotes reconciliation and unity in the Body of Christ. Bob seeks to bring about personal spiritual change and growth in the lives of believers, regardless of denominational persuasion. His unique style of humor is designed to keep you smiling so it isn't too painful when the truth of his teaching hits home. Such high intensity in the Holy Spirit, accompanied by his pointed and colorful delivery, enables him to impact his audiences with an unforgettable and life-changing experience.

Bob and his wife, Judith, can be reached through Lifechangers..

If you would like to receive information about Lifechangers, or a catalog of materials available, you can write Bob at:

LIFECHANGERS

PO Box 3709, Cookeville, TN 38502 U.S.A.

800.521.5676   931.520.3730

lc@lifechangers.org   www.lifechangers.org

Other Titles by Bob Mumford

BOOKS:

Fifteen Steps Out
Take Another Look at Guidance
The King & You
The Purpose of Temptation
Dr. Frankenstein & World Systems
Giving and Receiving Offense

BIBLE STUDIES:

The Agape Road
Breaking Out (also in Spanish)
Knowing, Loving & Following Jesus
Leading Leaders in Agape
Unshared Love

BOOKLETS:

Below the Bottom Line
Church of My Dreams
Correction Not Rejection
The Difference Between the Church and the Kingdom
Forever Change
Grace: God's Rubber Room
The Implications of Following Jesus
On Being Scandalized
Prison of Resentment
Psalm for Living
Renegade Male
Riddle of the Painful Earth
Standing in the Whirlwind
Three Dimensional Reality
Water Baptism
Why God?
(and many others)

In the right hands, This Book will Change Lives!

Most of the people who need this message will not be looking for this book. To change their lives, you need to put a copy of this book in their hands.

> *But others (seeds) fell into good ground, and brought forth fruit, some a hundred-fold, some sixty-fold, some thirty-fold* (Matthew 13:8).

Our ministry is constantly seeking methods to find the good ground, the people who need this anointed message to change their lives. Will you help us reach these people?

> *Remember this—a farmer who plants only a few seeds will get a small crop. But the one who plants generously will get a generous crop* (2 Corinthians 9:6).

EXTEND THIS MINISTRY BY SOWING
3 BOOKS, 5 BOOKS, 10 BOOKS, OR MORE TODAY,
AND BECOME A LIFE CHANGER!

Thank you,

Don Nori Sr., Founder
Destiny Image
Since 1982